AYURVEDA AND MARMA THERAPY

ENERGY POINTS IN YOGIC HEALING

AYURVEDA AND MARMA THERAPY
ENERGY POINTS IN YOGIC HEALING

Namarta Roy

ABD PUBLISHERS
Jaipur ■ New Delhi

ABD PUBLISHERS

Regd. Off. "Bony Residency", Gate No. 2
Opp. Tilak Public School, Vishweswariya Nagar,
Gopalpura Road, Jaipur - 302018, India
Ph: 0141 - 2761280, Telefax: 2761381
Email: abdpublishersjpr@gmail.com

Delhi Office: 102, 1st Floor, Satyam House,
4327/3, Ansari Road, Darya Ganj,
New Delhi - 110002, India
Ph: 011-45652440

visit us: www.oxfordbookcompany.com

Distributed By
KEYA INTERNATIONAL PRESS LLP
E-mail: keyainternationalpressllp@gmail.com

Published in India, 2025

ISBN : 978-81-19343-14-0

Typeset by Shivangi Computer, Jaipur

Printed and bound in India by Thomson Press Ltd.,
New Delhi

Contents

Preface

Ayurveda, the ancient system of holistic healing from India, and Marma Therapy, a specialized aspect of Ayurveda, offer profound insights into the interconnectedness of the body, mind, and spirit. Central to both traditions is the concept of energy points, known as "marmas" in Ayurveda and "chakras" in Yoga, which play a pivotal role in promoting health and well-being through yogic healing practices. In Ayurveda, marmas are regarded as vital junctions where the body's energy pathways intersect, influencing physical, mental, and emotional functions. These energy points are believed to be centers of consciousness and intelligence, housing the subtle essence of life force known as "Prana." By stimulating or balancing marmas, Ayurvedic practitioners aim to harmonize the flow of Prana throughout the body, thereby promoting health and vitality. Similarly, in Yoga philosophy, chakras are seen as energy centers located along the spine, each corresponding to different aspects of human experience and consciousness. Through yogic practices such as asana (physical postures), pranayama (breathwork), and meditation, individuals can activate and balance the chakras, facilitating the free flow of energy and promoting holistic well-being. The integration of Ayurveda and Marma Therapy with Yoga provides a comprehensive approach to healing that addresses the physical, energetic, and spiritual dimensions of health. By combining the therapeutic benefits of yoga postures, breathwork, and meditation with the precise manipulation of marmas, practitioners can unlock the body's innate capacity for self-healing and transformation.

Ayurvedic texts describe various marmas located throughout the body, each with its specific anatomical location, physiological functions, and therapeutic applications. Through gentle pressure, massage, and energy work, Ayurvedic practitioners stimulate these marmas to alleviate pain, improve circulation, and promote overall vitality. Additionally, herbal remedies, aromatic oils, and therapeutic sounds may be utilized to enhance the therapeutic effects of marma therapy. In the context of Yoga, the practice of asana, pranayama, and meditation serves to awaken and balance the chakras, allowing individuals to experience greater harmony and alignment on all levels – physical, energetic, mental, and spiritual. By integrating mindfulness, breath awareness, and subtle body practices, yogic healing fosters a deep connection between body and mind, facilitating healing and self-discovery. The synergy between Ayurveda, Marma Therapy, and Yoga offers a holistic approach to health and well-being that honors the interconnectedness of all aspects of the human experience. Through the exploration of energy points in yogic healing, individuals can tap into their innate healing potential, cultivate balance and vitality, and embark on a journey towards greater health, happiness, and wholeness.

Ayurveda and Marma Therapy is an essential reference guide for all students of Yoga, Ayurveda, massage or natural healing. This book is easy to understand and use even for the inexperienced students and practitioners.

— ***Namarta Roy***

Chapter 1

Introduction

Introduction to Marma Therapy

The word Marma is of Sanskrit origin 'Mrin Maranae'. The Sanskrit phrase, "mriyatae asmin iti marma" means 'there is likelihood of death or serious damage to health when these points are inflicted. Hence, these areas are called marma. Marma in Sanskrit also means hidden or secret. By definition, a Marma point is a juncture on the body where two or more types of tissue meet, such as muscles, veins, ligaments, bones or joints.

Ayurveda, the ancient system of holistic healing from India, and Marma Therapy, a specialized aspect of Ayurveda, offer profound insights into the interconnectedness of the body, mind, and spirit. Central to both traditions is the concept of energy points, known as "marmas" in Ayurveda and "chakras" in Yoga, which play a pivotal role in promoting health and well-being through yogic healing practices.

In Ayurveda, marmas are regarded as vital junctions where the body's energy pathways intersect, influencing physical, mental, and emotional functions. These energy points are believed to be centers of consciousness and intelligence, housing the subtle essence of life force known as "Prana." By stimulating or balancing marmas, Ayurvedic practitioners aim to harmonize the flow of Prana throughout the body, thereby promoting health and vitality.

Similarly, in Yoga philosophy, chakras are seen as energy centers located along the spine, each corresponding to different aspects of human experience and consciousness. Through yogic practices such as asana (physical postures), pranayama (breathwork), and meditation, individuals can activate and balance the chakras, facilitating the free flow of energy and promoting holistic well-being.

The integration of Ayurveda and Marma Therapy with Yoga provides a comprehensive approach to healing that addresses the physical, energetic, and spiritual dimensions of health. By combining the therapeutic benefits of yoga postures, breathwork, and meditation with the precise manipulation of marmas, practitioners can unlock the body's innate capacity for self-healing and transformation.

Ayurvedic texts describe various marmas located throughout the body, each with its specific anatomical location, physiological functions, and therapeutic applications.

Through gentle pressure, massage, and energy work, Ayurvedic practitioners stimulate these marmas to alleviate pain, improve circulation, and promote overall vitality. Additionally, herbal remedies, aromatic oils, and therapeutic sounds may be utilized to enhance the therapeutic effects of marma therapy.

In the context of Yoga, the practice of asana, pranayama, and meditation serves to awaken and balance the chakras, allowing individuals to experience greater harmony and alignment on all levels - physical, energetic, mental, and spiritual. By integrating mindfulness, breath awareness, and subtle body practices, yogic healing fosters a deep connection between body and mind, facilitating healing and self-discovery.

The synergy between Ayurveda, Marma Therapy, and Yoga offers a holistic approach to health and well-being that honors the interconnectedness of all aspects of the human experience. Through the exploration of energy points in yogic healing, individuals can tap into their innate healing potential, cultivate balance and vitality, and embark on a journey towards greater health, happiness, and wholeness.

107 Marma Points in Ayurveda for Healing

Marma therapy utilizes 107 points or "doorways" into the body and consciousness. The mind is considered as the 108th marma.

Major marma points correspond to the seven chakras, or energy centers of the body, while minor points radiate out along the torso and limbs. These points range in size from one to six inches in diameter. The points were mapped out in detail centuries ago in the ' Sushruta Samhita ', a classic Ayurvedic text.

The points cover both the front and back of the body, including

- 22 on the lower extremities
- 22 on the arms
- 12 on the chest and stomach
- 14 on the back, &
- 37 on the head and neck

Happens During Marma

In Marma therapy, a very light stimulation of points on the body is done. It removes blockages from the marma points giving physical and psychological relaxation and strength.

This is a powerful process and a therapy that works with these subtle and sensitive energy points to open the energy channels in the body are called srothas.

Marma points, when gently pressed on the skin can stimulate a chain of positive events.

Marma Great for You

Marma therapies are profound and work at many levels - physical, emotional, mental and spiritual and can create dramatic shifts in the body.

- Relief from chronic or acute pain, both locally and distally
- Detoxification at all levels.
- Significant improvement in bodily/organ functions, especially immunity, digestive, respiratory, neural & psychological
- Healthier skin and a radiant appearance
- Balances body temperature and can balance the doshas
- Releases neuro-chemicals such as serotonin, melatonin for improved cognitive function and deeper sleep

A more creative you with higher energy levels:

Here's a big secret to understanding marma:

Marma therapy can actually alter consciousness and change one's awareness. Through working on the marma points, we can control:

- prana (energy) levels
- our sensory and motor organs, and eventually
- the entire mind-body complex

This gives us easier access to higher realms of consciousness. From that place, a person can move forward with self-care, creativity and renewed energy.

Marma Points in Ayurveda Healing

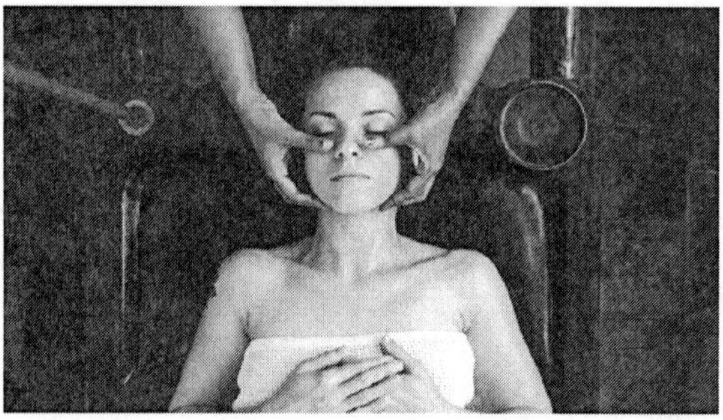

Ayurveda is a traditional Indian alternative medicine system that has a long, rich history of use. Under Ayurvedic medicine, it's believed that the five elements of the world have a huge impact on a person's health. Marma points are specific anatomical locations in your body through which the energy of these elements is believed to flow. Marma points therapy is the practice of stimulating these spots through gentle massage therapy. We explore where the marma points are located, what marma points therapy is, and the potential benefits of marma points massage therapy.

Marma Points

Ayurvedic medicine - and ideas about the existence of life energy and marma points - has been around since roughly 2 B.C.

In Ayurvedic medicine, marma points are anatomical locations in your body where a concentration of life energy exists. Marma points are said to contain the three doshas:

- vata (air and space)
- kapha (earth and water)
- pitta (fire and water)

These doshas are believed to be linked to your physical and emotional well-being.

Like traditional Chinese acupuncture, Ayurvedic medicine believes that stimulation of the marma points can improve your physical and mental health.

It's also believed that injury to the marma points can result in negative health effects in the body and in some cases, further injury and even death.

Location of Marma Points

It's said that there are 107 marma points in various locations around the human body:

- 11 marma points in your limbs
- 26 marma points in your trunk
- 37 marma points in your head and neck region
- 33 marma points located elsewhere in your body

Marma Points in Ayurveda Healing

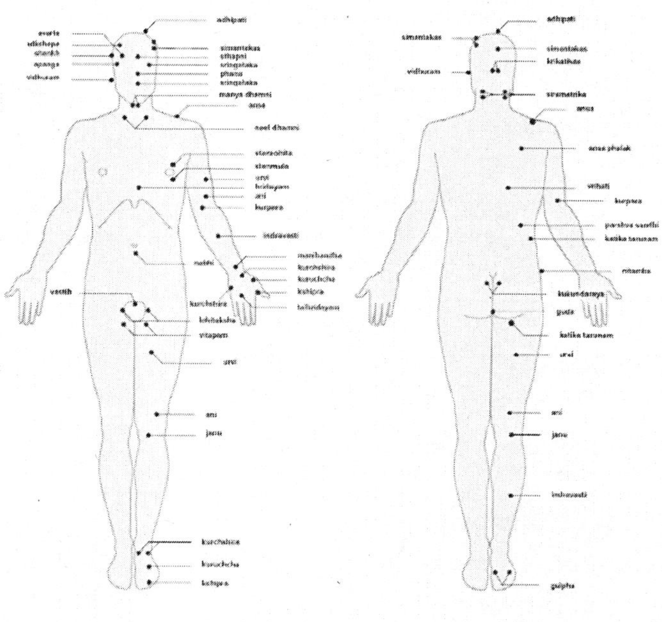

healthline

Marma Points Therapy

Ayurvedic medicine proposes marma points therapy as a method of changing or improving your biochemistry. It's believed to release stagnant energy and stimulate your internal organs, hormones, and other chemicals to help meet the needs of your body. Marma points therapy is done by gently stimulating the marma points around your body through massage therapy.

Generally, this is performed by a trained massage therapist who has experience with Ayurvedic medicine. These massage therapists have extensive knowledge of the locations and functions of the various marma points. Aromatic massage oils, sometimes infused with herbs, are typically used to increase the benefits of the massage.

The Benefits of Marma Points Therapy

There isn't much scientific research available on the benefits of marma points therapy, and the few studies that do exist are relatively small.

For example, one study from 2011 investigated the impact of the kurpara (elbow joint) marma as a vaikalyakara marma.

Vaikalyakara marma are marma points believed to have negative effects on your health when injured. Of the 80 participants in the study, those who experienced injury to the kurpara marma also reported significant damage to the rest of their arm, as well as a slew of other side effects.

Another small study from 2006 investigated the benefits of marma points therapy for stroke patients. In this study, standard post-stroke care was compared with the same care plus marma points therapy.

The researchers found that while the marma massage therapy was well tolerated, it didn't necessarily produce a significant difference in recovery scores for participants.

More research is needed to determine the exact benefits of marma points therapy.

Marma Points Massage

Marma points massage therapy can be both relaxing and invigorating. It can not only help loosen your muscles and tissues, but it's also thought to help promote the proper flow of energy around your body.

The good news is that you don't have to be a certified massage therapist to give yourself a marma points massage. Here's how you can massage your own marma points without a professional:

1. Use the tips of your fingers to gently but firmly stimulate each marma point listed below.

2. Massage each point in a clockwise circular motion for up to 5 minutes.
3. Optionally, use herb-infused massage oils during your massage.

Below, you'll find some of the more notable marma points that you can easily stimulate using the massage technique above.

Marma point	Location	Believed to affect
Sthapani marma	center of forehead	mind, brain, and nerves
Phana marma	either side of the nose at the base of the nostrils	sinuses, ears, sense of smell, and stress levels
Shringataka marma	center of the chin	eyes, ears, nose, tongue, and various nerves
Talhridayam marma	center of the palm of each hand	lungs
Manibandha marma	center of the spot where your inner wrist meets the palm of each hand	body stiffness
Nabhi marma	center of the navel	small intestines
Janu marma	lower inner point at the bottom of each kneecap	heart, liver, and spleen
Indravasti marma	center of each calf muscle	digestion and the small intestine
Kurcha marma	center of the ball of each foot, between the first and second toes	vision
Talhridayam marma	center of the sole of each foot	lungs (similar to the talhridayam marma points on the hands)

Key Takeaways

Marma points therapy is a traditional Ayurvedic massage technique that's believed to help sustain the flow of energy throughout your body.

Marma Therapy: What Is It, Types and Benefits to Promote Energy Flow and Healing

Ayurveda, the ancient Indian system of medicine, encompasses a wealth of therapeutic practices aimed at harmonizing the body, mind, and spirit. At the core of Ayurvedic healing lies Marma Therapy, a profound and intricate technique focused on vital energy points within the body. These marma points are considered to be junctions of life force energy (prana), where the body's subtle energies converge.

Marma Therapy

Marma Therapy, derived from the Sanskrit word 'marma,' meaning secret or hidden, involves the gentle manipulation or stimulation of these specific points to facilitate the flow of prana and promote healing. These points, totaling 107 in the body according to traditional Ayurvedic texts, are believed to be where physical, mental, and emotional elements converge. Each marma point holds a unique significance, connecting with specific organs, nerves, and subtle energy channels (nadis) throughout the body.

Through precise touch, massage, or application of gentle pressure, Marma Therapy aims to release blockages, balance energies, and encourage the body's innate healing abilities.

Beyond its physical implications, Marma Therapy takes a holistic approach, addressing not only the physiological but also the psychological and spiritual aspects of an individual. It is believed that by nurturing and balancing the flow of prana through these points, overall wellness and harmony can be achieved.

The Different Types of Marma Therapy

Marma Therapy is a profound technique within Ayurveda that involves the manipulation or stimulation of specific points in the body to promote healing, balance energies, and enhance overall well-being. There are various types or categories of Marma points based on their locations and functions within the body. Here are some of the different types of Marma Therapy:

Maha Marma: These are the major, vital points in the body where larger nerves, blood vessels, and ligaments converge. Stimulating these points can have significant effects on various physiological and psychological functions.

Sthana Marma: Referring to static or fixed points, Sthana Marma points are situated at specific anatomical locations, such as joints, where bones, muscles, and tendons meet. Manipulation of these points can alleviate pain and improve joint mobility.

Kshetra Marma: These points are associated with regions of the body and have a broader influence. They relate to organs, tissues, or functional systems. The activation of Kshetra Marma points aims to harmonize the functions of these areas.

Sadya Prana Harana Marma: Translating to "immediately life-threatening," these points are crucial in emergencies. When stimulated or injured, they can lead to immediate life-threatening situations. Therefore, caution is exercised around these points.

Kalantara Marma: Referring to temporary or transient points, Kalantara Marma points are where vulnerable structures temporarily become susceptible to injury. These points are associated with specific times or situations.

Bandha Marma: Bandha Marma points are linked to body energy locks (bandhas) and are manipulated to release tension, improve energy flow, and enhance vitality.

Utkshepa Marma: These points are associated with the concept of displacement. When affected or injured, they can lead to disorientation or displacement of bodily functions.

Procedure to Perform Marma Therapy

Performing Marma Therapy requires precision, knowledge of the specific points, and gentle manipulation techniques. Here's an overview of how Marma Therapy can be performed:

Step 1: Create a calm and quiet space conducive to relaxation and healing.

Step 2: Learn to locate the specific Marma points on the body. These points correspond to specific anatomical landmarks and are often located at joint spaces, nerve intersections, or other vital areas.

Step 3: Use gentle touch, massage, or light pressure on the Marma points. Techniques involve circular motions, light tapping, or holding the point with gentle pressure.

Step 4: Approach Marma Therapy with intention and focus. Cultivate a healing intention and mindfulness during the therapy session.

Health Benefits of Marma Therapy

Balances Energy Flow: By stimulating specific Marma points, the therapy aims to balance the flow of prana (life force energy) within the body. This balance is believed to support overall health and vitality.

Reduces Stress: Marma Therapy techniques, when applied gently, can induce relaxation, reduce stress, and promote a sense of calmness. It helps release tension held in the body.

Remedies Pain: Manipulation of Marma points may alleviate pain by releasing blockages in energy channels and stimulating the body's natural healing mechanisms. It's often used for musculoskeletal discomfort and joint issues.

Enhances Circulation: The therapy may improve blood and lymphatic circulation, aiding in the removal of toxins and promoting better overall circulation.

Emotional Balance: Some believe that working on specific Marma points can influence emotional states, helping to ease anxiety, uplift moods, and promote emotional balance.

Supports Healing: Marma Therapy is believed to support the body's innate healing processes. It can complement other healing modalities and therapies, aiding in recovery from various ailments.

Improves Energy Levels: By promoting the flow of prana and balancing energies, individuals may experience increased vitality, improved energy levels, and a sense of rejuvenation.

Points To Remember While Performing Marma Therapy

- Customize the therapy based on an individual's needs. Take into account their constitution, any imbalances (dosha), and specific health concerns.
- Practice with caution and care, especially around Sadya Prana Harana Marma points, which can have immediate life-threatening implications if manipulated incorrectly.
- Some practitioners may use herbal oils or formulations specific to certain Marma points to enhance the therapeutic effects.
- The duration of therapy and the frequency of sessions may vary based on individual needs and the specific Marma points being addressed.
- It's crucial to seek guidance and training from a qualified and experienced practitioner before attempting Marma Therapy. Proper training ensures accuracy, safety, and effectiveness in the application of these techniques.

Side Effects of Marma Therapy

Certainly, here are some potential side effects or considerations associated with Marma Therapy:

- Pain or Discomfort: Excessive pressure or incorrect manipulation of Marma points can cause discomfort or pain.
- Bruising or Sensitivity: Aggressive or improper techniques might lead to bruising or increased sensitivity in the treated areas.
- Allergic Reactions: Some individuals may experience allergic reactions to oils or herbal formulations used during the therapy.
- Risk of Injury: Incorrect manipulation, especially around sensitive points, can potentially lead to injury or aggravate existing health conditions.

- Not Suitable for Everyone: Certain individuals with acute health conditions, fractures, or specific medical histories might not be suitable candidates for Marma Therapy.

Marma Therapy, rooted in Ayurveda, offers a holistic approach to wellness through precise manipulation of vital energy points. By balancing energies, reducing stress, and aiding in pain relief, it promotes harmony of body and mind. With proper training and care, it holds potential for enhancing overall health and vitality.

An Introduction to Marma Points

What are the Marma points? Here's a quick overview and a 3-step self-massage you can do every day.

For centuries, practitioners have been mapping the human body and linking various limbs, organs, immune responses and even emotions to specific energy points.

These 'points' are referred to in Chinese Medicine as Acupuncture or Acupressure points, and in Ayurveda and yogic healing as Marma points. This isn't to say that the two systems discount each other - many books on marma points also speak of meridians and many books on acupuncture mention chakras. According to both Ayurveda and Chinese Medicine, energy (prana or chi) can stagnate in these points. Both systems have healing practices focused on freeing this energy, whether through acupuncture or acupressure, Ayurvedic massage or even visualisation - like in Esther's class below.

Marma points are energy points in the body used for healing in Ayurveda. They can be compared to acupuncture points in Chinese Medicine.

Literally translated, marma means 'a point that can kill', and indeed some of the marma points have been identified and used in martial arts, however in marma point massage, these points are only used for healing purposes! They're also identified as neurolymphatic points, stimulating the removal of lymph and enhancing the efficiency of the body's organs.

The focus of marma point massage is primarily to manipulate subtle energy or prana, but physically they're also very effective for relieving stiff muscles and boosting circulation. Marma therapy is used extensively throughout Ayurveda, and is considered important in self-care and self-healing practices. Just as many of us are (re)discovering through yoga, the key to greater health and happiness doesn't necessarily lie outside of us, but instead is quite literally at our fingertips.

There are said to be 107 marma points on the body, each serving a particular purpose, and each with its own name and specific way of massaging it. Different oils are used depending upon each person's Ayurvedic dosha type.

Marma points are measured in anguli or 'finger units'. For instance; the marma point Hridaya (meaning 'heart') is found at the sternum, and measures four anguli in size. It is best massaged in a broad and gentle way with the palm of the hand with sesame oil in order to calm the energy of the heart. Mustard oil can be used to enhance circulation, and acupressure at this point can help relieve stress and negative emotions. Try it for yourself - even just placing your hand here can have a calming effect.

How to Give Yourself a Marma Point Massage

One of the best things about knowing where certain marma points are located, is that you can utilise them and use a gentle self-massage technique wherever and whenever you are! Keep reading for three marma points you can massage daily to help you feel vibrant and well wherever you find yourself!

Talahridaya

Known as the point at the 'heart of the hand', this marma point is found at the center of the palm, and measures ½ anguli (half a finger unit) in size.

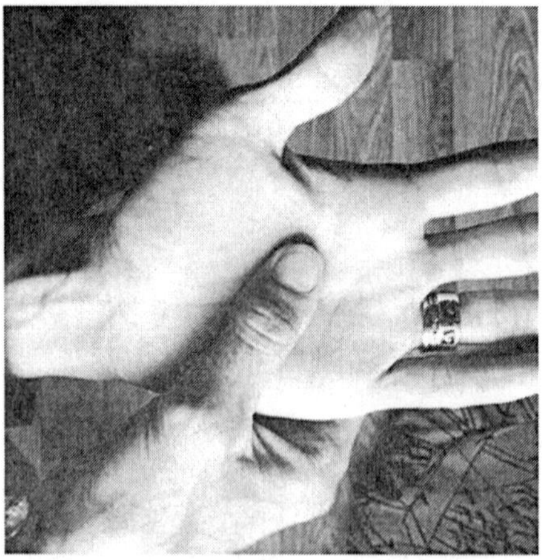

Figure: *Talahridaya marma point*

This point is closely linked to Anahata, the heart chakra, and is thought of as an important point in stimulating circulation throughout the whole body. It links closely to the lungs and respiratory health, and is also a vital marma point to work with regarding communication. Therapists who use their hands can also massage this point before a treatment to enhance the flow of prana to the palms.

Massage this point in a strong, circular motion for roughly five minutes. Sesame or almond oil is best used, with essential oils like eucalyptus for opening blocked sinuses or 'energising' the hands. You can also energise the point further by rubbing the palms together until they feel warm.

Indrabasti

Referring to the God Indra's arrow, this point is found at the center of the calf muscle, and measures approximately ½ anguli (half a finger unit).

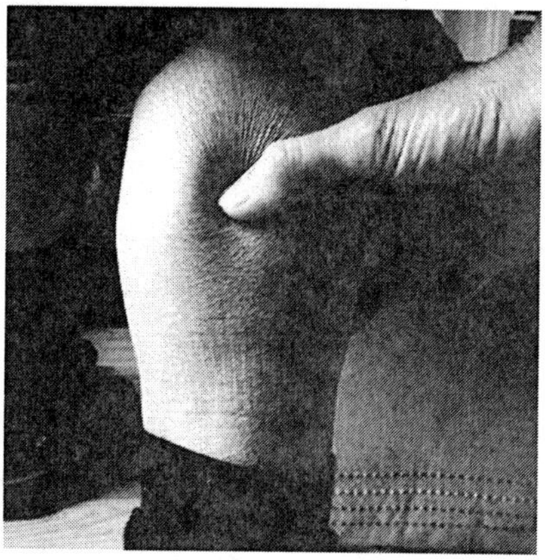

Figure: *Indrabasti marma point on the back of the lower leg*

Massaging the calves is important to do daily, as they can very easily become tight, but also because they're one of the most important parts of the body regarding blood flow! They are sometimes referred to as the 'second heart' pumping the venous blood back up to the heart through the veins as they contract and release through movement and exercise. When they're unable to work efficiently, the heart has to work a lot harder. Another reason to get up out of your chair as much as you can!

In Ayurvedic marma therapy, this point is said to control the digestive system and the activity of the small intestine. Massage this point with a strong, circular motion for roughly five minutes.

Acupressure here can increase agni or 'digestive fire' and digestion, especially when your massage oil is combined with essential oils like fennel, ginger, cinnamon or black pepper.

Phana

Meaning 'a serpent's hood' and found at the sides of the nostrils.

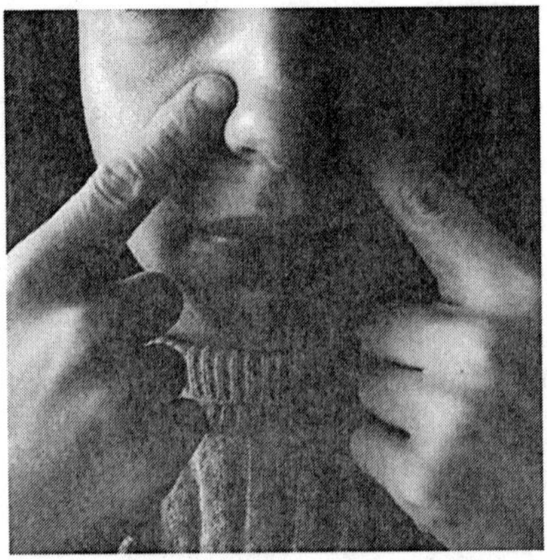

Figure: *Phana marma point on each side of the nostrils*

Each of these two points measures ½ anguli (half a finger unit) in size, and is located just outside the base of the nose, where the nostrils open out. These points are said to control the flow of prana through the subtle body, the sense of smell, and the sinuses.

To massage these points, use a strong and circular motion for about five minutes simultaneously. When using the index finger for acupressure at this point, it is said to help relieve headache symptoms and sinus congestion, and can be even more effective when coupled with aromatic oils like peppermint, eucalyptus or camphor. Choose a massage oil such as mustard or apricot oil if available.

Marma Chikitsa

The word 'marma' means 'hidden', or 'secret'.Marma points are very important elements of Ayurveda's healing power. Marma Analysis by our experts confirms your energy levels and decides treatments accordingly. Developed in India centuries ago, these 108 energy points profoundly affect the body, mind, and spirit and facilitate the deepest levels of healing.

Prana is the current of energy that infuses every cell within the body. Stimulating marmani (energy points) directly taps into this reservoir of energy and promotes health. in ancient Vedic times, marma points were called Bindu - a dot, secret dot, or mystic point. Like a door or pathway, activating a marma point opens into the inner pharmacy of the body.

The body is a silent, universal, biochemical laboratory operating every moment to interpret and transform arising events. Touching a marma point changes the body's biochemistry and can unfold radical, alchemical changes in one's makeup.

Stimulating these inner pharmacy pathways signals the body to produce exactly what it needs, including hormones and neurochemicals that heal the body, mind, and consciousness. This deep dimension of marma therapy has the potential to unfold spiritual healing. Ayurveda refers to the junctures in the body where muscles, veins, ligaments, bones, and joints intersect. Ayurveda also recognizes these points where the three life forces, referred to as the dosha resides in the body.

Benefits of Marma Therapy

Encouraging energetic stimulation through these subtle points results in a multitude of benefits which can be employed by a therapist or through self-care.

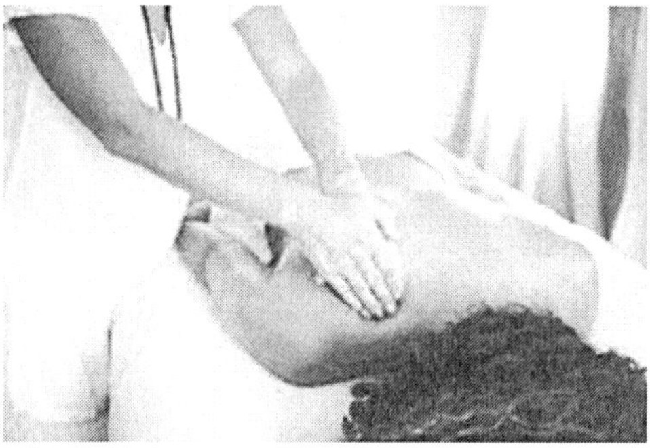

These include but are not limited to:

- greater energy
- enhanced immunity
- relief from localized pain
- relaxation
- sleep support
- increased energy to vital organs
- balancing dosha
- rejuvenation
- detoxification

While we share with you some points you can use for self-care at home, we recommend working with a trained marma therapist for treatment protocols.

How to do Marma Therapy

Techniques of Marma application can include using them in gentle oil massage; deep tissue massage; steady pressure; or application of heat to the marma area.

One nice way to begin is through gentle stimulation to the area. You can apply even pressure with your thumb or index finger. You want to press deep-not excessively-for stimulation, but not to the point of pain. This pressure can be held for 10-15 seconds or breaths. Some therapists like to do gentle circular movements in the area. Give both a try!

The Master Points

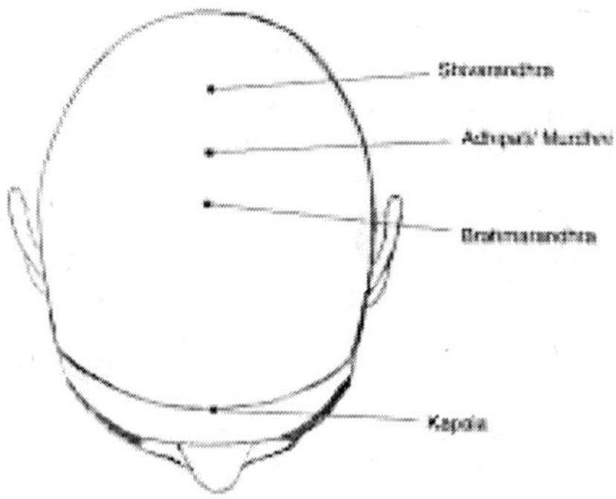

There are three main points known as the "master" points of Marma. They are recommended in every protocol for therapy and we highly recommend you give them a try at home. Use these daily before meditation, as a de-charge and re-charge from work or to wind down at the end of the day. Let us know how you feel!

Murdhni/Adhipati

Located on the vertex at the mid-line of the head

Regulates Prana and supports Prana and Apana Vayu to stabilize

Restores consciousness

Treats motor dysfunction and supports coordination

Supports memory stimulation, attention and concentration

Relieves headaches

Indicated for: stroke, muscle spasms, seizures, migraines, sinus headaches, tension headaches, insomnia, concentration, memory, ADD, nausea, vomiting, congestions, palpitations and emotional disturbances of all doshic origin.

The Vishnu point meaning "moment to moment". It supports mastery of the senses and leads to reduction in mental disturbances of all dosha. This point can also help one gain ESP. It stabilizes prana therefore can be used to balance unsettled energy and ADD in children.

Brahmarandra

Located at the midline of the head 2 anguli (finger widths) anterior to Murdhni

Regulates Sadhaka Pitta

Supports pituitary function

Supports cerebral circulation and activity

Assists creativity, mental function and memory

Calms the mind and emotions

Relieves headaches

Indicated for: migraines, sinus headaches, strokes, vertigo, insomnia, ADD, poor memory, hiccups and high emotions of any doshic origin

The opening of the creator, Brahma, as well as the unfolding of creative intelligence.

It calms the emotions for high vata and kapha nature, promotes creativity intelligence and memory; regulates sadhaka pitta and transforms the mind to a state of calm and expansive consciousness (Brahma Consciousness)

Shivarandhra

Located at the back midline of the head 2 anguli (finger widths) posterior to Murdhni

Regulates Tarpaka Kapha

Relieves headaches

Supports pituitary function and cerebral circulation

Supports memory and calms emotions and the mind

Indicated for: neck pain, spinal arthritis, ringing in the ear, vertigo, insomnia and ADD

The opening point of Shiva. It enhances positive memory and balances Vata disturbances like anxiety, stress and fear of loneliness. It brings a peaceful calm to the mind.

Marma therapy can be a powerful tool to add to your daily self-care practice. We find marma to be a lovely addition to our morning regimen (dinacharya).

Try adding these points to your self oil massage. If you practice full yogic breathing it's a nice time to add awareness to both practices and utilize the stillness of mind to dive into these vital energy points.

Combining Marma Therapy with other Energy Healing Techniques

Marma Therapy can be studied and practiced as its own discipline, though it is best combined with its greater Ayurvedic body of knowledge. There are several other practices in Ayurveda that address the Marma points:

Massage Therapy: Marma is a form of touch therapy and therefore seamlessly translates into massage.

Yoga: One of the objectives of Yoga is to increase and balance the flow of Prana through the mind-body system.

Therefore, working with Marma points complements the practice of the most commonly known Yogic practice of Asana, by emphasizing specific poses or breathwork.

It can also be used as a tool for supporting energy flow with clients in a Yoga Therapy practice.

Marma Therapy: Marma points are stimulated by massage to achieve healing effects to specific areas of the mind-body system. Marmas are sensitive areas so massage should be done carefully.

The duration of the Marma point stimulation should be at least 3-5 minutes.

Panchakarma: The eightfold detoxification process of Panchakarma involves many different types of bodywork therapies for addressing systemic, deeply rooted imbalances and injuries. Panchakarma Therapists can incorporate physiological information about Marma points to support healing and avoid injury during practice.

Surgery (Ancient Context): Sushruta, author of Sushruta Samhita and considered the father of surgery, emphasized the importance of the knowledge of Marma in surgical practice.

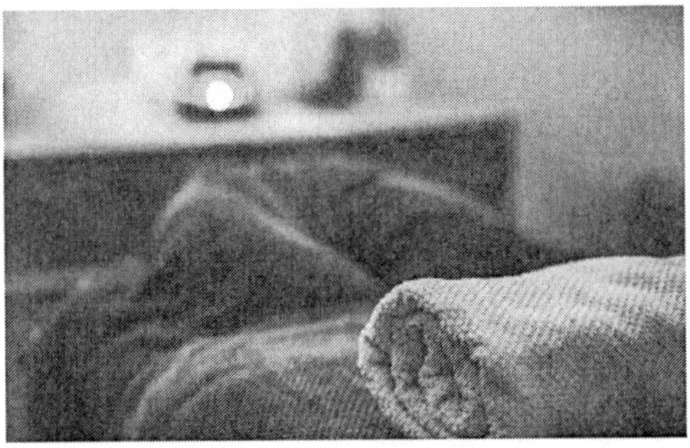

How to Train in and Implement Marma Therapy

Training in Marma Therapy like our Marma Therapy for Energy Healing workshop includes knowledge transfer and hands-on practice. The traditional principles of Marma Therapy include wisdom from Sushruta, Charaka, and Vagbhata. Marma Therapists must learn and memorize the 107 locations of the points, as well as how to conduct a therapeutic stimulation of these points.

In addition to the technicalities of this process, advanced practitioners are trained in assessing an individual's constitution and imbalances for applying clinical Marma support. Because Marma Therapy is a touch-based practice, in order to run a professional Marma practice, the practitioner may be required to possess a license to touch. This requirement is stipulated by state or county and varies across locations.

Although it may seem surprising that a healing tradition like Marma Therapy is so closely linked to practices used in battle, it's important to remember that the Kalari warriors were part of why Ayurveda itself survived colonization. Part of why Ayurveda stands the test of time is due to how holistic in nature it is, encompassing mind, body, and soul, both light and darkness. Just as the Marma points themselves contain all the Doshas, the path of healing is not separate from the wound. Without the wound, there can be no healing.

Marma Point Therapy in Ayurvedic Healing: Expert Explains the Healing Potential of Vital Energy Points

Marma point therapy addresses the mental, emotional, and spiritual facets by concentrating on the body's essential energy points.

With roots in India more than 5,000 years ago, Ayurveda is an age-old holistic healing system that provides a holistic approach to health and wellness. Marma point therapy is a system of healing that targets important energy points in the body to restore balance, promote health, and alleviate a wide range of physical and mental ailments. It is one of its lesser-known but incredibly effective techniques.

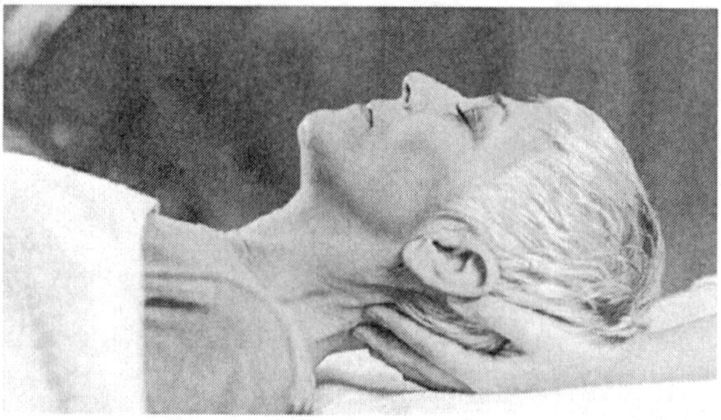

Historical Roots of Marma Point Therapy

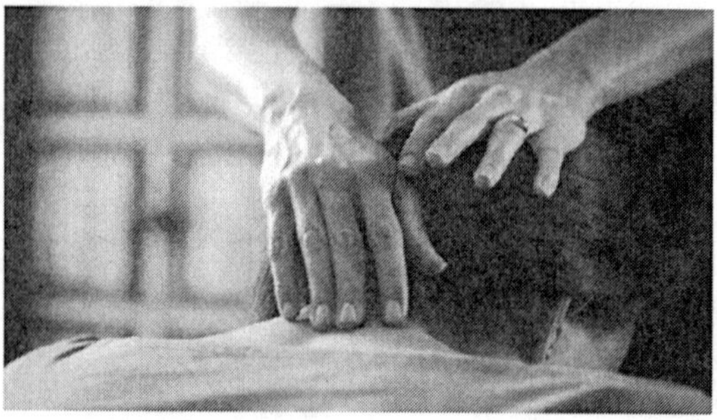

The origins of Marma point therapy can be found in the old Ayurvedic texts, such as the Sushruta Samhita and Charaka Samhita, which provide a thorough understanding of marma points and their therapeutic applications. "According to these writings, the aarmas are crucial locations where a person's metaphysical and physical selves come together. "Marma" itself comes from the Sanskrit word 'mri', which means 'to kill' or 'to die'. This emphasises how crucial these points are and how susceptible they are to damage", said Dr Verma. In traditional Ayurveda, marma points were associated with both physical and spiritual well-being. They were considered to be the meeting points of life force energy, or 'prana' and played a pivotal role in maintaining harmony within the body, mind, and spirit. Marma point therapy was used not only for healing but also in martial arts, as the knowledge of marmas could be used to incapacitate an opponent.

The Philosophy of Marma Point Therapy

The three doshas (Vata, Pitta, and Kapha) and the Ayurvedic concept of balance are the foundations of marma point therapy. Dr Verma informed, "Ayurveda teaches that while imbalances result in diseases, harmony and balance among these doshas produce good health. It is thought that marma points play a crucial role in controlling prana flow and, by extension, the doshas. Incorrect alignment or blockage of these points can result in both physical and psychological disorders."

Key Principles of Marma Point Therapy

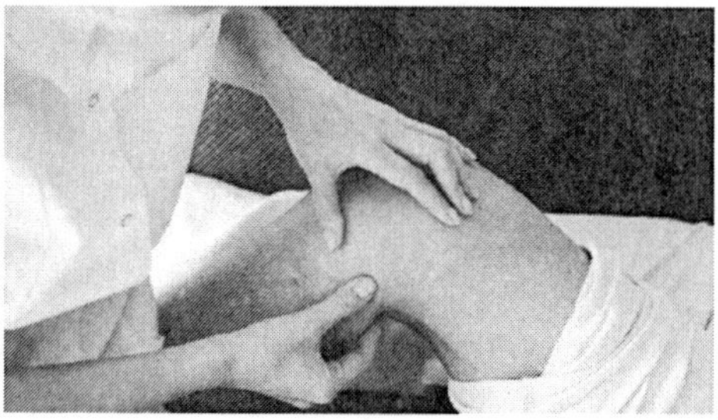

- Prana Flow: Marma points are believed to regulate the flow of prana within the body, ensuring its proper distribution and preventing stagnation.
- Dosha Balance: By stimulating specific Marmas, Ayurvedic practitioners aim to balance the doshas and correct imbalances that may be causing illness or discomfort.
- Holistic Healing: Marma point therapy approaches healing holistically, addressing the physical, mental, and spiritual aspects of an individual's well-being.
- Energy Transformation: The therapy focuses on the transformation of energy, channelling it from imbalanced or blocked points to restore health and harmony.

The Anatomy of Marma Points

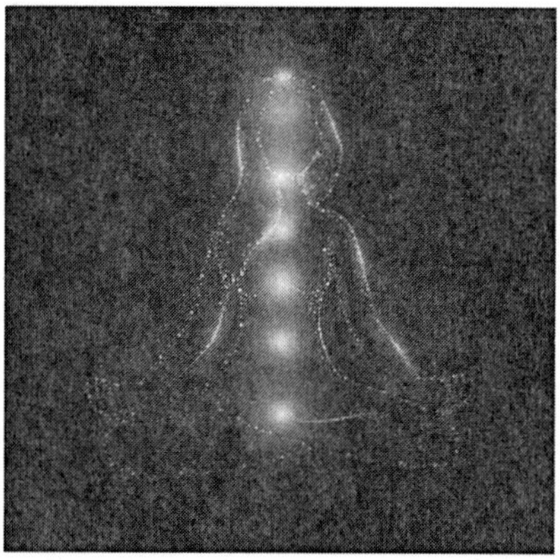

"Marma points are strategically located throughout the body, and they correspond to various anatomical structures such as bones, joints, muscles, and internal organs. They are categorised into different groups based on their anatomical location, which influences their therapeutic applications", highlighted Dr Verma.

Major Categories of Marma Points

- Sthana Marma: Associated with specific organs and anatomical locations
- Bala Marma: Related to the strength and stability of the body
- Kshetra Marma: Concerned with the fields or regions within the body
- Indriya Marma: Tied to sensory organs and their functions
- Mano Marma: Linked to the mind and emotions.

"Every marma point is linked to specific physiological and psychological processes and has a distinct purpose. To balance emotions and enhance emotional well-being, for instance, stimulation of the 'Hridaya Marma', which is situated at the heart centre, is thought to be beneficial", said Dr Verma.

Techniques of Marma Point Therapy

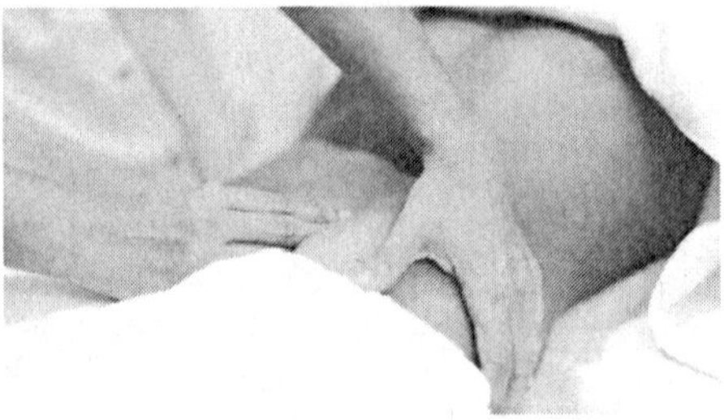

Marma point therapy employs various techniques to stimulate or calm specific Marma points, each with its therapeutic benefits. These techniques may include:

- Massage: Gentle or firm pressure is applied to stimulate the Marma point, releasing blocked energy and promoting relaxation.
- Herbal Poultices: Herbal pastes or poultices are applied to Marma points to alleviate specific conditions and imbalances.
- Acupressure: Specific pressure points are pressed and released to enhance energy flow and alleviate discomfort.
- Essential Oils: Therapeutic oils are used to massage or anoint marma points, providing additional benefits through aromatherapy.

- Meditation and Pranayama: Meditation and controlled breathing techniques can be used to balance marma points, as they are deeply connected to the mind and emotions.

Benefits of Marma Point Therapy

Marma point therapy offers a wide range of physical and mental health benefits. Some of the key advantages include:

- Pain Relief: Marma point therapy can effectively alleviate pain in various parts of the body, such as headaches, joint pain, and muscular discomfort.
- Stress Reduction: By balancing prana and harmonising the doshas, marma therapy helps reduce stress and promote relaxation.
- Improved Circulation: The stimulation of marma points enhances blood and lymphatic circulation, supporting overall health.
- Enhanced Digestion: Certain marma points can be used to improve digestion and alleviate gastrointestinal issues.
- Emotional Balance: By addressing marma points associated with the mind, emotions, and senses, this therapy can promote emotional balance and mental clarity.
- Detoxification: Marma point therapy can aid in the elimination of toxins from the body, thereby promoting detoxification.
- Enhanced Energy: The therapy can revitalise and energise the body, combating fatigue and restoring vitality.

Applications of Marma Point Therapy

Marma point therapy can be used to address a wide range of conditions, including but not limited to:

- Musculoskeletal Disorders: Arthritis, back pain, and muscle tension.

- Neurological Disorders: Headaches, migraines, and nerve pain.
- Gastrointestinal Disorders: Indigestion, constipation, and bloating.
- Emotional and Psychological Issues: Anxiety, depression, and stress.
- Skin Conditions: Eczema, psoriasis, and acne.
- Respiratory Disorders: Allergies, asthma, and bronchitis.
- Women's Health: Menstrual irregularities, PMS, and menopausal symptoms.
- Chronic Fatigue: Low energy, weakness, and lethargy.

Chapter 2

Marma Chikitsa: Unlocking Holistic Healing

Introduction

In a world where modern medicine often takes center stage, there's a growing interest in holistic and traditional healing practices too. Marma Chikitsa (Marma therapy), an ancient Indian healing technique, has gained popularity for its remarkable benefits.

Marma Chikitsa finds its roots in ancient India, dating back thousands of years. The term "Marma" refers to vital or sensitive points on the body, and "Chikitsa" means therapy or treatment. This holistic healing system is closely associated with Ayurveda, the ancient Indian science of life and wellness. It is believed that Marma Chikitsa was initially developed by sages and healers who sought to harness the body's natural energy flow to promote healing and vitality.

Marma Therapy: Unlocking Ancient Energies for Holistic Healing

In the rich tapestry of ancient Indian Ayurveda, Marma Therapy emerges as a sacred thread woven into the fabric of holistic healing. With roots stretching back 5,000 years, this time-honored practice is grounded in the profound understanding that within our bodies lie vital energy channels waiting to be awakened. At the heart of Marma Therapy is the Sanskrit word "marma," signifying vulnerable points, where the convergence of energies holds the key to unlocking healing for the body, mind, and spirit.

Marma Therapy transcends the physical and delves into the subtle energies that flow through these marma points. These energy channels, when activated, facilitate a harmonious balance within the individual, promoting overall well-being. The practitioner of Marma Therapy is akin to an artist, skillfully navigating the body's intricate map to release blocked energies and restore the natural flow of life force.

The fundamental principle of Marma Therapy is to stimulate and balance the flow of prana, or life force, through these vulnerable points. As these energy channels are opened, a cascade of healing is unleashed, addressing not just physical ailments but nurturing the interconnected aspects of mind and spirit.

The therapeutic potential of Marma Therapy spans a spectrum of benefits. From alleviating physical pain and promoting organ health to soothing emotional imbalances and fostering mental clarity, Marma Therapy stands as a holistic approach to healing. By understanding the intricate network of marma points, practitioners can tailor treatments to address specific concerns and promote a profound sense of well-being.

The sacredness of Marma Therapy lies not only in its ancient roots but in its adaptability to the modern world. As individuals seek holistic approaches to health, Marma Therapy provides a bridge between traditional wisdom and contemporary well-being practices. It serves as a reminder that within the ancient lies the timeless, and the energies harnessed through Marma Therapy continue to be a source of profound healing in our fast-paced lives.

In conclusion, Marma Therapy beckons us to explore the subtle realms of our being, tapping into the intricate network of vulnerable points that hold the key to holistic healing. As we embark on this journey, we embrace the wisdom of the ancients and invite the transformative energies of Marma Therapy to weave their magic, restoring balance and vitality to the body, mind, and spirit.

Understanding the Principles

Marma Chikitsa is based on the principle that there are 108 vital points or "marma" scattered throughout the human body. Marma points are vital where muscles, veins, ligaments, bones, and joints meet. These points are considered to be the seats of vital life energy, or "prana," and are believed to have a significant impact on a person's physical and mental well-being.

The prana points are considered the junctions where the mind, body, and consciousness meet. They are believed to be interconnected by energy channels known as "nadis," and any disruption in the flow of energy can lead to physical or emotional imbalances.

The Techniques of Marma Chikitsa

1. Diagnosis through Pulse Reading Marma Chikitsa practitioners often begin by reading the pulse to identify imbalances (Vata, Pitta and Kapha doshas) in the body's vital energy. This diagnostic method helps them pinpoint specific marma points that require attention.
2. Gentle Pressure and Massage Once the imbalances are identified, practitioners use gentle pressure and specialized massage techniques to stimulate or soothe the marma points. This process encourages the free flow of energy throughout the body.

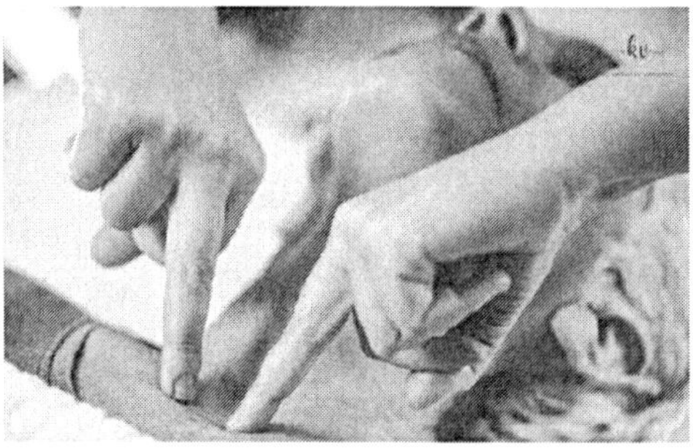

3. Herbal Remedies In conjunction with marma point stimulation, herbal remedies are often prescribed to support the body's natural healing processes. These remedies are tailored to an individual's unique constitution and health needs.

The Benefits of Marma Chikitsa

Marma Chikitsa offers a wide range of benefits for both physical and mental well-being:

1. Pain Relief: Marma Chikitsa is often used to alleviate various types of pain, including joint pain, muscle pain, and headaches. By stimulating specific marma points, it can help release blocked energy and reduce discomfort.
2. Stress Reduction: The therapy involves gentle touch and manipulation, which can induce deep relaxation. This helps in reducing stress and anxiety, promoting mental clarity and emotional balance.
3. Improved Circulation: By working on marma points, Marma Chikitsa can enhance blood circulation and lymphatic flow. This can aid in the removal of toxins from the body and improve overall health.

4. Enhanced Energy Flow: Practitioners believe that marma points are connected to the body's energy channels (nadis). Stimulating these points is thought to balance the flow of energy (prana), promoting vitality and overall well-being.
5. Boosted Immunity: Regular Marma Chikitsa sessions may support the immune system by improving the body's energy balance and reducing stress, which can weaken immune function.
6. Improved Digestion: Marma therapy can be used to address digestive issues by stimulating marma points related to the digestive organs. This may help improve digestion and alleviate gastrointestinal discomfort.
7. Better Sleep: Many people report improved sleep quality after Marma Chikitsa sessions. The relaxation induced by the therapy can help individuals sleep more deeply and peacefully.
8. Enhanced Mental Clarity: The therapy is believed to clear mental blockages and enhance cognitive function. This can lead to improved focus, concentration, and mental clarity.
9. Balanced Emotions: Marma Chikitsa is thought to help balance emotions and relieve emotional imbalances. It can be beneficial for those dealing with stress, depression, or mood swings.
10. Holistic Healing: Marma Chikitsa takes a holistic approach to healing, addressing both physical and energetic aspects of health. It can complement other healing modalities and traditional medical treatments.

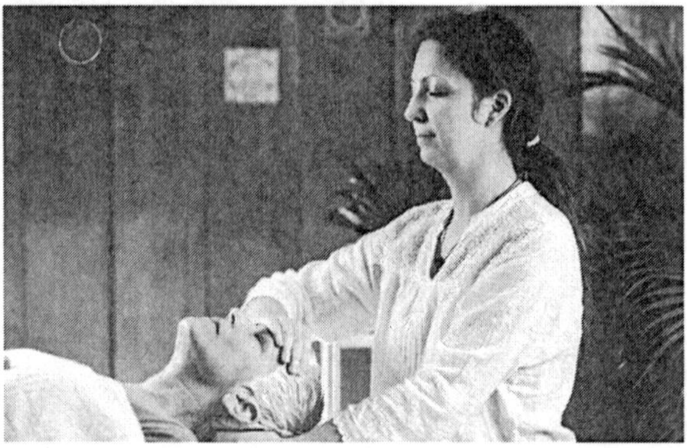

Incorporating Marma Chikitsa into Your Life

If you're interested in exploring the benefits of Marma Chikitsa, it's essential to seek guidance from a qualified practitioner. They can create a personalised treatment plan tailored to your specific needs and health goals. Marma Chikitsa offers a unique and holistic approach to healing that has stood the test of time.

Its rich history, therapeutic benefits, and potential to enhance overall well-being make it a valuable addition to anyone's journey towards optimal health. Whether you're seeking pain relief, stress reduction, or improved energy flow, Marma Chikitsa has much to offer. Consult professional Marma chikitsa experts at Vardhan Ayurveda. Embrace this ancient healing art and unlock the secrets to holistic well-being.

Experience the Power of Marma Chikitsa

In the era of holistic healing, Marma Chikitsa is an important practice in Ayurveda. Derived from the Sanskrit words "Marma" (meaning vital point) and "Chikitsa" (meaning treatment), this ancient therapeutic technique targets specific energy points in the body to promote healing and balance.

Understanding Marma Chikitsa

Marma points are junctions where various tissues, such as muscles, veins, ligaments, and bones, meet. They are considered vital energy centres that govern the flow of prana (life force energy) within the body. Marma Chikitsa involves the gentle manipulation and stimulation of these points to restore balance and alleviate imbalances.

Benefits of Marma Chikitsa

Pain Relief: By addressing specific marma points associated with pain, this therapy can offer relief from chronic discomfort, whether it's related to muscles, joints, or internal organs.

Stress Reduction: Marma Chikitsa helps release stored tension and stress from the body, promoting deep relaxation and a sense of calm.

Improved Circulation: By targeting marma points related to blood flow, this therapy can enhance circulation, promoting better nutrient and oxygen delivery to tissues.

Enhanced Energy Flow: Balancing the flow of prana through marma points revitalizes the body's energy, leaving you feeling rejuvenated and invigorated.

Emotional Balance: Certain marma points are associated with emotional well-being. Stimulating these points can help balance emotions and promote mental clarity.

Immune Support: Marma Chikitsa can support the immune system by ensuring that vital energy flows freely through the body, strengthening its natural defence mechanisms.

Finding the Best Marma Chikitsa Near Me

The search for "Marma Chikitsa" is a journey towards holistic well-being. It's essential to choose a reputable Ayurvedic clinic or practitioner who specializes in Marma Chikitsa. Look for qualifications, experience, and client testimonials to ensure you're in the right hands.

A reputable Marma Chikitsa practitioner will conduct a good assessment, considering your unique constitution and any specific health concerns. This personalized approach ensures that the therapy is compatible with your individual needs.

The Marma Chikitsa Experience

During a session, you can expect gentle and precise manipulation of specific marma points using fingers, hands, or specialized tools. This process is typically painless and deeply relaxing. The therapist will guide you through the experience, creating a safe and nurturing environment.

Post-Treatment Care: After a Marma Chikitsa session, it's advisable to take some time for rest and relaxation. Hydration and a light, nourishing meal can further support the body's healing process.

Embarking on the quest for "Marma Chikitsa" is a step towards holistic healing and well-being. This ancient practice offers a unique approach to balance and vitality, targeting vital energy points within the body. By choosing a qualified practitioner and experiencing the personalized benefits of Marma Chikitsa, you open the door to a journey of self-care and rejuvenation. Remember, it's essential to consult a certified Ayurvedic practitioner for personalized advice and treatments.

Asana (Postures) and Effect on Marma

The word asana can be commonly translated as posture. Its literal meaning is the seat or posture adopted during meditation, which promote the mental concentration. As a rule a healthy mind lives in a healthy body, and these postures give a positive effect on health and may cure a number of diseases.

As you know we adopt some postures for different routine or specific works. As for cycle or motorcycle driving we have to adopt a specific posture, or office work or computer work needs sitting posture on a chair, in the same way, during self-marma therapy we have to adopt specific postures to derive maximum benefit from the technique.

How do yogic postures and pranayama affect the body and mind? What is the scientific explanation of it? How one can reenergize the body and mind by adopting some specific postures for a few minutes? These are few questions, which come in the mind of a yoga student or practitioner.

In reply to these questions it is very important to understand the importance of marma points. These marma have control on different body functions and any trauma to these parts may give rise to many complications. By yogic postures and pranayama, by their stretch, pressure, vibration and rhythmic movement, the activity of marma get affected. It also affects the functioning of the organ related to the particular marma. It is apparent that the yogic postures and pranayama affects the body and mind by the stimulation of marma. All the yogic postures in which the body is moved forward and backward affect the marma of abdomen, chest and back. These marma can be energized by regular practice of yoga and pranayama.

One can achieve the same benefits of exercises with the selfmarma therapy. As we know that exercise is necessary for the body strength and normal body functioning, we can say that self-marma therapy is a short cut key to the yoga, pranayama and other physical exercises.

The important yogic postures and pranayama are discussed with their effects.

Lotus Pose (Padmasana):-

In this posture the base of the legs looks like a lotus. So it is known as Padmasana. Tomake the proper lotus pose sit on the floor with crossed legs. Raise the left foot up onto right thigh, as near to the anterior part of right hip joint as possible; place right foot on the left thigh, near to the anterior part of the left hip joint. During this posture the knee should be placed on the surface and the soles should be in upward direction. Keep the head, neck, and spine in a straight line; hands should rest on knees. This is the best pose for meditation. During this pose breathe naturally. Women are suggested to reverse the legs, placing the left foot on top.

Benefits:- Regular practice of Lotus pose calms the mind and pushes the prana into sushumna. The position of the crossed legs holds the spine in its natural curve; allows the vital organs to fall into correct position; gives rest to the heart; and makes hips, knees and ankles flexible. Regular practice of padmasana improves the psychosomatic functions. It purifies the whole nervous system of the body by the energy accumulated at muladhara chakra. When the whole nervous system gets purified it is helpful to keep the body Healthy physically and mentally. So this posture is useful in many psychosomatic disorders and helps in a number of sexual ailments.

In this posture both heels are paced over the vitapa marma. During lotus pose continuous pressure over vitapa marma is helpful in inguinal hernia, hydrocele, varicocele and it improves the function of the urogenital system. When a person practices the aswini mudra during lotus pose it stimulates the central nervous system and it cures haemorrhoids, prolapsed rectum, prolapsed uterus, benign prostatic hyperplasia and atony bladder. For self-marma therapy it is the most suitable pose for the stimulation of marma of lower extremity especially kshipra, tala hridaya, kurca and kurcasira. This postures stimulates the marma of lower extremity especially gulpha(ankle joint) and janu (knee joint).

It is the most popular pose of yogis. Regular practice of adept's pose provides many physical and spiritual gains. After sitting on crossed leg posture place left heel under the testicles and lift the right heel resting on the genitalia and over the left heel. Head, neck and spine should be in a straight line. There should be no extra pressure on the genitalia and testicles. Women should place left heel in front of anus, right heel on top of left. Keep head, neck, and spine in a straight line and breathe naturally.

Benefits:- Adept's pose purifies the nervous system. It helps in maintaining celibacy or continence. It pushes vital energy, prana, into susumna. In this posture the heels provide pressure on guda and vasti marma and it is helpful to eradicate the diseases of anorectal region and urogenital system. It is very useful in atony bladder, retention of urine, urinary incontinence, benign prostatic hyperplasia and anorectal disease. After the age of 45 years every person should practice adepts pose regularly to avoid the urogenital problems. This pose is highly recommended for meditation.

Cow's Head Pose (Gomukhasana)

To adopt Cow's Head pose sit with right leg folded over left; as a result the right knee will be above the left knee. Try to bring the feet towards the back, resting at the side of the hips. Raise right arm overhead and bend the elbow so that the hand hangs down at the back. Place left hand behind back and take hold of right hand. Breathe in slowly and extend by pulling up with right arm and down with left arm. Hold the breath during pose, keeping spine, neck and head in straight line, right arm up and held down with left arm. Breathe out slowly, reversing legs and arms. Repeat the pose on the other side in the same manner. Persons who cannot clasp the hands may bring together the upper hand and lower hand as much as possible

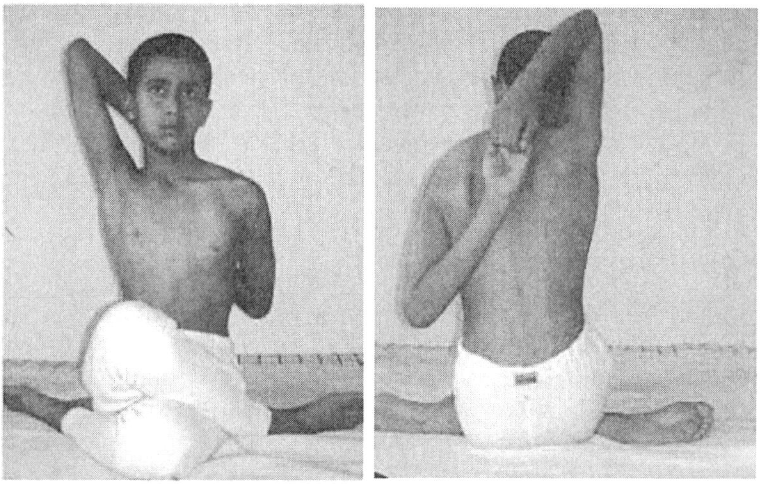

Benefits:- Regular practices of Cow's Head pose strengthens the spine. It aids in celibacy, helps remove muscular pains in the back and shoulders, cures abdominal weaknesses, andalleviates indigestion and insomnia. In this pose, marmas of the back, thorax and abdomen, and upper and lower extremities get affected.

Shoulder Stand Pose (Sarvangasana)

To adopt this pose lie flat on the back with arms parallel to body. Raise legs slowly until they make a right angle with the body trunk. Then with the arms flat on the floor raise the body straight up on shoulders with the head and shoulders resting on the ground, balance on the shoulders and breathe naturally. One can support the back with the hands during this pose

Benefits:- it strengthens the entire body. It regulates the functions of thyroid and parathyroid glands. It improves the metabolic activities of the body and the function of endocrine system, cardiovascular system, respiratory system and nervous system. One can get all benefits of headstand pose. In this pose the blood circulation increases in chest, neck and brain. In this posture amsa, amsa phalaka, vrihati, parsvasandhi, hridaya, stanamula, stanarohita, apalapa, all marms of neck and head get affected.

Plough Pose (Halasana):-

In continuation of the Shoulder Stand pose, lower the legs over the head keeping knees and arms straight. Touch the floor with the toes. After a few seconds inhale slowly and return back to shoulderstand pose. In the same way ear-knee pose (karnapidasana) can be adopted by bending legs and bringing knees forward and towards the ears. Hold the breath out in the pose; then inhale slowly and return to shoulder stand and inhale slowly, then exhale into the ear-knee pose. The plough pose is complementary to the bow pose.

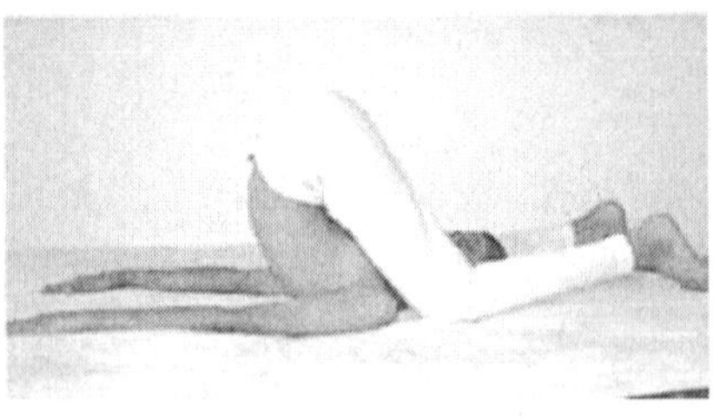

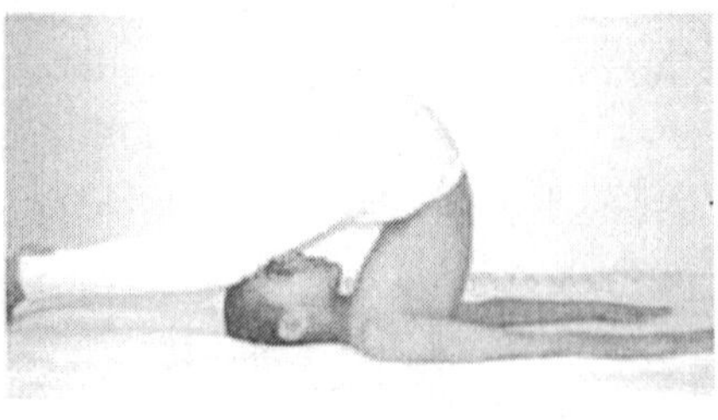

Benefits:- In addition it tones spinal nerves, muscles of the back, and the sympathetic nervous system. Makes the spine flexible, prevents laziness, and relieves constipation. In this posture amsa, amsa phalaka, vrihati, parsvasandhi, hridaya, stanamula, stanarohita, apalapa, all marmas of neck and head get affected. Krikatika marma is very much affected during the flexion of neck over the chin.

Wind-Releasing Pose (Pavanmuktasana):

To adopt this pose lie on the back, inhale slowly and fold the left knee onto the chest, pulling it firm by clasping the hands around it, trying to touch head to knee, keeping the right leg straight. Hold the breath during pose; subsequently exhale while lowering leg and head. Repeat with right leg; and then with both legs together.

Benefits:- Releases abdominal flatulence, improves indigestion, and reduces abdominal fat. It gives positive effect on the inflammatory lesions of large intestine and other abdominal organs. In this posture vitapa, lohitaksha, vasti and nabhi and thorax marma get affected.

Fish Pose (Matsyasana):-

To adopt this pose lie on the back with arms at the sides; then, by pushing down on the floor with the elbows, inhale slowly and curve the back so that the top of the head rests on the floor. Try to raise the chest as high as achievable. Place hands on chest, palms together, with fingers pointing towards chin. Hold breath in pose; then exhale slowly and return to starting position. The Fish pose is a counter pose for the Shoulder stand, and is complementary to the Rabbit Pose (sasakasana).

Benefits:- Regular practice of the Fish pose expands the chest, strengthens the lungs, and brings oxygenated blood to the thyroid and parathyroid glands. It is useful for asthma and bronchitis. In this posture kakshadhara, vitapa, lohitaksha, vasti and nabhi and thorax marma get affected. It also affects the krikatika, adhipati and simanta marmas.

Cobra Pose (Bhujangasana)

To adopt this pose lie face down on the floor. Place palms on floor at the side of shoulders. Inhale and slowly raise head and chest, arching the neck in hyper extension looking up and back. Hold breath during pose; subsequently exhale and come down slowly. This pose is complementary to the back-stretching exercises.

Benefit:- Regular practice of Cobra pose makes the spine stretchy; relieves gastro-intestinal disorders; expands the chest, in this manner strengthening the lungs and heart; awakens kundalini. The cobra pose is recommended for women after childbirth because it strengthens the reproductive organs and other organs of thorax and abdomen. In this posture kakshadhara, vitapa, lohitaksha, vasti and nabhi, thorax marma and marma of lower extremity get affected.

Bow Pose (Dhanurasana)

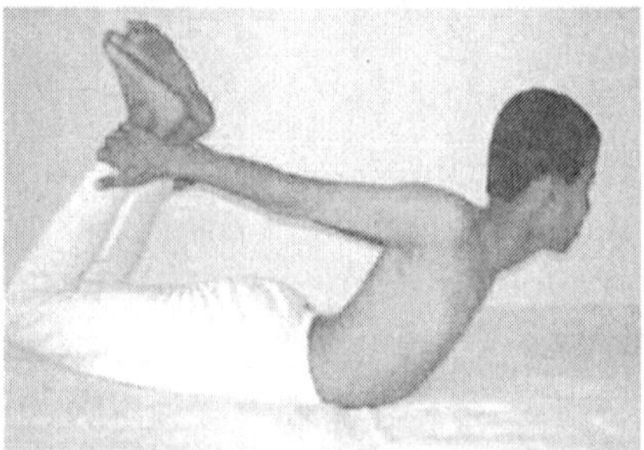

To adopt this pose lie face down on the floor. Bend the knees, try to reach back and hold the ankles with hands. Inhale and try to lift head, chest, and thighs as high as possible, stretching the body into a bow shape. Try to keep the head back. Hold breath during pose; subsequently exhale slowly releasing legs and coming down. The Bow pose is opposite to the Plough pose.

Benefits:- Regular practice of the Bow pose strengthens the spine, intestines, liver, and kidneys; improves digestion; reduces fat; and makes the body flexible. In this posture vitapa, lohitaksha, vasti and nabhi and thorax marma and marma of lower extremity get affected.

Wheel Pose (Chakrasana)

To adopt this pose lie on the back, put the hands beside the ears, palms down and fingers pointing towards the feet. Try to bend the knees and pull the feet close to the hips. Subsequently inhale slowly and raise body up and try to balance on hands and feet. Hold breath during pose; afterwards exhale at the same time as lowering the body back to floor.

Benefits:- Regular practice of Wheel pose affects the whole body, especially the spine; strengthens the upper and lower extremities. It gives vitality, strength, energy and sensation of lightness. In this posture vitapa, lohitaksha, vasti and nabhi and thorax marma and marma of back and both extremities get affected.

Half Spinal Twist Pose (Ardha Matsyendrasana)

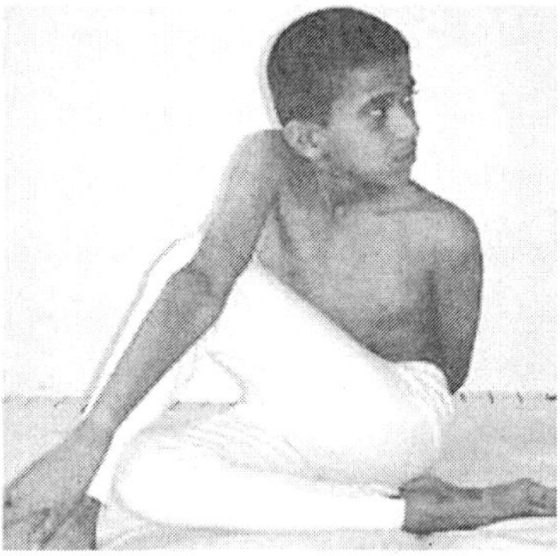

To adopt this pose sit with right heel folded at the side of the left hip. Try to raise the left knee, cross left foot over the folded right leg. Put left foot flat on floor beside the right thigh. Try to bring right upper arm around to the outside of left knee and grab left foot with right hand. Bend left arm behind back, inhale, and twist spine and head to the left, looking back over the left shoulder as far as possible. (Straighten spine, neck, and head by stretching torso upward before twisting.) Hold breath during pose; afterwards exhale and untwist slowly. Reverse legs and arms and repeat.

Benefits:- Regular practice of Half Spinal Twist pose gives strength, flexibility to the body and oxygenated blood supply to the spine and abdominal organs. It increases appetite, metabolic process and digestion. Retards aging; tones the nervous system; and strengthens the reproductive glands. In this posture vitapa, lohitaksha, vasti and nabhi and thorax marma and marma of back and both extremities get affected.

Yogamudrasana

Sit in Lotus pose. Cross arms behind the back and grab the left big toe with the left hand, and the right big toe with right hand, or simply grip left wrist with right hand behind the back. Inhale deeply, then exhale and slowly bend forward, resting forehead on the floor. Hold breath out in pose; then inhale and sit up. When used as a meditation posture, breathe naturally and concentrate on ajna chakra.

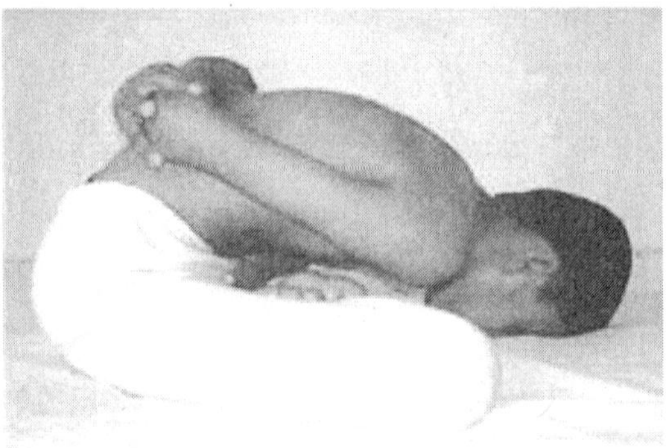

Benefits:- It intensifies the benefits of Lotus pose. It also increases memory and gastric fire; strengthens the spine, waist, lungs, heart, and abdomen. In this posture vitapa, lohitaksha, vasti and nabhi and thorax marma and marma of back and both extremities get affected.

Nobility Pose (Bhadrasana)

Sit on the floor. Bring soles of feet together, clasp hands around feet, and pull heels in as close to the body as possible. Inhale slowly and press knees down towards the floor, keeping spine, neck, and head in a straight line. Hold breath in pose. Concentrate on ajna chakra. Exhale slowly and release. In a variation hands are placed on the knees, pressing them down gently. The Nobility pose can be used as a meditation pose, breathing naturally.

Benefits:- Relieves urinary disorders and sciatic pain; keeps the kidneys, prostate, bladder, and ovaries functioning properly; strengthens the reproductive glands and aids in celibacy.Recommended for women, as it helps regulate the menstrual cycle; also recommended during pregnancy. In this posture vitapa, lohitaksha, vasti and nabhi. guda and thorax marma and marma of back and both extremities get affected.

Frog Pose (Mandukasana)

To adopt this pose sit in Thunderbolt pose and close the hands by putting thumbs inside. Now place both the closed hands around the umbilicus and try to bend forward, exhaling breath and keeping sight forward. Keeping this pose for a while come back to the Thunderbolt pose. This can be repeated three to five times.

Benefits:- during this pose there is direct pressure on abdominal organs. It improves the function of the pancreas. It increases the amount of insulin and improves the quality of gastric and liver juices. It is good for abdominal ailments. It improves the function of heart and lungs. In this posture vitapa, lohitaksha, vasti and nabhi and thorax marma and marma of back and both extremities get affected.

Peacock Pose (Mayurasana)

Kneeling on the floor, with arms resting in front of the body on the palms, inhale and bring head off the floor by shifting the body slightly towards the feet. Then raise the legs by shifting body forward again. Hold breath while balancing on the hands; then exhale slowly lowering head and feet. Either return to kneeling position or relax in the Reverse Relaxation Pose. (Uttana Shavasana).

Benefits:- Increases digestive fire, alleviating indigestion and constipation; is helpful for diabetes, haemorrhoids, and inflammation of the intestines or liver; stimulates circulation of blood in the abdomen; tones the lungs; rouses kundalini; and strengthens the wrists, arms, and abdominal muscles. In this posture vitapa, lohitaksha, vasti and nabhi and thorax marma and marma of back and both extremities get affected.

Thunderbolt Pose (Vajrasana)

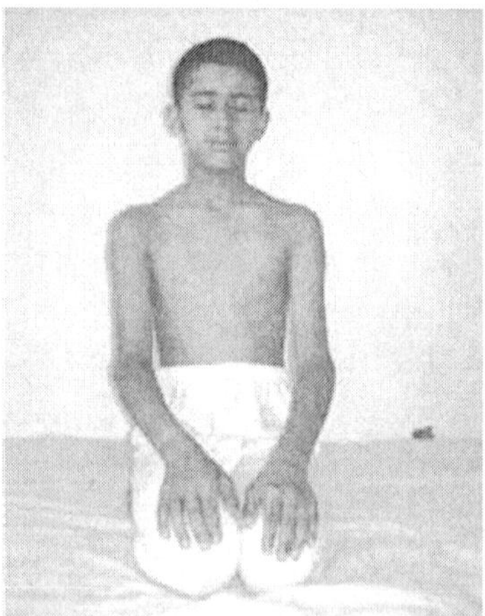

Kneel and sit on calves, knees together. Place hands on knees, keeping arms and back straight. Either close the eyes, or focus on the tip of the nose. Breathe slowly and deeply. This pose can be used for meditation. This is the one asana that may be practiced directly after eating.

Benefits:- Calms the mind; aids digestion. In this posture vitapa, lohitaksha, vasti and nabhi and thorax marma and marma of back and both extremities get affect.

Lying Thunderbolt Pose (Supt vajrasana)

To adopt this pose sit in Thunderbolt pose and try to lie on the back. In this posture bot thighs should be placed together. Hands should be kept on thighs. During the reversal of pose take the support of elbows and hands.

Benefits:- Regular practice of Lying Thunderbolt pose gives stretch on lower abdominal part and lower extremity. It stimulates the function of large intestine and regulates the bowel. It is useful in hemorrhoids, constipation and the diseases of urogenital system. In this posture vitapa, lohitaksha, vasti and nabhi and thorax marma and marma of back and both extremities get affected.

Relaxation Pose (Shavasana):-

To adopt this pose lie flat on the back like a corpse, keeping arms at the sides and head rolled slightly to one side. Close eyes and relax; breathing should be natural. The mind should be calm and thoughtless. Practice the Relaxation pose after each series, or after several strenuous poses, for fifteen to twenty seconds. At the end of asana practice, do this pose for five to ten minutes. It is also recommended to practice this after pranayama and meditation.

Benefits:- The Relaxation pose facilitates blood circulation; it relieves fatigue and reduces stress and depression. Practice of Relaxation pose gives soothing effect on total body marma.

Conclusion about Marma and Yoga

In concluding this section on Yoga and Marma, we can therefore see the close and astounding inter-relationship between the two practices, the practice of Marma being inherent in the Yogic postures. In all the higher yogic practices as well, like the various pranayama and mudras, as well as concentration / meditation on the chakras, various marma points get affected and stimulated. Thus, it can be remarked, extending this perception, that self-marma therapy in itself can be considered as a Yogic practice.

Enhancing Your Vitality with Marma Therapy: Rejuvenate Your Body and Mind

In a fast-paced world where stress and ailments take control, ancient wisdom holds the key to rejuvenation and holistic healing.

Ayurveda, the timeless Indian system of medicine, and its profound companion, Marma Therapy, provide a harmonious blend of knowledge and practice.

Marma Therapy

Marma therapy is an integral part of Ayurveda, which deals with the stimulation of vital points in the body known as "marma points." Marma can be translated as hidden or vital points according to Ayurveda. These points are considered the intersections of energy channels (nadis) and are believed to be the seats of the life force (prana) in the body. There are 107 marma points throughout the body, and each of them has a specific therapeutic value. Gently stimulating certain areas along the body helps to rejuvenate the body, eliminate any negative energy, and promote physical circulation, all of which improve the functioning of specific body components.

The Benefits of Marma Therapy

The therapy offers immense benefits to Individuals suffering from various ailments. The holistic therapy act as a gateway to relief from pain and discomfort, a journey to rejuvenating the body, and a path towards enhancing circulation and overall well-being. Continue reading the blog 'Enhancing Your Vitality with Marma Therapy: Rejuvenate Your Body and Mind', as we delve into the therapeutic advantages that encompass stress reduction, relaxation, and even improved sleep quality.

- Balancing energy flow Marma points are considered the extremely vital energy centres in an individual's body. So the therapy will stimulate the points which aid to balance the flow of energy and help to promote good energy and overall health.
- Relieves Pain and Discomfort This therapy is quite effective in helping with various types of pain and discomfort such as headaches, joint pain, muscle tension and general body aches. During the procedure, experienced practitioners will try to stimulate the marma points. Besides Marma therapy also helps to relieve blocked energy and reduce inflammation and the body's natural pain relieving mechanism.
- Rejuvenates the body In Ayurveda, marma therapy is thought to renew and revitalise the body by restoring the equilibrium of the three doshas - Vata, Pitta, and Kapha. When these doshas work together harmoniously, the body operates properly and the ageing process is slowed. The therapist can trigger the body's self-healing capacities by targeting specific marma spots,

resulting in enhanced vitality, improved energy levels, and a sense of overall well-being.

- Enhances Circulation Stimulating marma points during therapy will enhance both blood and lymphatic circulation. It also has a direct impact on the immune system too. Marma therapy can assist in breaking up stagnation and congestion in the blood and lymphatic systems, increasing overall health and preventing numerous circulatory illnesses.
- Stress reduction and Relaxation Marma therapy is quite known for its soothing calming efforts on the body and mind. The therapy can induce deep relaxation by targeting certain areas of marma points associated with stress relief like the forehead and temples. It will also help with our hormone levels, lowering blood pressure and even helps with tension and anxiety issues.
- Improves Sleep Quality Marma points are also connected with promoting better sleeping and even balancing your nervous system. People can incorporate marma therapy into their wellness routine and can improve their sleep patterns and get a good night's sleep.

Diseases Which can be Treated Using Marma Therapy

- Muscle and joint pains
- Respiratory Diseases
- Digestion related issues
- Nervos system problems
- Headaches
- Ageing disorders
- Migraine
- Psychological issues
- Muscle Strains
- Low energy
- Carpel Tunnel Syndrome
- Paralysis like Bell's palsy

In summary, Marma Therapy presents a myriad of benefits for the body and mind. Starting from pain relief to rejuvenation and enhanced circulation, this ancient practice offers transformative results. You can experience relaxation and reduced stress by activating vital energy points by professional and experienced practitioners.

Chapter 3

Ayurvedic Treatment and Principles of Marmas

Introduction

Ayurveda, the ancient holistic system of medicine, offers a comprehensive approach to healing that encompasses various modalities, including the manipulation of vital energy points known as "marmas." These marmas are pivotal in Ayurvedic treatment, serving as gateways through which the body's vital energy flows. Understanding the principles of marmas is essential for practitioners and enthusiasts alike, as they play a significant role in promoting health and well-being.

At the core of Ayurvedic philosophy lies the belief that optimal health is achieved when there is a harmonious balance of the three doshas - Vata, Pitta, and Kapha - along with proper digestion, elimination, and a robust immune system. Marmas contribute to this balance by facilitating the smooth flow of Prana, the life force energy, throughout the body. Any disruption or imbalance in these energy points can lead to physical, mental, or emotional disturbances. The concept of marmas is not exclusive to Ayurveda; it is also integral to Yoga and other traditional Indian healing systems.

In Yoga, these energy points are referred to as "chakras" and are associated with spiritual awakening and personal transformation. However, in Ayurveda, marmas are primarily considered from a therapeutic perspective, with specific emphasis on their anatomical location, physiological functions, and therapeutic applications. Ayurvedic texts classify marmas based on their location, depth, and the impact of their manipulation. There are 107 marmas distributed throughout the body, with varying degrees of vulnerability and significance. Some marmas are relatively superficial and easily accessible, while others are deep-seated and require precise knowledge and skill to manipulate safely.

The therapeutic principles governing the manipulation of marmas are guided by the individual's unique constitution, known as Prakriti, as well as their current state of imbalance, or Vikriti. Ayurvedic practitioners assess these factors to determine the most appropriate treatment approach, which may include gentle pressure, massage, herbal remedies, or energetic techniques.

The therapeutic benefits of marma manipulation are manifold. By stimulating or calming the flow of Prana through these vital energy points, Ayurvedic treatments can alleviate pain, improve circulation, enhance organ function, and promote overall vitality. Additionally, marmas are believed to influence the mind and emotions, making them valuable tools for managing stress, anxiety, and other psychosomatic conditions. One of the fundamental principles of Ayurvedic treatment is the concept of "do no harm" (Ahimsa). Therefore, practitioners must approach marma therapy with caution and respect for the body's innate intelligence.

Proper training, anatomical knowledge, and a deep understanding of Ayurvedic principles are essential prerequisites for working with marmas safely and effectively. Ayurvedic treatment and the principles of marmas offer a holistic approach to health and well-being that integrates body, mind, and spirit. By harnessing the inherent wisdom of the body and its subtle energy pathways, Ayurvedic practitioners can facilitate profound healing and transformation. Whether used as a standalone therapy or as part of a comprehensive treatment plan, marma therapy holds immense potential for promoting optimal health and vitality in individuals of all ages and backgrounds.

Marma Points of Ayurveda

Ayurvedic Body Techniques, Ayurvedic Medicine

Based on centuries of intuitive wisdom and field-tested knowledge, marma chikitsa (therapy) is an essential hands-on Ayurvedic practice that often delivers profound mind-body benefits. This practical application of ancient Ayurvedic principles is defined by the renowned Ayurvedic physician Dr. Vasant Lad as "the precise art of touching an individual in exactly the right place at a critical moment in time for the purpose of healing." Similar to the acupoints described in Chinese medicine, marma points, or marmani, are specific locations on the body where our mental and physical energies can be accessed and adjusted or redirected.

These access points occur in areas where veins, arteries, bones, tendons, or joint intersect. In Sanskrit the word marmameans "mortal or vulnerable point," suggesting that these areas may be tender, weak, or sensitive. Located along the nadis-the energy channels that prana(the life-force) flows through-marma points are used in Ayurvedic medicine to promote communication between the body and mind as well as between cells, maintaining and coordinating their functional activities and transmitting healing energy to organs and tissues.

Stimulation of a marma point that relates to a particular tissue can be used to not only help maintain the normal functioning of that tissue but also to address a specific imbalance (vikruti) in our elemental makeup by either increasing or reducing the predominance of a particular dosha, thus restoring our constitution (prakruti) to its natural intended state. The activation of marma points also produces a powerful response in the mind, helping to calm it while increasing the clarity of perception and empowering more effective communication.

Often these points are used as a mechanism of pain relief. Pain is generated when tension and stagnation in the body block the flow of prana to a particular part of our body, disrupting the delicate equilibrium of the doshas associated with that area. Marma chikitsa alleviates this pain by stimulating the flow of prana to the affected area, pacifying the accumulated dosha.

There are 117 primary marma points that are classified according to their location; constituent elements; degree of vitality; and associated doshas, tissues (dhatus), bodily wastes (malas), organs, and physical channels (srotamsi). The power of the marmani is intimately connected with the basic components of the vital essence of life (ojas, tejas, and prana). Marma chikitsa is rarely used in isolation; more often it's employed as a part of a comprehensive, multifaceted treatment program.

To design this type of program, an Ayurvedic practitioner must have a broad and deep understanding of the etiology and symptomatology of disease and the stages of pathogenesis as well as sensitivity and skill in Ayurvedic diagnosis. However, marma chikitsa can also be used for immediate pain relief, long-term pain management, and first aid. Although marma therapy alone may not eradicate the disease process completely, it can give temporary symptomatic relief and may prevent serious complications from arising.

Marma points reflect the qualities of the region of the body where they reside and the internal and external features of the corresponding doshas and subdoshas.

Sushruta, an expert Ayurvedic surgeon in ancient India, described marmani according to the six major parts of the body: the four extremities, the trunk, the head and the neck. He also defines the points in relation to the five principal components of the body's physical structures: mamsa(muscle), sira(veins), snayus(ligaments), asthi(bone) and sandhi(joints).

The marmani on the scalp are connected to the brain as well as to organs situated in other parts of the body. On the chest and upper back, the points are connected with the heart and lungs. The points on the lower back are connected with the kidneys, stomach, and the digestive organs. Each of the areas where marmani reside is associated one of the five constituent elements of the body (space, air, fire, water, and earth), and each marma point activates the energy of the element associated with its location.

The language of the doshas is absolutely key to understanding the Ayurvedic viewpoint on health and disease. Knowing how marma points affect the dosha that predominates in a particular region of the body is crucial to achieving excellent therapeutic results. For example, chest and lung marma points stimulate kapha, umbilical points affect pitta, and colon points will influence vata.

There are eight great marma points that are essential to life. These marmani house the greatest concentration of vital energies of all the points. Sushruta described how injuries at these marma points, whether superficial or deep, can disrupt the flow of prana, decreasing vitality and even causing life-threatening damage.

These points are known as the sadyah pranahara marmani: murdhani(crown), brahmarandhara (anterior to crown), shivarandhra(posterior to crown), ajna(third eye), shanka(right and left temple), hrdayam(heart), habhi (umbilicus), and uda(anus). The illustration below shows these eight marmani, as well as five other vital points-kantha, griva, basti, vrushana, and yoni jihva-that can cause death or serious injury when traumatized.

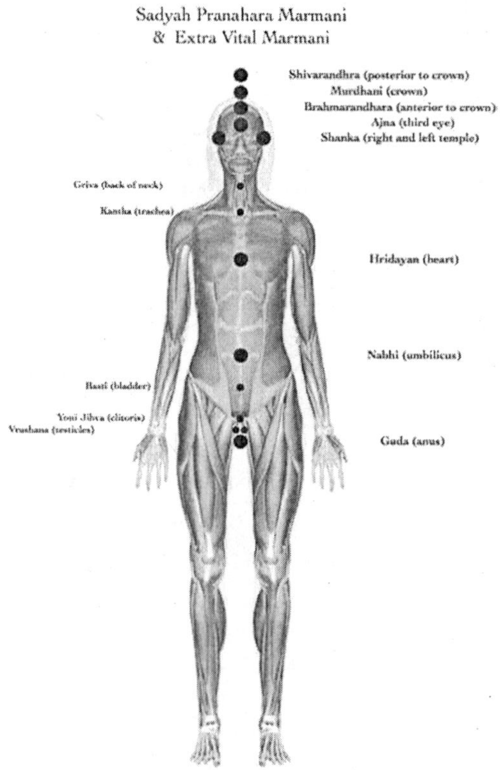

While marma points are the most vulnerable areas of our body, they also hold great potential to improve our health and well-being. Each of the following marma points provides access to specific health benefits:

- Anja - benefits the eyes and nose, regulates hormones, and improves pituitary function
- Shivarandhra - stimulates memory, calms the mind, and balances emotions
- Hrdayam - directs the healing energy of love to the heart
- Nabhi - enkindles gastrointestinal agni(digestive fire)
- Murdhani - stimulates blood flow in the cerebral cortex and the circulation of the cerebrospinal fluid
- Brahmarandhara - relieves headache and optimizes the functioning of the pituitary gland
- Shankha - strongly pacifies pitta, relieves stomach pain and excess acidity, improves speech

- Griva - boosts circulation of plasma and lymphatic fluid, benefits the throat and thyroid
- Guda - balances strength, vitality, and stability

In general, stimulating the marmani enhances the flow of prana. The manipulation of marma points can be quite effective when used on its own to treat mild and short-term illnesses and dysfunctions. As the complexity of a disease increases, other Ayurvedic therapies become essential. These may include herbal or dietary recommendations, panchakarma, and exercise and lifestyle changes.

Marma Therapy for a Beautiful Skin and Peaceful Mind

When was the last time you took a break and listened to your mind and body? Well, it won't be surprising if you say it was long ago. Our lives in this modern age are so chaotic that we don't have time to focus on ourselves. And with so much information on health and wellness, it can be difficult to determine which tips are reliable and which are merely another fad. In general, though, the most trustworthy option is to choose the one that has been tried and tested for decades.

A treatment method based on the principle of universal interconnectedness is what you need to eradicate impurities and reduce the impact of diseases on your body. Ayurveda, an ancient form of Indian medicine, is one such treatment method. This system of Ayurveda delves into the science of life itself, what it is made of, how it functions, and the plethora of physical and energetic tools that can be used to realize it more thoroughly.

Ayurveda and Massage Therapies

Ayurveda, like other Eastern medical systems such as Traditional Chinese Medicine, strives to prevent disease rather than simply treat symptoms of illness. The Ayurvedic approach maintains that each individual is both unique and an essential component of nature. It considers health to be a state of being balanced and in tune with our internal and external environments. For example, if you ask an Ayurveda practitioner to cure a sore knee or frozen shoulder, he or she will focus on more than just the knee. Your entire being is evaluated, including your digestive system, the dosha balance you now have, your food habits, your lifestyle, and the health of your mind, body, and spirit, as they are all likely to have an impact on the external layer of the physical body.

Ayurveda Marma Message-Is it Beneficial

Ayurveda recommends massage therapy as one of the cornerstones of longevity. It helps to balance the Vata dosha, which dries us out as we age, resulting in everything from wrinkled skin to constipation and more. Ayurveda marma massage is one of the most efficient methods for reducing stress, slowing the skin's aging process, improving blood circulation, and removing toxins from the cells. It works on a cellular level to detoxify, nourish, and tone the skin by combining ancient Ayurvedic herbs with oils. It stimulates lymphatic drainage, inhibits free radical activity, and detoxifies the body. The herbs used in Ayurvedic marma massage therapy have natural anti-oxidants and anti-bacterial and anti-inflammatory properties.

In Ayurveda, the body's energy centers, known as marma points, are used for healing, which is similar to acupuncture points in Asian medicine. Our body has 107 marma spots, each of which has a unique name and method of massage and serves a specific function. During marma chikista, these points are massaged therapeutically. The marma points are also known as neuro-lymphatic sites, and it promotes lymphatic drainage and improves the performance of internal organs. Marma massages primarily focus on utilizing subtle energy, or prana, but they are also excellent for physically easing sore muscles and increasing circulation. Marma treatment is a common practice in Ayurveda and is significant in self-care and self-healing techniques.

Ayurveda and Treatment

The ancient intuitive India that brought to being the brightest and the most inspired of eternal spiritual songs on the struggles and problems of active life in this terrestrial world in relation to the highest End of Existence which Self-realisation is, and embodied them in the four Vedas, could not resist its native many-sided tendency not merely to subject the entire nature of man to a process of dynamic spiritualisation, but literally to seek the health, strength, vim, vitality, longevity of the third of the triune aspect of man,-the physical body, which is recognized as the indispensable and perfectible vehicle for both the enjoyment of temporal happiness and supreme spiritual felicity. This tendency of an essentially intuitive mind, towards an integral development of life, towards a complete blossoming of the whole man even while living in a physical form in this material world, this impassioned affirmation of positive living, this acceptance of the body as the best instrument for the realization here on earth, of the best blessings of the profound spiritual realms, resulted in the obtainment of the yet unmatched, deepest insights, the subtle determining vital powers and secrets in the human system that govern its radiant health and longevity and in the creation of a yet another Veda, the Ayurveda. Ayurveda is a perfect science of life and consists of a body of most remarkable knowledge on the internal mechanism of human health and longevity, on medicinal herbs and therapeutic roots, on the efficacious treatment of human ills by eradicating from the human system the very sources of their causation. This great medical science and humanity's most ancient and finest preventive school of practical medicine, which has been practised in India, century after century for over four thousand years, by expert Vaidyas well-versed and highly trained in its lore, should now receive, as a matter of immediate practical necessity, the increasing and the best interest of modern free India. To those who claim to have a knowledge of this ancient medicinal science enriched by the happy results of the researches and advancement made by eminent Vaidyas in succeeding ages, its superior merits over the Western systems of medicine, and its immense value, do not need any delineation. Such names of the great pioneers who added to the development of the science of Ayurveda, as Vagbhata, Madhava, Jivaka and Bhava Mishra of Banaras are well-known, and the almost miraculous results that the medicinal herbs prescribed by Ayurveda have brought into the systems of those who have used them, are more than sufficient proof of its unique value. The amazingly wide scope and the genuine scientific nature of Ayurveda received much enthusiastic appreciation by such Westerners as Sri William Hunter, too, and the recent researches show that the early Greeks owed much of their knowledge on the physiology of man and medicine, to Ayurveda. The interest of Government of India, in Ayurveda is indeed most encouraging, but the private bodies and the public too should come to an increasing recognition of its importance and value, and as a first step begin trying its drugs.

To deal with nicotine, tar and other toxic compounds in the channels, consider these recommendations:

Drink plenty of water, better yet if it is kept in a container made of copper, which scrapes away ama (toxic deposits). Perform neti kriya morning and night (with the help of a neti pot, allow room-temperature normal saline solution to enter one nostril and flow out the other; then, reverse.).Practice bhastrika pranayama, morning and night, to expel contaminants in the upper airways (any good hatha yoga manual will have simple instructions). For nicotine, tar and other toxic compounds already deposited in the dhatus: take three tablets or one tablespoon of triphala every night, before bedtime.

Toning herbs include Ashwagandha, Shatavari, Bala, and Ginseng. Take a constitutionally appropriate rasayana every morning, which will help detoxification. Rasayana 'Chyavanaprash' is suitable for person of any constitution.

Diet: Very best to stay away from alcohol, sugar and coffee the first week or longer, as these tend to stimulate the desire for a cigarette. Avoid fatty foods, as metabolism will slow down a bit without the nicotine, and may gain weight even eat the same amount as before quitting. So discipline about diet is extra important now. No one ever said acquiring new habits would be easy! Take vegetarian low fat diet to increase the Sattvic quality of mind. All fresh foods contains, prana and they increase ojas. Nibble on low calorie foods like celery, apples and carrots. Chew gum or suck on cinnamon sticks.

Exercise: Exercise is an obvious way to help avoid gaining weight after quit. Studies show that smokers have an easier time quitting when they add exercise to their smoking cessation plan. There are some other benefits of exercise including: stress reduction

Help from Yoga: Yoga is a form of relaxation and exercise that incorporates stretching, meditation and the knowledge of the body's full potential. It helps relieve tension and stress, and helps increase strength and vitality.

Corpse pose (Shavasana): The corpse pose, or Shavasana in Sanskrit, is the classic relaxation Yoga Pose, and is most restful pose in yoga. It's the final pose used in most yoga classes, but can also be done on its own to facilitate meditation or relaxation. It looks deceptively simple, but it is in fact, one the most difficult Yoga Asanas and one which changes and develops through practice.

AIDS

AIDS is an acronym for the 'Acquired Immune Deficiency Syndrome'. AIDS is not a single disease but it is a syndrome- a set of diseases, which results from the destruction of the body's defences by human immune deficiency virus, HIV. The virus that causes ' Aids' - HIV belongs to a family of viruses known as retroviruses. HIV looks like a rolled up porcupine. It contain two snakes like single strands of RNA along with reverse transcripts firmly wrapped up in a core, giving HIV its characteristic appearance.

On entering the white blood cells known as CD 4 cells, HIV produces its own DNA and sees to it that this gets inserted into the DNA of the host cell. The viral DNA has enough power and i to direct the destiny of the cell. It can force the cell to manufacture several new copies of HIV. However due to certain trigger and regulatory mechanisms, the viral DNA lies dormant in the host cell for several years before it begins to do the damage.

People infected with HIV may take 7 - 10 years to develop AIDS.

Ayurvedic Perspective: According to Ayurveda the AIDS disease may be correlated with "Kshaya' or "Ojakshaya' meaning loss of energy. The Symptoms and causative factors and treatment for the latter are found mentioned in many ancient Ayurvedic tests like, Charaka Samhitha, Bhavaprakasha, Vaidyachin-tamani and Chakradatta etc., Shosha is another condition, which results from loss of energy that is similar to AIDS.

The disease is caused by the dominant kapha dosha along with the other doshas tends to block the path for the flow of rasadi dhatus in their respective locations thus resulting in the deterioration of saptha dhatu Rasa(plasma), Rakta (blood cells),Mansa (muscular tissue), Meda (adipose tissue), Asthi (bony tissue), Majja (bone marrow) and the Shukra (reproductive tissue). thus resulting into the disease.

The major symptoms are: Loss of appetite, Drastic loss of weight-emaciation fatigue and lethargy, susceptibility to allergies and contagious diseases, skin irritations, bronchial disorders, often leading to tuberculosis of the lungs, damage to intestinal flora resulting in diarrhoea, dysentery, gastritis and wide fluctuations in body temperature. prolonged fever sleeplessness etc.

Treatment of Aids According to Ayurvedic System: All seems not lost for the HIV infected persons as the Ayurvedic supplements are proven to be harmless without any side effects and there can only be improvement and not deterioration.

Treatment Plan: The first step to stem the disease is to ensure a good and healthy atmosphere for the patient. He should be surrounded by well meaning friends and relatives who must affirm that the disease state is totally curable. Nothing negative should be discussed before the patient.

The patient should be given nourishing food which is easily digestible. He should be encouraged to do easy exercise which does not strain his fragile health. He should be kept engaged in fruitful activities which strengthen the good tendencies inherent in him.

Initially, the patient is given tonics and rejuvenators (Rasayanas) to boost immunity levels and to strengthen the system and stimulate appetite. After gaining some strength, shodhana (elimination) techniques are used to expel toxins from the body through enemas, purgation and emesis. The medications administered at this stage are not hard or drastic, but soft, ghee-based so that the patient withstands them with ease.

Secondly the blood is purified with appropriate medications. Liver corrective measures also play an important role. A strengthening diet along with medicated ghee preparations and soups is recommended. But spicy, oily and acidic foods are to be avoided. A little alcohol is recommended as anupana (carrier) to aid the digestive process, and also remove blockages in the flow of Rasadi dhatus, i.e. srothorodha.

Patient is advised to do regular exercise. If the patient is incapable of exercising or running due to weakness, then steaming (swedanam) is also recommended. reason behind this is 'Heated blood is said to weaken, and even destroy, the virus in some cases'. Experience has shown that certain herbo-mineral compounds prepared as per the formulae prescribed by sages like Agasthya, Charaka, Sarangadhara and others for the treatment of Kshaya have brought about significant results in improving the condition of AIDS patients. The Rasayana and Vajikara effects of the these medicines are good for the patients.

Some of the propritery ayurvedic medicines achieving good improvement in the quality of life of patients include 'Chyavanprash', 'Raktavardhak' for Immunity building and 'Sookshma triphla tabs' to keep awaythe the infection.

Chyavanprash

An Ayurvedic remedy which may be of use in the treatment of persons diagnosed with AIDS is 'Chyavanprash'. 'Chyavanprash' is most useful and most popular rejuvenator tonic(Rasayana) of Ayurveda.

This is an Ayurvedic herbal formula which increases ojas, and restores the digestive, eliminative, respiratory and sexual systems. It is frequently employed in wasting conditions where it has been clinically shown to improve health and assist with weight gain. The main ingredient in Chyavanprash is 'Amalaki'- the Indian gooseberry (Emblica officinalis), which has the highest yield of natural source vitamin C, with 3000 mg per fruit. It is also a rich source of naturally occurring anti-oxidants including bioflavonoids, vitamin B-complex and carotenes (vitamin A). Studies suggest that this berry possesses antifungal, antibacterial and antiviral properties. It assists digestion, lowers high blood pressure and lowers blood cholesterol. Clinical research has shown that it accelerates repair of muscle and skin and enhances natural anti-inflammatory substances. Chayvanprash also contains about 35 others herbs which amplify and augment the effects of its main ingredient; such a powerful formulation may indeed be helpful in the treatment of persons who have been diagnosed with AIDS.

Infertility

Infertility Introduction: Incapability of the woman to conceive, after one year of regular sexual union without contraceptives, or to retain the fetus till childbirth is called as infertility. It is a problem, which not only affects the physical life of the woman but also disturbs the social and emotional life of the couple. According to some experts about half the childless marriages are due to abnormalities in the male partners though women are traditionally blamed for sterility. Infertility is also assigned to factors relating to non production of sperms or to other reasons relating to quality.

Factors Involved in Creating a Healthy Child: According to Ayurveda, conception takes place due to healthy sperm, healthy ovum, and a healthy uterus. For both men and women, reproductive health depends on the health of the shukra dhatu, or reproductive tissue. In women the shukra tissue creates the ovum as part of the monthly cycle, and in men the semen is formed due to sexual stimulation.

The shukra tissue itself is created as part of a long chain of metabolic transformations, starting with the digestion of food and including the transformation of food to nutrient fluid, blood, muscle, fat, bone, bone marrow and finally, to shukra tissue. Healthy shukra tissue, then, according to ayurveda, depends on the health of all the other tissues in the body.

Allergies

Allergies occur when a hypersensitive immune system reacts to a common or unusual substance. In some people it is hereditary, but one can also develop an allergy at any time in his or her life. Any substance, whatever its origin, is a possible allergen. Foods, chemicals in foods, medicines, and environmental factors, including pollen, parasites, dust, animal hair, and chemical toxins, can all cause allergic reactions almost anywhere in the body.

Ayurveda sees ama (toxins) and low immunity as the primary causes of most allergies. Ama can settle at the digestive level or in the various tissues, with different symptoms at each level. Ama toxicity aggravates blood and Pitta, or it can aggravate Kapha, with different symptoms.

Hay Fever: Most of us are familiar with the symptoms of hay fever, or seasonal allergies, whether we have them ourselves or know someone else who does have- runny nose, sneezing, itching eyes, scratchy throat, and itching, swelling, or hives on the skin. Often, people seem to have a cold. With more severe reactions, one might suffer from asthma and other breathing difficulties, aches and pain, gastrointestinal reactions or rapid or irregular heartbeat.

Seasonal allergies can occur anytime, but they occur most often during spring and early summer, when plants and trees are flowering and producing pollens, the most common allergens. Seasonal allergies are also fairly common in the fall - many people are sensitive to the molds produced by decaying leaves and other plants. Animal feathers, hairs and dust cause similar symptoms. Ayurveda sees hay fever as a Kapha-Pitta disorder; however, people with a Vata constitution suffer most from it, because it is also due to immune disorder and hypersensitivity of the nervous system:

Symptoms and Dosha Predominance: Vata aggravation often produces headache, insomnia, and anxiety. Pitta aggravation produces yellow nasal discharge, feverish feeling, burning eyes, and skin rashes. Kapha aggravation produces whitish sputum and heaviness and dullness in the body. If the sinuses are congested, there may be a dull headache around the region of sinuses.

General Treatment

A. Home Therapies In all cases, nasal medication is recommended for controlling and preventing seasonal allergies. Use medicated sesame oil made with licorice, agaru (aquilaria agallocha), bilva (aegle marmalos), kantakari (solanum xanthocarpum), lotus, and nutgrass. Then put one drop in each nostril at bedtime. Use this for 4 weeks. Medicated oil specialy prepared for Nasya ' Amrut Bindu' is very effective.

B. Herbs For Vata & Kapha - Take trikatu (dry ginger, black pepper and long pepper powder in equal amount) 20 mgm.+ basil 250 mgm. + 10 mgm. cloves, camphor, and coriander each. It is advisable to take this mixture 3 times a day with warm water. Start before hay fever season. & take the mixture till the season is over.

C. Diet Avoid heavy foods, cold drinks, and dairy products (including cheese and yogurt), that increase Kapha and decrease digestive fire. Also, follow diets that rebalance own pattern of doshic imbalance.

Vata Treatment

Home Therapies: Follow the " Unit increase/unit decrease "Rasayana treatment described in the section on asthma.

Pitta Treatment: During an attack with Pitta aggravation, take a tea made with licorice, cardamom, and santalum album. For making tea - take equal proportion of dried herbs + 4 times water. Boil it. Reduce till 1/4th. For Pitta pacification, bitter herbs & blood cleansing herbs like dandelion, barberry or echinacea should be taken. Take any of these herbs in dose of 1 to 3 gms. a day for 2 weeks.

Home Therapies: Inhale medicated vapour made with water, basil leaves (holy basil, if possible), and eucalyptus oil. Do nasya (nasal medication) with coconut oil 2 times a day. Put 2 -3 drops of oil in the nose at bedtime.

Kapha Treatment

a. Herbs Take 50 mg. of camphor and cloves and 1 gram of basil twice daily for 2 months.

b. Prepared Medicines To ease Kapha aggravation, take 2 tablets of guduchi, three times daily with a tea made from basil, cloves, and camphor for 2 weeks.

c. From the Ayurvedic Physician An Ayurvedic physician would recommend medicated therapeutic vomiting to balance Kapha and prevent the recurrence of seasonal allergies.

d. Yoga and Breath Therapy It is common for hay fever to start with symptoms that are similar to colds and sinus problems. To prevent symptoms such as runny nose, sneezing and congestion, practice nasal cleansing with water (jala neti) regularly to purify the entire upper respiratory tract and prevent recurrence of allergic attacks. Use a special pot with a spout - a neti pot - available for this purpose, and make nasal cleansing a regular part of daily hygiene.

Deep breathing or regular practice of [anuloma viloma pranayama] can also prevent attack. When hay fever allergies are chronic, practice (Kapalabhati) regularly to increase the patient's stamina.

ASTHMA -(SHWAS ROGA)

In today's stressful modern urbanised living, incidence of Asthma is considerably increasing. The rapid industrialisation, excessive crowding, Increasing pollution are some of the factors responsible for this increase in incidence of Bronchial Asthma. It has been stated that 15% of Indian population suffers from Asthma and in developed countries like USA every year there is 10% increase of Asthmatic patients Every now and then we come across patients of Asthma seeking Ayurvedic treatment and advice.

This is because of the versatile approach of Ayurveda to root cause of the problem and it's belief in preventing the disease rather than treating it.

Ayurvedic Concept: In Ayurveda, Asthma is known as 'Swas Roga' Samprapti (Pathogenesis): The vitiated 'Pranvayu' combines with deranged 'Kapha dosha' in the lungs causing obstruction in the 'Pranavaha srotasa'(Respiratory passage). This results in gasping and laboured breathing. This condition is known as 'Swas Roga'

Types: Five types of 'Swas Roga' are described in Ayurvedic texts

1. Maha-shwas
2. Urdhva-shwas
3. Chinna-shwas
4. Tamak-shwas
5. Kshudra-shwas

Among these five types first three are not curable. 'Tamak-shwas is 'yapya'(Controllable) and is difficult to cure. The last one is curable. More than 75% of the cases belong to last two catagories.

Cause

A. Factors Related to Diet: Excessive indulgence in lablab beans,black grams, raw milk, soar curd, excess salt, flesh of aquatic and wet land animals. Excessive use of 'Ruksha'(dry) and 'Guru'(heavy) diet, excessive use of cold water and cold drinks. Excessive use of 'Abhishandi'(Kapha producing) diet, Excessive use of not easily digestible and irritant food.

B. Factors Related to Work: Excessive exposure to dust and smoke. Excessive wind, cold, cold bath or excessive heat, sun bath. Exhaustive exercise, walking, excessive sexual activities. Supression of natural urges Psychological factors

C. Other Factors: Trauma to vital organs viz. - chest, throat

Asthma may be as a sequaelae in other diseases like:

Fever, Long standing common cold, Tuberculosis, Anaemia, Heart disease, Poisoning etc.

Treatment

A. During Attacks Apply warm 'Til tail' over chest and back.Apply fomentation Take 'sunth powder'1/4 tea spoon+'Kali mirch' 6+'Kala namak 1/4 teaspoon+ 5 leaves of 'Tulsi' Boil this mixture in 200 ml water reducing it to 50 ml. Filter and sip it. Medicines: Ayurvedic medicines are very safe and cure the problem to a great extent. Few common medicines are -Swaskuthar ras, Sitopaladi choorna, Vasavleha etc.

B. Treatment in between Attacks 'Rasayan-chikitsa is advocated for'Pranvaha shrotasa' (Respiratory system

Lung Tonic: Make paste of Black resin,dates, long pippali and honey,in equal quantity.Take one teaspoonful of it morning and evening with warm milk.

Panchakarma especially 'Vaman' is advocated before rainy season

Simple Home Remedies: Express the juice from garlic. Mix 10 to 15 drops in warm water and take internally for asthma relief.

Mix, onion juice ¼ cup, honey 1 tablespoon and black pepper 1/8 tablespoon. Mix licorice and ginger together. Take ½ tablespoon in 1 cup of water for relief from asthma. Drink a glass of 2/3 carrot juice, 1/3 spinach juice, 3 times a day.

Add 30-40 leaves of Basil in a liter of water, strain the leaves and drink the water throughout the day effective for asthma.

Fibromyalgia [Cfs]

Fibromyalgia is a recently recognized disorder that is regarded as a chronic condition associated with the experience of non-inflammatory pain and tenderness in muscles, ligaments, joints and fatigue. Fibromyalgia is a relatively common condition, estimated to affect about four percent of the general population.

It is very similar to chronic fatigue syndrome (CFS); Only point of difference is presence of musculoskeletal pain in fibromyalgia and that of fatigue in CFS. Low level of Serotonin is considered to be most important biochemical criteria. The primary treatment goals should include raise serotonin levels, improve sleep quality, and assure adequate magnesium levels.

"Symptoms: Generalized aches or stiffness at many sites for more than three months.

Generalized fatigue

Chronic headache including migraines

Sleep disorder, particularly timings of cycles

Neuronal and psychological complaints

Swelling

Numbness/ tingling sensations

Ayurvedic View: It can be described as 'Mansa Dhatugat and Mansavrut Vata' Fibromyalgia is perceived as a Vata imbalance. Vata is the main imbalance and Aggravated Vata destabilizes the nervous system and can create hypersensitivity leading to pain and tenderness. Accumulation of Ama (toxins) and shrotorodha are also contributory factors.

Ayurvedic Approach of Fibromyalgia and CFS Treatment: The aggravation of Vata dosha and accumulation of Ama (toxins) are the primary causes and should be treated mainly. Associated weak digestion, constipation, and effects of chronic stress should also be tackled.

Panchakarma Therapy: Pre-purification Measures namely 'snehan' and 'swedan are very useful to balance 'Vata' and to loosen the toxins. Snehan is the Herbalized Oil Massage. This oil is applied to the entire body with a particular type of massage. Swedan is sudation or sweating and is given immediately following the snehan. An herbal concoction may be added to the steam to further enhancement of effect.

Daily herbalized oil massage also provides a deeply soothing and balancing effect to the entire nervous system. The motion of massage creates heat and friction which enhances circulation and helps cleanse the areas of chemical impurities that could be aggravating and hypersensitizing nerve tissues.

Diet and Nutrition: Following is the diet suggested for the patients suffering form Fibromyalgia and CFS

Vegetable juices and soups, Coconut water and Coconut milk, Juice of carrot, Cucumber, Beetroot, Cooked vegetables, Spices like cumin, coriander, ginger asafetida. Green salad with a dressing of lemon juice and a little salt, Khichadi

The patient of Fibromyalgia and CFS should avoid the following:

Eating hot, spicy and fried foods, Too much tea, coffee, alcohol, Sleeping during the day and staying up late at night, Mental tensions

Yoga for Stress Management and Improved Mental and Emotional Function:

It is well documented that fibromyalgia is often worsened by heightened stress, anxiety and mental fatigue. Meditation,Yoga, Pranayama and studying of spiritual philosophy are all recommended for supporting personal healing and relaxation of the mind. Efforts should be made to increase the Sattvic quality of mind.

Yogasana: Various stretching exercises are known to have a positive effect on fibromyalgia. Yogic breathing practices will also create a state of restful alertness in mind and body. Progressive deep relaxation, i.e., shavasana is recomended

Lifestyle and Daily Routine: Regularity in our daily routine is effective in reducing Vata imbalances.

Ayurvedic Herbs: Decoction of the roots of ten herbs 'Dashamularishtam' is useful Daily use of the Ayurvedic compound 'Triphala choorna' is recommended to cleanse the colon. Half a teaspoon of turmeric powder with warm water helps to reduce pain and inflammation in Fibromyalgia. Garlic is useful for detoxification and to enhance immune system function. Guggul is a very helpful herb for relief of pain.

Licorice root supports the glandular system and acts in the body like cortisone. Use with caution. Ginger Tea. Ginger is a good alternative to aspirin to relieve minor aches and pains. Generic preparations available in market such as Dashamularishtam, Triphala guggul, Maharasnadi quath, Vata Vidhwans Rasa etc. can be taken under the guidance of a ayurvedic physician

The Treatment of Cholesterol

Alfalfa (Medicago satina) Alfalfa is effective in treating problems of the arteries. It helps in clearing arteries congested with cholesterol.

Arjuna (Terminalia arjuna) Arjuna has been used since centuries in the treatment of heart related problems such as heart attacks. The bark of the arjuna when taken in powder form has beneficial properties. This can dissolve the cholesterol that accumulates in the coronary artery and reduce the possibility of heart attacks.

Coriander (Coriandrum sativum) Coriander is a very good diuretic. It makes the kidneys perform their functions of excretion better. Therefore the kidneys flush out the excess unneeded cholesterols from the body.

Garlic (Allium cepa) Garlic is very beneficial to people with cholesterol problems that affect the heart. Eating two to three cloves of garlic a day helps to reduce or even completely eliminate the harmful cholesterol in the blood. Garlic can disintegrate the blood cholesterol and hence free up the arteries.

Guggulu (Commiphora mukul) This is a traditional Indian herb which has become very popular in the Ayurvedic treatment of cholesterol-related heart problems. It contains guggulsterones which have been proven to reduce the levels of cholesterol on regular use. 25 mg of these guggulsterones are prescribed for intake thrice a day.

Holy Basil (Ocimum sanctum) Holy basil has the capacity to dissolve the accumulated cholesterol from the arteries into the person's bloodstream. From here they are eliminated by the kidneys.

Dietary Treatments for Cholesterol

The various dietary regimes which will help to reduce the buildup of cholesterol in the arteries are as follows:-

Keep a careful watch on the amount of calories are consuming. Say no to chocolates, ice creams, red meats and all such foods that can increase the calorie count.

Sources of fats such as fried foods are to be avoided. Groundnut oil must be strictly prohibited. But fat sources such as cow's milk, cow's ghee and cow's butter are recommended. Buffalo dairy products are to be avoided.

Consume more fresh vegetables and fruits. Green leafy vegetables are needed since they would provide roughage for the elimination of the waste materials. Soy and soy products are very beneficial for the proper utilization of cholesterol. Drink lots of water. Water will help to remove the toxic buildup in the arteries.

Smoking and alcoholism must be avoided as they interfere with the proper utilization of cholesterol in the body.

Ayurvedic Treatment for Cholesterol

Ayurvedic treatment for high level of cholesterol is to prescribe the various herbs that have properties to reduce the buildup. One popular herb in Ayurvedic medicine is arjuna. It is prescribed in several forms such as Arjunarishta and Arjuna Ghritam. Other popular medicines are Hridayarnava Rasa and Prabhakara Vati. If the cholesterol amount is very profuse, then Mrigamadasava is prescribed.

Yoga is also very beneficial in proper circulation and elimination of the cholesterol buildup in the body. Some of the useful asanas are:- a) Ardhamatsyendrasana b) Shalabhasana c) Padmasana d) Vajrasana

Home Medications: Drinking coriander in water everyday helps in the reduction of cholesterol in the body. This regime must be continued for about a month. Then the cholesterol levels must be checked again. Boil a glassful of milk with a piece of garlic in it. This will reduce the cholesterol and take care of cardiac pains.

It has to be continued for a few days before the method begins to show its effects. Have cold hipbaths twice daily. These have been shown to have positive effects in the reduction of cholesterol when taken on a regular basis. A simple remedy is to have a single piece of garlic every morning. This takes time to show results, but the results are positive. Consume some almonds and walnuts on a daily basis.

Uniqueness of Ayurveda

There are several aspects to Ayurveda that are quite unique:

Ayurveda offers points for managing treatment decisions specific to each case. Ayurvedic theory is profoundly useful in analysing individual patient constitution and understanding variations in disease manifestation. The Ayurvedic framework can be used to structure working models of the unique state of each patient, and to project a vision or goal for a whole state of health, again unique to each case.

Ayurveda offers specific recommendations to each individual on lifestyle, diet, exercise and yoga, herbal therapy, and even spiritual practices to restore and maintain balance in body and mind. Ayurveda sees a strong connection between the mind and the body. This understanding that we are all unique individuals enables Ayurveda to address not only specific health concerns but also offers explanation as to why one person responds differently than another.

Marma Treatment

Classical Ayurveda treatment can be separated into eight parts: Salyam, Shalakayam, Kayacahikilsa, Bhoothavidya, Kowmarabrithya, Agathathandram, Rasanayana, Thandram and Vajeekaranam. Of these it it Salyam that deals specifically with marma treatment.

To those uneducated in the ways of Ayurvedic medicine the marma points can seem extremely mysterious. The mystery behind the critical points is only increased by the fact that their locations are kept a closely guarded secret by those that know them. The knowledge of these points - the mistreatment of which can cause critical damage and even death - would be very dangerous if it fell into the wrong hands. For this reason, the doctors and Kalari masters who hold the information will only pass it on to those they know to be mature and responsible enough to learn it.

The origins and science behind marma treatment date back many hundreds of years. The first mentions of it in classical scriptures come from two sources of traditional legends: the Ayurveda legend of Susrutha Maharshi and the Sidha legend of Agasthya. In ancient times, in the early days of Kalaripayattu, students would frequently suffer injuries due to impact to the marma points. As a way to counter this a branch of Ayurvedic medicine was developed that sought to treat marma specific injuries - this eventually became known as marma treatment or Kalari treatment.

Alongside the physical therapy of marma treatment there developed a life philosophy. The idea is that it should not matter how long you might live, whats important is how long you can remain healthy. Taking care of the marma points is a way of prolonging healthy living for as long as possible. Too much hard work and the wrong kind of routines can have a negative effect on the well being of the marma points and cause imbalances within the body. Marma treatment can solve these problems and result in the body being empowered and re-energised.

Marma

Marma in Sanskrit means "hidden or secret." In Malayalam literature, the term is used to indicate, "the most important or vital factor." Marma points also known as the vital energy points are the junctions where two or more tissues overlap(different muscles,tendons, ligaments, veins etc.). These points on the body grant access to the body's vital energy more directly than in other parts of the body.

Healer's and martial artists, use their knowledge of such points to heal or harm, respectively. This energy is also known as Prana in India and Chi ,KI or Qi, in China and Japan. In China and Japan, the marma system is closely related to the meridian system of Accupressure(Shiatsu)/Acupuncture system, also used widely by healers and martial artists who have studied these concepts.

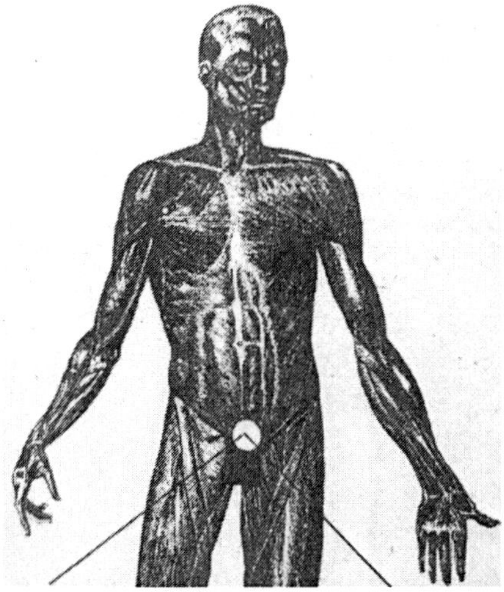

In India, Prana(vital life force) and Lord Shiva are considered to be one and the same. Shiva(Siva) is a member of the triumvirate of gods in the Hindu pantheon. The three main gods are known as Brahma the creator, Vishnu the preserver and Shiva the destroyer. Shiva in this context refers to his immense power to destroy the impurities and transform the mind/body.Injuries, such as falls, strikes and cuts to these marma points were observed to result in physical problems or death. The ancients observed this and realizing the body's energy(prana) could be affected not only to harm but to heal, and in India it became an integral part of Ayurvedic medical studies.

In our body, the prana passes through the 72,000 nerves known as nadis and 3000 marma and are connected to the chakras. There are said to be 114 chakras but most of us are familiar with 7. When the nadis meet at certain parts of the body, we refer to them as chakras(wheel)According to Yogic and Ayurvedic Science, there are two nerve currents in the spinal column, known as Ida(left side) and Pingala(right side) and a center hollow channel called the Sushumna. When the kundalini(the latent form of female Divine energy also known as Shakti, which is the balancing force to that of Shiva)which is located at the base of the spine(Earth) awakens, it begins to rise through this hollow column of Sushumna, on its way towards the crown chakra(Universe) allowing theone to become detached from mind and body and allowing the soul to be liberated.

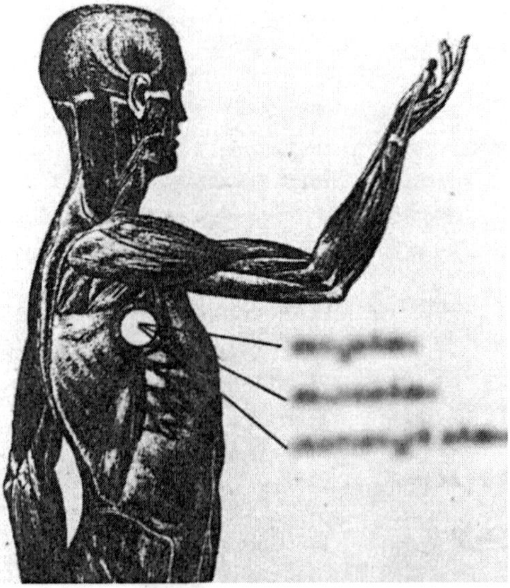

Tamil medical science holds there are 108 marma points that are considered to be particularly important. That number in Ayurveda is 107. Marma points are also used in assessment of possible imbalances as a tool to decide which course of action may address and correct these imbalances. In Ayurveda, there are said to be 25 marman in the face and head, 12 in the neck, 9 in the chest, 3 in the abdomen, 14 in the pelvic region and buttocks and 44 in the arms and legs

The 108 points of Tamil are divided into two parts: Padu marmam and Thodu marmam. The knowledge of these points is used most skillfully by the kalaripayattu Master for combat or for healing.

Padu Marmam

Related to the cartilage and bones there are 12 marmas in this category. Injuries to these marmas are considered the most dangerous to the individual. The ancients being aware of this, began to develop armor to specifically protect these points.

Thodu Marmam

Related to the nerves(nadis) and joints there are 96 marmas in this category. If injury occurs to these marmas, the nervous system will be disrupted and may invoke a collapse of the body and even bring about death. The striking of these specific marmas is called Marma Adi. Comparable to the Chinese and Japanese Dim Mak, or death touch

5 Effects of Attacking the Marma

Sadhyo Pranaharam: When striking these points death is instantaneous. There are 17 sadhyo pranaharam.

Kalanthara Pranaharam: When striking these points death is certain but may not occur sometime after the attack has occurred. There are 33 kalanthara pranaharam.

Visalya Pranaharam: If these points are penetrated by a weapon, upon removal, death is immediate. There are 3 visalya pranaharam

Vikalya Pranaharam: When striking these points the individual may become disabled/handicapped. there are 44 vikalya pranaharam

Rujakara Pranaharam: If these points are struck a steady intense pain will be produced.

Benefits of Marma Treatment

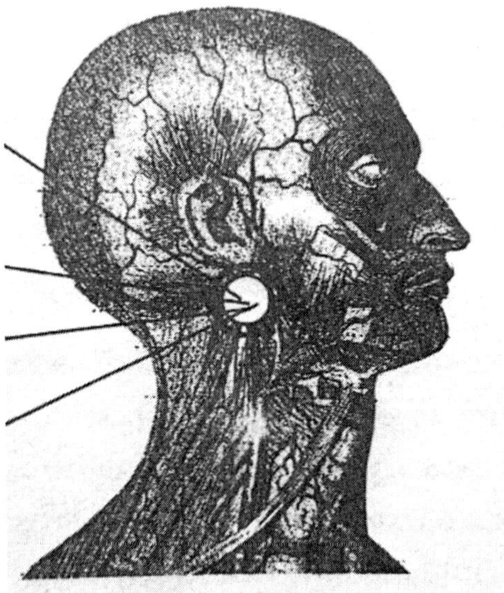

Marma treatment improves the range of motion of the joints by working directly on the soft tissues(muscle, tendon, connective tissues etc).

The lessening or disappearance of pain by relaxing the nervous system and releasing tension in soft tissues as well as removing waste by-products cause by injury. Reduces physical and mental stress(

known to be the precursor to most disease. Dis-ease means not being at ease) also effected through relaxation of the nervous system and soft tissues of the body.

Increases blood flow(blood circulation), which in turn promotes healing. For example: In areas that have been injured, the blood flow is diminished. Increased blood circulation can help to remove the waste by-products caused by the inflammation response of the body when injury occurs(white blood cells, lymphocytes, etc).

Improves muscle and nerve function. Just as blood circulation is improved, so are all fluids circulation(lypmh, cerbrospinal fluid) and other energies such as the bio electrical(Prana, Chi...) improved. When there is less or no obstruction to the chemical and electrical signals that the Nervous system uses to control every facet of the mind/body, then the overall function of all systems are also improved.

Improves immune system function. As mentioned, with increased circulation through the removing of obstructions (such as will occur through tension, injury or disease) than the functioning of the entire system will increase. The immune system is the body's built in self-defense. When the Immune System is operating at a high level, one"s ability to fend off disease and to heal itself is dramatically raised.

Marma treatment promotes a more healing, restful sleep. Each of the aforementioned benefits will all affect a person's ability to relax, release tensions and increase the chances of deep sleep, which is when much of the body's healing occurs.

Helps elimination of toxins through increased performance of the Circulatory and Immune Systems.

Marma treatment strengthens the tissues and organ systems. Vigorous massage often returns organs and tissues back to their normal positions, which mat have moved due to injury or incorrect body positioning through out the day over a lifetime. It will also return the organs and tissues back to their more natural elastic and dynamic state.

Ayurvedic Treatment Methods

Ayurveda prescribes individual life-style health regimens designed with regard to age, sex, climate, vocation and other factors. We cannot expect to be healthy if we don't have a good diet, if we lack proper exercise or if we are filling our minds with disturbing influences. We create our own health or disease by our daily actions. So too, without changing these habitual activities, we cannot improve our health in a lasting manner.

Ayurveda shows the health benefits of the Indian style of cooking, like how the right spices can help us digest food. It teaches us the dynamic effects of each food article for health and disease. While modern medicine is only now beginning to accept the role of food and disease through an examination of phytochemicals, Ayurveda has long regarded diet as the basis of health. We are not only what we eat but also how we eat and with whom we eat. Food preparation is as important as food types.

Food is the first form of God, the Anna Brahma of the Upanishads. Without honouring this form of divinity, the other forms may not be able to manifest in our lives. In this regard Ayurveda recommends vegetarian foods to promote higher (sattvic) qualities of compassion and understanding, under the idea that food not only nourishes the body but also the mind and emotions.

Ayurveda contains many important herb and mineral preparations that reflect the botanical wealth of the Indian subcontinent and thousands of years of experience with plants. It has what is perhaps the most complex and intricate herbal pharmaceutical industry in the world with pills, powders, resins, extracts, confections, and oils not to mention Ayurvedic cosmetics, toothpastes and soaps. Such Ayurvedic products can improve our lives in many ways.

Ayurveda works along with Yoga to prescribe helpful asana, pranayama, mantra and meditation methods for optimal health and spiritual development. The asanas that are good for one person or good for one season, just like the food articles, may not be good for another. Pranayama has its energetic effects. By strengthening Prana or the life-force we can improve perception and circulation and add more energy to counter all diseases. Indeed Prana is the second form of God, the Prana Brahma of the Upanishads.

Mantra and meditation practices have their energetics that should be adjusted according to individual needs and capacities. Mantra helps us energize the mind and clear the subconscious. Meditation helps us open our higher awareness potentials so that we can deal with our lives with more insight and detachment.

Ayurveda has an extensive system of detoxification called Pancha Karma. Pancha Karma includes a system of oil massage, sweating therapy, and various internal cleansing processes to remove the doshas from the tissues, which can effectively eliminate disease-causing toxins from the body so that they can no longer promote the disease process. A number of Pancha Karma centres are now functioning in the West and most Ayurvedic clinics in India offer this service.

Ayurveda has a special science of rejuvenation or rasayana. It recognizes that the body contains a secret potential to renew itself in old age, just it does daily in the state of deep sleep. Ayurveda contains specific exercise, diet, and meditation regimens to facilitate the rejuvenation of body and mind. As the baby boomer generation gets older, which has been very active physically and has pioneered the new interest in alternative medicine, this rejuvenation approach is bound to become much more sought after.

Perhaps most importantly, with its broad basis, Ayurveda provides a good model for integrating all the worlds different medical systems in a harmonious manner. It recognizes the importance of surgery, particularly for larger tumors, but also its limitations, its weakening of our internal energy.

It recognizes the importance of drugs, particularly for acute pain relief, but also their limitations, their tendency to dull the mind and depress our energy. It accepts the healing power of food, herbs, massage and other natural healing methods and shows their applicability and long term healing power.

Yet while respecting all healing modalities Ayurveda also shows us how we can heal ourselves. What we do for ourselves on a regular basis, through the food, thoughts and lifestyle we choose creates who we are and shapes where we are going in life. To think that an outside force, person or treatment can suddenly heal what has taken perhaps years to create, is a delusion. It is an abdication of responsibility for our choices moment by moment. In Ayurveda, the practitioner can make recommendations, but it is up to the client to implement them on a regular basis.

The Future of Ayurveda

Ayurveda is one of the main world systems of natural healing and mind-body medicine, with a popularity spreading to America, Europe and East Asia, a trend that has been steadily developing over the last fifteen years. However, in America Ayurveda is mainly being taken up by the general population. Few Indians, particularly the many medical doctors, are supporting it or even adequately informed about it.

The current Prime Minister of India, Atal Bihari Vajpayee, has mentioned the importance of Ayurveda for proper medical care in India, particularly for disease prevention. The same comments extend to the West where acute disease is no longer the main issue but rather how to improve our vitality and awareness for more creative and fulfilling lives.

As we move into a new millennium and a global age, Vedic knowledge of all types, with its universal vision, is becoming increasingly important. This includes Ayurveda, Yoga, Vedic Astrology, Vedanta and Sanskrit. But as we are first of all physical creatures and as our health needs are radically changing in the computer world, Ayurveda may be the main vehicle through which Vedic knowledge expands again today. Through the Vedic approaches of Ayurveda, Yoga and Jyotish (Vedic Astrology) we have an elaborate system for self-healing, self-understanding, and self-realization. This marvelous heritage should not be forgotten, particularly in India.

Herbs and Ayurvedic Remedies for Cholesterol Treatment

Cholesterol buildup in the coronary arteries leads to the condition known as Hridaya roga in Ayurveda, which literally means heart disease. This is similar to atherosclerosis. When the cholesterol collects in the arteries leading to the heart, their lumen becomes narrow and the amount of blood entering the heart is insufficient. Due to this the heart needs to pump harder, causing several kinds of cardiovascular diseases, the worst of which is the fatal angina pectoris.

Cholesterol is present in fatty acids. Some cholesterol is needed for the proper utilization of foods in the body, formation of the hormones and the bile, etc. This is known as the high-density cholesterol, or simply, the useful cholesterol. The rest of the cholesterol simply builds up in the arteries without any apparent function. This is the low-density cholesterol, or the bad cholesterol.

The buildup of cholesterol can be reduced by several Ayurvedic treatments. Cholesterol reduction means safety from the various cardiovascular diseases, which are the leading causes of deaths in the world today.

Ayurvedic Diagnosis Processure

Ayurvedic Examination Process

To confirm, evaluate and treat a disease, physicians need to perform clinical examinations of patients ? wherein textual knowledge (aptopadesa), direct perception (pratyaksha) and inference (anumana) are all very important components. The examination of patients can be carried out in the following manners:

Three (Tri) fold (Bidha) Examination (Pariksha) Covers a general examination of the patient.

Involves: Visual observation (darshana)

Tactile perception (sparshana)

Questioning (prashna)

Eight (Asht) fold (Bidha) Examination (Pariksha)

Provides a clear picture of nature of ailment and patient's general condition.

This involves the examination of pulse, tongue, voice, skin, eye, general appearance, urine & stool.

Examination of the Pulse (Nadi Pariksha): The foremost clinical art in ayurvedic diagnosis it can provide deep insights into the history of the patient. The ideal time for pulse examination is early morning in empty stomach. But in case of emergency, it can be examined at any time of the day or night. An experienced ayurvedic physician can assess body nature (prakriti), pathological state (vikruti), imbalances of body type, very subtle observations & even prognosis of disease through the pulse.

Examination of the Tongue (jivha pariksha):: Assessed through its doshic state, a Vata aggravated tongue is dry, rough & cracked, Pitta suffered tongue is red with a burning sensation and Kapha influenced it is wet, slimy and coated. Suggesting the state of the digestive system.

Examination of the Voice (Sabda Pariksha): Healthy and natural when the doshas are in balance, the voice will become heavy when aggravated by Kapha, cracked under Pitta effect and hoarse & rough when afflicted by Vata.

Examination of Skin (Sparsha Pariksha): Also used for assessing the state of organs and tissue, palpation is an important clinical method for examination of skin. Noted for doshic influences, a Vata aggravated skin is course & rough with below normal temperature, a Pitta influenced one has quite high temperature and Kapha effected it becomes cold & wet.

Examination of Eyes (Drka Pariksha): Vata domination makes the eyes sunken, dry and reddish brown in colour. On aggravation of

Pitta, they turn red or yellow and the patient suffers from photophobia and burning sensations. High Kapha makes them wet & watery with heaviness in the eyelids.

Examination of general appearance (akriti pariksha): The doshic influences that reflect on the face of the patient enables physicians to gauge the basic constitution and the nature of the disease.

Examination of Urine (Mutra Pariksha): Both examination of urine sample and questioning of patient are important for assessing doshic influence. A modification of this is the oil (taila) drop (bindu) test (pariksha) in which the effect of an oil drop on urine sample suggests the curability of disease.

Examination of Stool (Mala Pariksha): If digestion & absorption of food are poor, the stool carries a foul odour and sinks in water. Vata aggravated, the stool is hard, dry and grey / ash in colour. Excess Pitta makes it green / yellow in colour and liquid in form. And high Kapha lines it with mucus.

Ten (Dash) fold (Bidha) Examination (Pariksha)

Related to the patient: Covers body constitution, pathological state, tissue vitality, physical build, body measurement, adaptability, psychic constitution, capacities for digestion & exercise and age.

Body Constitution (prakriti): Determined by relative predominance of doshas during foetal development the prakriti can be any of vatika, paittika, Kaphaja, Vata paittika, Vata Kaphaja, Pitta Kaphaja or samdoshaja.

Pathological State (vikriti): Related to the biological history of the diseases in its entirety, it enables physicians to consider the signs & symptoms of the disease in order to assess the strength of the disease, the causes, the doshas, the affected body elements, body constitution, time and strength of an individual.

Tissue Vitality (sara): Broadly speaking, there are seven vital tissues, namely lymph (rasa), blood (rakta), muscle (mamsa), adipose (meda), bone (asthi), bone marrow (majja) and reproductive tissue (shukra). Lymph in the skin is assessed by its smoothness, softness, clearness, thinness and whether the skin is covered with short, deep rooted and delicate hair. Percentage of blood in body is evaluated from the condition of the eyes, mouth, tongue, lips, nails and soles of the feet. When muscles are in perfect condition, the temples, forehead, nape of the neck, shoulders, belly, arms, chest, joints of the body, jaws and cheeks are covered firmly with the skin. People with healthy adipose tissue have oily skin and healthy hair, nails, voice and teeth. The health of bones is determined by pliable but firm forearms, chin, nails, teeth, ankles, knees and other joints of the body. Healthy bone marrow leads to good complexion and stout, long, round & stable joints. Those in whom the semen is perfectly healthy, are strong and cheerful.

Physical Build (samhanana): Body examination is carried out by direct perception ? a healthy body being well- built with symmetrical bones, strong & stable joints and enough flesh & blood.

Body Measurement (pramana): In Ayurveda, body measurement is given in terms of finger breadth and any person in close proximity to the ideal measurements is termed as normal and healthy.

Adaptibility (satmya): Indicating substances intrinsic to the body, it refers to two types of people - those that are strong, adjust easily to difficulties and have excellent digestive capacity and those that are generally weak, intolerant to change and can have only few food options. Psychic Constitution (sattwa): Refers to the mind which controls the body in contact with the soul (atma). Depending on degree of mental strength, it is considered to be high, moderate or low. To know more about body type.

Digestive Capacity (ahara sakti): This has to be judged from the individual?s capacity to ingest and digest food substances. Capacity for Exercise (vyayama shakti): Assessed by capacity for hard work, it is either low, moderate or high.

Age (vaya): Broadly categorized into childhood, middle age and old age, it provides vital clues for the diagnosis & treatment and is a must consideration in clinical examinations.

Ayurvedic Diagnosis - Six

Stages of Disease

The imbalance of doshas and the course they follow to cause disease is termed samprapti or pathogenesis. Since diseases develop in distinct stages, a good knowledge of those helps in early recognition of disease. Ayurveda thus elaborates a six stage process for diagnosis called kriya (action) kal (time). The first 4 stages being unique to Ayurveda in that they permit recognition and elimination of the disease before it ventures into differentiated clinical symptoms.

One who knows the various stages of pathogenesis accumulation (sanchaya), provocation (prakopa) spread or migration (prasara), deposition or augmentation (sthana samshaya), manifestation (vyakti) and the differentiation (bheda) is entitled to be a physician.

Stage One: Accumulation (Sanchaya)

Weak digestive power and excess of dosha is responsible for such a condition. Here toxins (ama) produced by improper digestion collects in the gastro-intestinal (GI) tract. Toxins resulting from a Kapha imbalance accumulates in the stomach, those associated with a Pitta imbalance collects in the small intestine, and that related to Vata malfunction amasses in the colon.

Due to the presence of one of these toxins, mild and ill-defined symptoms may show. We should recognize and eliminate the cause instead of ignoring or suppressing it. Causes aversion to similar things and attraction for contraries.

Stage Two: Aggravation (Prokapa)

The accumulated, stagnant doshas are now 'excited? by factors as ahara, vihara & seasons.

The toxins amass in such degree to get provoked in the site of production in the GI tract.

Stage Three: Spread (Prasara)

In this stage, the toxins accumulated in the GI tract start overflowing. Generally, up to this stage the damage is entirely reversible and restoration of doshic balance can be achieved with proper measures. Or there may be spontaneous prashama (remission) influenced by seasonal changes. Thus there is sanchaya of Pitta in rainy season, prakopa in fall and prasara in early winter. Based on degree of excitation, it might even passed the stages of prashama or prasara.

Stage Four: Agumentation (Sthana Samshraya)

Overflowing toxins migrate, entering and taking refuge in localized, weak or defective dhatus thereby leading to malfunction and structural damage. It is from here that specific degenerating disease and susceptibilities to serious infections begin.

Stage Five: Symptom Manifestation (Vyakti)

Differentiated symptoms first begin to appear from the location.

Manifested symptoms being used by modem medicine for classification & diagnosis of disease.

Stage Six: Complications/Differentiation (Bheda)

The disease having taken years or even decades to reach this final stage, becomes chronic.

Offers detailed understanding of the group of symptoms thereby making clear nature of disease. Might act as predisposing factors for the spread of other diseases.

Diagnosis of Disease in Ayurveda

Indian medicine names three main causes of disease 'overuse', 'disuse' or 'misuse? of faculties; 'errors in judgement'; and influence of seasonal changes. According to Ayurveda all human diseases can be classified into the seven broad categories, namely:

1. Genetic (Adibalapravritta): Consists of ailments as obstinate skin diseases, hemorrhoids, diabetes, tuberculosis and asthma that arise primarily due to defects in the sperm (shukra) of the father ? when it is called pitrija or the ovum (sonita) of the mother ? when it is termed matrja.
   Undigested food, abnormal behaviour, addiction of any type and stressful situations affect the reproductive elements of both the male and female, resulting in a defective foetus.
2. Congenital (Janmabalapravritta): Caused essentially due to nutritional disorder (rasakrita) and unfulfilled cravings of the mother during pregnancy (dauhrdya)
   If diet and / or conduct of the mother aggravates Vata, the foetus might end up with deformities as kyphosis (hunchback), blindness and dwarfism; increased Pitta may cause alopecia and yellowish pigmentation of skin; and enhanced Kapha might result in albinism.
3. Constitutional (Doshabalapravritta): Arise out of any dietary or behavioural disturbance brought about by an imbalance in any one of the three vital physical energies (tridosha) or the three vital mental energies (triguna).
   Thus constitutional disorders are of two types: somatic (Sharirika) & psychic (Manasika).
4. Traumatic (Sanghatabalapravritta): Undergoing any trauma causing experience. external or internal. leads to this. External trauma is induced by injuries inflicted by sharp instruments and bites of animals or venomous insects. Tress and overstrain lead to internal trauma.
5. Seasonal (Klabalapravritta): Brought about by changes in the

nuances of seasonality. Sometimes the body fails to adjust itself to the sudden and abnormal climatic changes ? extreme cold might lead to frostbite and rheumatic disease. While extreme heat may cause sunstroke or fever.

6. Infectious and Spiritual (Daivabalapravritta): Either born out of natural calamities as lightning, earthquakes, floods and the invisible, malignant forces of nature. Or contacted through sexual & physical intimacy and sharing of food, plates, bed, clothes, towels and cosmetics with effected friends & relatives. Or as a result of sheer jealousy.
7. Natural (Swabhavbalapravritta): Even the healthiest of people are struck by hunger, thirst, sleep, death or senility. Brought about by functional, organic and natural changes in the body.

In Ayurveda, physicians try to assess the symptoms of these diseases as much as the nature of ailment and its root causes (nidana). This is of utmost importance in ensuring correct choice of remedial & preventive measures for treatment of the disease. For otherwise, even after therapy, one might not get the desired response and there would remain a chance of recurrence.

The early signs and symptoms (purvaroopa) provide useful warnings and the opportunity for taking necessary action before a disease can assume dangerous magnitudes. The main signs and symptoms (roopa) reflect the true nature and intensity of the disease. Another oft used method of diagnosis is exploratory therapy (upasaya) which uses diet, medicines and routines to detect diseases otherwise difficult to diagnose. Acting either against the cause of disease or the disease itself or producing relief. a swelling that is alleviated by an oily & hot massage, is obviously caused by an imbalance of Vata.

Basics of Determining Dosha

Diseases, according to Ayurveda are caused by the imbalance in the three doshas. The predominance of a dosha in an individual?s constitution indicates his or her vulnerability to a particular disease. Diseases in Ayurveda are classified according to thee origin of their causes. Diseases which originate from factors within the human body, including psychosomatic diseases, are called adhyatmika. Adhyatmika diseases are further divided into hereditary diseases, congenital diseases and those caused by the aggravation of the doshas. adhibhautika diseases are those whose origin can be traced to external physical factors such as germs and accidents. adhidaiveka diseases are caused by the seasons, planetary influential, providential causes and so forth. The physician diagnoses a disease in an individual by an examination of the patient based on three general methods. These methods are common to understanding any phenomenon in the universe.

Direct observation or pratyaksha: This is done through the senses: seeing, hearing, smelling, touching and tasting. A direct contact between the senses and the object of examination is thus established. Inference or anumana: Just as one deduces that there is a fire when one sees smoke, one can make deductions in the observation of certain substances under the microscope. For instance, the examination of stool under a microscope will give clues about the state of the health of a person. Authoritative statement or shabda: Experts have bequeathed to us a legacy of authoritative statements regarding diseases. The patient is interrogated closely to determine the exact nature of the diseases. The client's relatives too are questioned for in this way the client?s previous history of diseases can be recorded. Fortified with the knowledge from previously recorded cases and the findings of experts, the physician can make a dosha determination.

Liver Care

The liver is the largest glandular organ in the body, and has more functions than any other human organ. A person's entire blood supply passes through the liver several times a day, and at any given time there is about a pint of blood there. The Liver has a pivotal role in human metabolism.

The liver produces and secretes bile (to be stored in the gallbladder until needed) that is used to break down and digest fatty acids. It also produces prothrombin and fibrinogen, both blood-clotting factors, and heparin, a mucopolysaccharide sulfuric acid ester that helps keep blood from clotting within the circulatory system. The liver converts sugar into glycogen, which it stores until the muscles need energy and it is secreted into the blood stream as glucose. The liver synthesises proteins and cholesterol and converts carbohydrates and proteins into fats, which are stored for later use.

It also produces blood protein and hundreds of enzymes needed for digestion and other bodily functions.The liver also produces urea, while breaking down proteins, which it synthesises from carbon dioxide and ammonia. It is eventually excreted by the kidneys.The liver also stores critical trace elements such as iron and copper, as well as vitamins A, D, and B12.The liver is also responsible for detoxifying the body of poisonous substances by transforming and removing toxins and wastes. There are five main sources of body toxins and wastes that the liver deals with: toxins from food (traces of pesticides, preservatives)and alcohol; toxins from outside (drugs, adulterants, and environmental pollutants); internally produced chemicals, such as hormones, that are no longer needed; nitrogen-containing waste left over from protein re-use; and energy production. These toxins and wastes are converted into less harmful substances by the liver and then eliminated from the body.

Because of the significant role the liver plays in maintaining our health, we must do all we can to keep it functioning properly.

Symptoms of a "sluggish liver"

These are fatigue, general malaise, digestive problems, blood sugar regulation disorders (such as hypoglycaemia), high cholesterol, psoriasis, allergies and chemical sensitivities and constipation. Extreme cases of liver problems would be jaundice, hepatitis and cirrhosis.

Hepatitis

Among the many diseases that can affect the liver the most common is hepatitis (a viral infection of the liver). Hepatitis can be caused by drugs, viruses, bacteria, mushrooms, parasites like amoebas or giardiasis. The most common hepatitis viruses affecting the liver are named for letters of the alphabet: hepatitis A, hepatitis B, hepatitis C, hepatitis D, and hepatitis E.

Hepatitis A: Takes 14 to 21 days after infection to cause symptoms. It is transmitted through food. Once infected with HAV, some symptoms such as dark yellow urine and fatigue will begin to appear within 25 days.

Hepatitis B: Is on the increase world-wide. It is transmitted through direct contact with blood, serum, saliva, faeces, urine, and sexual contact.

Hepatitis C: is a truly serious disease with no known effective treatment. It is transmitted through blood and body fluids in transfusions, injections, the sharing of IV needles with drug users, and possibly by sexual contact with exposed partners.

Hepatitis D: Only occurs in the presence of Hepatitis B virus

Hepatitis E: Is another common type of hepatitis in developing countries. It occurs in epidemics. The infection route for it is faecal-oral, the same as the route for Hepatitis A virus; therefore, again, very careful in eat and drink.

Treatment of Hepatitis

Usually Hepatitis A is self-limiting. Most of the Hepatitis A virus patients will return to normal in between four to six weeks time. The antibodies that the body's immune system develops kill the infection and also produce immunity to Hepatitis A virus.

But with Hepatitis B virus and Hepatitis C virus, many people will go into a chronic phase that leads to chronic phase. With chronic HBV and HCV, 30% of patients develop cirrhosis of the liver or hepatocellular carcinoma.

In modern medicine, the only protection against hepatitis are the HAV and the HBV vaccines. There is nothing available for HCV protection so far. Therefore, limiting our exposure to hepatitis is the best prevention. We have to take the responsibility for prevention of hepatitis ourselves. This means using safe sexual practices, taking precautions when exposed to blood and blood products; avoiding the sharing of IV needles; taking care to eat in restaurants that enforce hand-washing policies among their employees; and avoiding scavenger seafood. These measures can cut chances of being infected with hepatitis to a minimum.

Cirrhosis

Cirrhosis of the liver is a chronic, diffuse degenerative liver disease in which the parenchyma (the functional organ tissue) degenerates, the lobules are infiltrated with fat and structurally altered, dense perilobular connective tissue forms, and areas of regeneration often develop.Cirrhosis is the seventh leading cause of death by disease in the United States. In most cases, though, there is a loss of liver cell function, and an increased resistance to blood flow through the damaged liver tissue (a condition known as portal hypertension) leading to oesophageal varices. Severe cirrhosis leads to ammonia toxicity, hepatic coma, gastrointestinal haemorrhage, and kidney failure. As liver cells are destroyed, they are systematically replaced by scar tissue.

The most common cause of cirrhosis is believed to be alcohol abuse Though it affects many organs, alcohol is especially harmful to the liver, and is a factor in about three-fourths of the cases of liver cirrhosis. Alcohol must be metabolized, and the liver performs most of that job, suffering serious damage in the process. Not only does alcohol destroy liver cells, it also robs them of their ability to regenerate. Such cofactors as hepatitis C virus can increase the risk of cirrhosis

Treatment of Liver Cirrhosis

More than half of all liver disease could be prevented if we acted on the knowledge we already have. Avoiding or limiting the use of alcoholic beverages. Man-made chemicals also pose an extreme threat to the liverOnce cirrhosis has been diagnosed, sodium and fluids should be restricted, and all alcohol consumption must cease. Antiemetics, diuretics, and supplemental vitamins are prescribed. Patients should avoid exposure to infections and eat small but frequent meals of nutritious foods. The liver is the only organ that can generate healthy, new tissue. It is therefore possible to regenerate a cirrhosis-damaged liver if extraordinary therapies are followed and the underlying cause of the cirrhosis is eliminated.

Interferon-alpha, a powerful antiviral, may reduce the risk of cancer in some cirrhosis patients. In cases of total liver failure, transplantation has been successful.

Ayurvedic Medicine in Treating Liver Disease

Hepatitis A virus can be taken care of very easily with herbs. Many of the Ayurvedic herbs have shown remarkable results in clinical trials and studies. One of these is Eclipta Alba (Bhringaraj), others are Boerhavia diffusa (Punarnava), and Picrorhiza kurroa (Katuki). It is recommend that people take these herbs on a prophylactic basis when travelling to parts of the world where hepatitis infection is a risk.

HBV and HCV are more serious infections. We must be careful how we use Ayurvedic herbs for prevention of HBV and HCV. The herbs mentioned earlier have shown a protective action in HBV, and using them on a regular basis may be a good way to prevent HBV. Ayurvedic medicines play a significant role in protecting the liver from cirrhosis and from liver cancer. Animal and clinical studies done with Phyllanthus Amarus, Phyllanthus Niruri, and Eclipta Alba have proven their ability to reverse HBV infections in approximately 60% to 70% of patients. More significantly, with these herbs we are able to stop the process, which leads to cirrhosis and cancer of the liver. This means that even if we are not able to make some patients negative for HBV and HCV, we can still protect them from cirrhosis of the liver, in which the liver stops functioning, and liver cancer. Take very good care of health. To protect liver, avoid alcohol and caffeine. Drink green tea, exercise, reduce stress, and use the herbs mentioned above. Give this hard-working and essential part of body a rest and a tune-up, and will be rewarded with better health, more energy and higher disease resistance.

Principle of Marma Therapy

Marma Chikitsa stands as a highly potent therapeutic approach within Ayurveda, offering a comprehensive healing experience. "Marma" signifies the vulnerable points within our body, totaling 108 in number. These points hold a crucial role, and they are instrumental in the flow of vital energy (Prana) through intricate pathways called Nadis. The essence of energy and intelligence emanates from these Marma points. Among the 108 points, 64 are deemed as vital, capable of either healing or harming the body. These Marma points are spread across muscles, bones, joints, and nerves. Any injury to these points can lead to potential deformities or even fatality. Central to this treatment is the utilization of oil therapy. Various forms of medicated warm oils and herbal oils are skillfully applied to massage the Marma points. Marma Chikitsa seamlessly integrates principles from neuromuscular and orthopedic sciences. This renders it highly effective in addressing issues such as dislocated discs, shoulder and ankle concerns. Furthermore, it extends its scope to correct paralysis and musculoskeletal deformities.

Marma Ayurveda practitioners leverage the marma points to identify imbalances in energy within tissues and organs, facilitating enhanced diagnosis and treatment. The activation of marma points brings about a boost in cellular intelligence, metabolism, and immune function. By promoting the unhindered flow of mental energy, the activation of metabolic fire is encouraged, accelerating cellular circulation, nutrition, and rejuvenation. Marma therapy triggers neural pathways from the brain to specific body areas, strengthening and purifying energy channels throughout the body. Consequently, traditional Ayurvedic treatments are significantly enhanced with Marma therapy acting as a supportive element.

Incorporating Marma into Ayurvedic Treatment: Individual Marma Activation: The chief physician administers personalized energy channel activation for each patient. This demanding practice necessitates years of dedicated experience in Marma therapy.

Marma Meditation and Yoga: Meditation and Yoga sessions are structured with a focus on energy channels. Marma meditation and Marma yoga, passed down through generations, are integral here. The term "Marmayogi" was used to refer to the chief physician's grandfather due to his expertise in this domain.

Self-Care Techniques: Patients are taught specific marma activations related to their ailment, enabling them to continue the therapy at home. This empowers them with long-term benefits post-treatment. In essence, Marma Ayurveda Marma Ayurveda serves as a tool to amplify the free flow of mental energy across the body, profoundly heightening the effectiveness of traditional body-focused Ayurvedic treatments.

Our approach entails a meticulously structured treatment plan that incorporates alignment correction alongside systematic Marma massage. Following treatment, adherence to post-treatment instructions becomes imperative. This holistic process culminates in the complete restoration of health, reinstating overall well-being.

Marma Massage

Marma massage is a very important massage therapy in Ayurveda where the vital points of the body are stimulated with mild pressure. The vital points of the body are known as marma in Ayurveda. Ayurveda says, there are 107 marma points in the whole human body. Marma, the word is taken from Sanskrit.

The meaning of marma is hidden or secret. It ensures mind, body, spirit relaxation and those who undergo marma point massage therapy gets complete satisfaction in every aspect. The traditional marma massage therapy of Ayurveda is now globally acclaimed and hundreds of abroad tourists are coming every year to experience the unique marma massage therapy.

Marma therapy is an important part of Ayurveda that helps to maintain health by cleansing blocked energy. In Marma therapy, a very light stimulation of points on the body is done. It removes blockages from the marma points giving physical and psychological relaxation and strength.

This is a powerful process and a therapy that works with these subtle and sensitive energy points to open the energy channels in the body are called srothas. Marma points, when gently pressed on the skin can stimulate a chain of positive events.

Benefits of Marma Therapy

- Strengthens the organ systems and tissues.
- Regenerates & nourishes the tissue.
- Helps to remove excess toxins & strengthens muscles and ligaments.
- Prevents aging & stimulate Immunity of the body.
- Improves lymph circulation.
- Nourishes the body and improve blood circulation.
- Increases the protection from vata disorders.
- Encourages good sleep & relieves stress.
- Reduces pain, inflammation in joints.
- Improves physical stability.
- Balances the dosha.
- Detoxification of the whole body.
- Helps to release blocked energy helping prevent diseases.
- Balances emotional disorders.
- All the benefit of traditional massage.

Chapter 4

Principles of Yoga Therapy and Benefits of Massage

Introduction

Yoga therapy, rooted in ancient yogic principles, is a holistic approach to healing that integrates various yogic techniques to promote physical, mental, and emotional well-being. Central to yoga therapy is the belief that the body has an innate ability to heal itself when provided with the appropriate tools and practices. By combining yoga postures, breathwork, meditation, and mindfulness, along with the therapeutic benefits of massage, practitioners aim to address imbalances and alleviate ailments in a holistic manner.

The principles of yoga therapy are guided by the understanding that each individual is unique and requires personalized care. Practitioners assess the client's physical condition, emotional state, lifestyle, and personal goals to develop a tailored treatment plan that addresses their specific needs. This approach emphasizes the importance of self-awareness, self-empowerment, and self-care in the healing process.

Yoga therapy recognizes the interconnectedness of the body, mind, and spirit and seeks to restore harmony and balance on all levels. Through the practice of yoga postures (asanas), individuals can improve flexibility, strength, and posture while releasing tension and promoting relaxation. Breathwork (pranayama) is incorporated to calm the mind, reduce stress, and enhance vitality by regulating the flow of prana, or life force energy, throughout the body.

In addition to yoga practices, massage therapy plays a complementary role in promoting healing and well-being in yoga therapy sessions. Massage techniques such as Swedish massage, deep tissue massage, and Thai yoga massage are utilized to release muscular tension, improve circulation, and facilitate the flow of energy throughout the body. The therapeutic benefits of massage extend beyond the physical realm to include mental and emotional relaxation, stress reduction, and enhanced overall vitality.

One of the key benefits of incorporating massage into yoga therapy is its ability to enhance the effectiveness of yoga practices by preparing the body for movement and deepening the relaxation response. Massage helps to release muscular tightness and restrictions, allowing individuals to move more freely and comfortably in their yoga postures. It also helps to calm the nervous system, making it easier to enter a state of deep relaxation and meditation.

Furthermore, massage therapy can address specific physical issues such as chronic pain, injury recovery, and musculoskeletal imbalances, making it an invaluable tool in the treatment of various health conditions. By combining the therapeutic benefits of yoga and massage, individuals can experience profound healing and transformation on all levels - physical, mental, emotional, and spiritual.

The principles of yoga therapy emphasize the importance of holistic healing and self-care in promoting health and well-being. By integrating yoga practices with the therapeutic benefits of massage, individuals can address imbalances and ailments in a comprehensive and holistic manner. Whether used as a standalone therapy or in conjunction with other healing modalities, yoga therapy and massage offer powerful tools for cultivating vitality, resilience, and inner peace.

We set the intention to use Yoga in a therapeutic way, we are given the opportunity to explore many modalities on our way back to health and wholeness. We do the best we can, given all the unique variables to our situation (environmental, genetic, and karmic).

These are a few of the principles that Yoga Therapy applies:

- Presence, awareness, and conscious intention: Through body work and breath work, we become more 'tuned in' to our internal environment. This presence and awareness can be practiced throughout the entire Yoga Therapy session, and the modalities used.
- Deep, Slow, Rhythmic Breath: Breath is the golden thread that we weave through all our practices. The ability to use our breath for healing is key in Yoga philosophy. Metabolic and

anabolic activities in the body can regulate. Physical, psychological, and spiritual layers to our being can unify.

- Right Diet: An exploration of diet through Ayurvedic enquiry will help get the bodies natural healing ability on track. Diet is a critical element to recovery and health maintenance.
- Conscious Relaxation: Stress can debilitate the body, mind and spirit. Learning how to relax deeply can have a positive affect on every cell in your body. This can increase our immunity, and give us the much needed rest and rejuvenation for mental/ emotional and spiritual well-being.

These are a few of the principles that we will begin to explore in a Yoga Therapy setting. There are many more principles that will give us the ability to wield vital energy (prana) in specific ways. By doing so we can increase our self confidence, self-reliance, and fortify ourselves against environmental stressors.

Modalities of Yoga Therapy

- Physical: The correct use and application of Yoga Asana (postures) to gently stretch, strengthen and soothe the body. These postures have a healing effect on many systems in the body including: respiratory, circulation, digestion, and elimination. Joints and muscles are massaged to help release tension from the physical layer of our being. Postures also lend healing energy at a cellular level, stimulating organs, as well as endocrine functioning.
- Mental: Relaxation techniques are key to re-aligning your peace of mind. There are many techniques offered through the various paths of Yoga, including Hatha, Jnana, and Raja Yoga that can help ease the mind back into harmony and balance.
- Emotional: Swadhyaya, Pranayama, Pratyhara, Dharana, and Dhyana (if these terms are new to you, not to worry!). These are all very practical and effective ways to help stabilize the emotional turmoil that you may be experiencing. Emotional balance, much like right diet is a critical step on your road to recovery.
- Spiritual: Everything mentioned above has a direct effect on our sense of spiritual well being. With practice, Yoga starts to reveal the subtle spiritual nature of who we are, and we can continue to explore this natural experience indefinitely.

- Preventive and Rehabilitative: Yoga Therapy gives us a chance to practice Yoga with a therapeutic intention. Whether our intention is to prevent illness, disease, and/or suffering, or if we are working to rehabilitate an injury and minimize recovery time, Yoga Therapy offers many modalities to explore. Once the Yoga 'Therapy' is concluded, we can continue on the journey through various means of learning about Yoga in our everyday lives. Remember, Yoga is a lifestyle; one that seeks to bring peace, and joy back into our lives.
- Pain Relief: Too many people are living and suffering with chronic pain (be it physical, mental/emotional an/or spiritual), and it doesn't have to be this way. We can reduce pain, work to eliminate it and improve our pain tolerance if conditions do not present a cure. Pain can be experienced in many ways. Everyone has felt some form of pain at one time or another. Sometimes it goes away, but sometimes it can linger for years. Mental/Emotional and Spiritual pain can be just as agonizing as physical pain. Grief and the loss of a loved one can be unbearable, debilitating fear can paralyze the system, lack of energy or loss of interest in being alive can leave one feeling hopeless and helpless. It is normal to experience pain, it comes with the territory of being human. But with Yoga we can manage symptoms, work towards eliminating them, and re-energize our spiritual connection for a more balanced, loving and joyful life.

Benefits of Massage

The general massage, dealing with all parts of the body, is highly beneficial in many ways. It tones up the nervous system, influences respiration and quickens the elimination of poisons and waste material from the body through the various eliminative organs such as the lungs, skin, kidneys and bowels. It also boosts blood circulation and metabolic processes. A massage removes facial wrinkles, helps to fill out hollow cheeks and neck and eases stiffness, sore muscles and numbness.

Peer-reviewed medical research has shown that the benefits of massage include pain relief, reduced trait anxiety and depression, and temporarily reduced blood pressure, heart rate, and state anxiety. Theories behind what massage might do include blocking nociception (gate control theory), activating the parasympathetic nervous system which may stimulate the release of endorphins and serotonin, preventing fibrosis or scar tissue, increasing the flow of lymph, and improving sleep but such effects are yet to be supported by well designed clinical studies.

Acupressure

Acupressure is an ancient healing art that uses the fingers or any blunted objects to press key points called as 'Acu Points' (Energy stored points) on the surface rhythmically on the skin to stimulate the body's natural self-curative abilities. When these points are pressed, they release muscular tension and promote the circulation of blood and the body's life force to aid healing.

Acupuncture and acupressure use the same points, while acupressure uses the gentle but firm pressure of hands or any blunted objects, but acupuncture employs needles, Acupressure has been practiced as a healing art for at least 5,000 years. This complete health system has been documented for use in treating over 3000 conditions. Now acupoints are commonly treated utilizing transcutaneous electric nerve stimulation (aka TENS) and laser light from laser or LED diodes in specific wavelengths shown to have rapid and lasting effects.

Acupressure philosophy and acupoint stimulation is based on the same principles as Acupuncture. By using pressure, electric stimulation or laser light instead of needles, it works to stimulate specific reflex points located along the lines of energy which run through the body, called meridians. There are 14 main meridian lines, each of which corresponds to an individual organ of the body. When the vital energies are able to flow through the meridians in a balanced and even way, the result is good health. When you experience pain or illness it is an indication that there is a block or leak in the energy flow within your body.

To find the appropriate point, gently probe the area until it is found that point which gives a "funny bone" feeling or is sensitive, tender or sore. Then press hard enough to make the point hurt. Stimulation is given by steady pressure or five seconds on and five seconds off rotating pressure. Usually one minute is sufficient for each treatment session.

Acupressure can be effective in helping relieve headaches, eyestrain, sinus problems, neck pain, backaches, arthritis, muscle aches, and tension due to stress, ulcer pain, menstrual cramps, lower back aches, constipation, and indigestion, anxiety, insomnia.

There are also great advantages to using acupressure as a way to balance the body and maintain good health. The healing touch of acupressure reduces tension, increases circulation, and enables the body to relax deeply. By relieving stress, acupressure strengthens resistance to disease and promotes wellness.

Acupuncture

Acupuncture is the procedure of inserting and manipulating fine filiform needles into specific points on the body to relieve pain or for therapeutic purposes. The word acupuncture comes from the Latin acus, "needle", and pungere, "to prick".

According to traditional Chinese medical theory, acupuncture points are situated on meridians along which qi, the vital energy, flows. There is no known anatomical or histological basis for the existence of acupuncture points or meridians. In China, the practice of acupuncture can perhaps be traced as far back as the Stone Age, with the Bian shi, or sharpened stones. Acupuncture's origins in China are uncertain.

The earliest Chinese medical text that first describes acupuncture is the Yellow Emperor's Classic of Internal Medicine (History of Acupuncture) Huangdi Neijing, which was compiled around 305-204 B.C. Some hieroglyphics have been found dating back to 1000 B.C. that may indicate an early use of acupuncture.According to one legend, acupuncture started in China when some soldiers who were wounded by arrows in battle experienced a relief of pain in other parts of the body, and consequently people started experimenting with arrows (and later needles) as therapy.Acupuncture spread from China to Korea, Japan and Vietnam and elsewhere in East Asia. Portuguese missionaries in the 16th century were among the first to bring reports of acupuncture to the West.

Traditional Theories of Acupuncture

In Traditional Chinese medicine, "health" is considered a condition of balance of yin and yang within the body. Some have compared yin and yang to the sympathetic and parasympathetic nervous systems. Particularly important in acupuncture is the free flow of Qi, a difficult-to-translate concept that pervades Chinese philosophy and is commonly translated as "vital energy". Qi is immaterial and hence yang; its yin, material counterpart is Blood (capitalized to distinguish it from physiological blood, and very roughly equivalent to it). Acupuncture treatment regulates the flow of Qi and Blood, tonifying where there is deficiency, draining where there is excess, and promoting free flow where there is stagnation. An axiom of the medical literature of acupuncture is "no pain, no blockage; no blockage, no pain."

Traditional Chinese medicine treats the human body as a whole that involves several "systems of function" generally named after anatomical organs but not directly associated with them. The Chinese term for these systems is Zang Fu, where zang is translated as "viscera" or solid organs and fu is translated as "bowels" or hollow organs.

In order to distinguish systems of function from physical organs, Zang Fu are capitalized in English, thus Lung, Heart, Kidney, etc. Disease is understood as a loss of balance of Yin, Yang, Qi and Blood (which bears some resemblance to homeostasis). Treatment of disease is attempted by modifying the activity of one or more systems of function through the activity of needles, pressure, heat, etc. on sensitive parts of the body of small volume traditionally called "acupuncture points" in English, or "xue" in Chinese. This is referred to in TCM as treating "patterns of disharmony."

Most of the main acupuncture points are found on the "twelve main meridians" and two of the "eight extra meridians" (Du Mai and Ren Mai) a total of "fourteen channels", which are described in classical and traditional Chinese medical texts, as pathways through which Qi and "Blood" flow. Other tender points (known as "ashi points") may also be needled as they are believed to be where stagnation has gathered.

Series of diseases, symptoms or conditions for which acupuncture has been demonstrated as an effective treatment:

- Allergic rhinitis
- Depression
- Headache
- Nausea and vomiting including morning sickness
- Pain in the epigastrium, face, neck, tennis elbow, lower back, knee, during dentistry and after operations
- Primary dysmenorrhea
- Rheumatoid arthritis
- Sciatica

- Cervical and Lumbar Sponsylosis
- Bronchial Asthma
- Insomnia

Chromo Therapy: Seven colours of Sun rays have different therapeutic effects. These colours are-Violet, Indigo, Blue, Green, Yellow, Orange and Red. For being healthy and in treatment of different diseases, these colours work effectively. Water and oil exposed to sun for specified hours in coloured bottles and coloured glasses, are used as devices of Chromo Therapy for treating different disorders. The simple methods of Chromo Therapy help in the process of recovery in a very effective manner.

Air Therapy: Fresh air is most essential for good health. The advantage of air therapy can be achieved by means of Air bath. Everybody should take an air bath daily for 20 minutes or longer if possible. It is more advantageous when combined with morning cold rub and exercises.

In this process, one should walk daily after removing the clothes or wearing light clothes at a lonely clean place where adequate fresh air is available. Another alternate method is in a constructed room without roof and surrounded by shutter like walls so as to allow free passage of air but prevent any view of the interior.

Mechanism: In order to react against the chilling effect of cold air or water, the nerve centers, which control the circulation, send the blood to the surface in large quantities, flushing the skin with warm, red, arterial blood. The flow of the blood stream is greatly accelerated and elimination of morbid matter on the surface of the body is correspondingly increased.

Benefits: Air bath has soothing and tonic effect upon the millions of nerve endings all over the surface of the body. It has good results in cases of nervousness, neurasthenia, rheumatism, skin, mental and various other chronic disorders.

Therapeutic Value of Massage

Massage is an excellent form of passive exercise. The word is derived from the Greek word 'massier' which means to knead. It involves the scientific manipulation of the soft tissues of the body. If correctly done on a bare body, it can be highly stimulating and invigorating. As far back as 400 B.C., the great Hippocrates, the father of medicine, employed massage and manipulation in healing his patients. Since then it has been used as a mode of treatment for many ailments and it has restored many a sufferer to health and vigour.

Various Movements

There are five fundamental modes of manipulation in massage and these are: effleurage (stroking), friction (rubbing), petrissage (kneading), tapotment (percussion) and vibration (shaking or trembling):

- Effleurage: This involves sliding with the hands, using long even strokes over the surface of the body. Effleurage is performed in five ways, namely stroking with (I) palms of two hands; (ii) the palm of one hand; (iii) the knuckles; (iv) the ball of the thumb and (v) the finger tips. Effleurage increases blood circulation and soothes the nervous system. It also warms and relaxes. It is very helpful in atrophied condition of the skin.
- Friction: The movements, which are circular in nature are performed with the help of the thumb and tips of fingers or the palm of the hand towards the joints or around the joints. Friction limbers up joints, tendons, and muscles and facilitates the removal of deposits by breaking them. It also helps in reducing swelling after nerve inflammation.
- Petrissage: This is the process of kneading, pressing and rolling of the tissues and is performed with one or both hands, with two thumbs or with thumbs and fingers. One should apply heavy pressure for deep kneading and light pressure for superficial kneading. Petrissage is a treatment of the muscles. It increases nutrition, strengthens muscles, relieves intestinal congestion and helps elimination of the poisons. It boosts long activity and cellular respiration, eliminates fatigue poisons and tones up nerve endings.
- Tapotement: This involves hacking, tapping, clapping and beating and is achieved by striking the body rapidly. Short and quick blows are generally given from the wrist. Tapotement helps in atrophied condition of the muscles. It increases blood supply, soothes nerves and strengthens muscles.
- Vibrations: This is achieved by rapidly shaking the pressing movements by use of the hand or fingers on he body. Vibrating hand should move constantly. This is beneficial in neuritis and neuralgia after the inflammatory stage is over. It stimulates

circulation, glandular activity and nervous plexuses. It also helps in bowel movement. Another form of massage helpful in most elements is the vibratory massage. This can be done by trained persons only. The vibratory muscles is more efficiently administered by a special, electrically operated machine.

Material for Massage

Cotton seed oil is most commonly used for massaging, but butter is used for filling out cheeks and the neck and also for breast enlargement. If the patient is averse to oil, talcum powder may be used. Oil should not be used by persons with excessive body hair. General body massage may be done for 40 to 45 minutes and local body massage for 10 to 15 minutes. The oil should be washed off completely after massage.

Therapeutic Uses: Massage can be used with advantage as a method of treatment for many common ailments. The various forms of massage and their usefulness in various diseases are described here in brief.

Massage of the Joints: Stiff and swollen joints can be cured by massage combined with mechanical movements. Massage is, however, not recommended in serious inflammatory cases of the joints and in tubercular joints. It should also be avoided in infectious diseases like diphtheria and gonorrhoea which cause formation of pus as massage may spread the pus to the entire system. Sprains and bruises can be cured by massage.

In these cases, affected parts should first be bathed with hot water for 15 to 30 minutes. Next the massage should be done for a few minutes. Gentle stroking and kneading is recommended on and around the injured tissues. Fractures can also be treated through massage. This form of massage is of great help in atrophy of the muscles which usually follows if the muscles are not used for any length of time.

This condition may also be brought about by injuries, diseases of the joints, inflammation of the muscles and nerves, and by too long use of cats, bandages and splints. A human being carries one -half of the weight of his body in the form of muscular tissues.One-fourth of the blood supply circulates in the muscles.

When one gets a good massage treatment, the muscles get regenerated and are then capable of holding half of the blood supply. Massage thus provides additional nourishment to feed the muscular tissues, helping them to grow strong. Tapping, striking, and vibrating help the muscle to develop its contractile power. Muscle massage is brought by first effleurage, kneading, followed by tapotement. Later, active and passive movements are given. Massage is employed for eliminatng muscle contraction and for breaking of adhesions. A little moderate kneading, and percussion cause muscles to contract and become stronger. Deep circular kneading and vibration loosens the muscles. Kneading under and round the muscles breaks up adhesions.

Massaging the Nerves: Massage benefits many nerve problems. In case of acute inflammation of the nerves, massage should be done carefully. Light and gentle stroking are recommended. Deep pressure should not be used on swollen nerves for it will increase the inflammation.

All that is needed is just a gentle tapotement or beating of the nerve. Nerve compression is recommended for soothing nerves. Grasp the limb with both hands, and create firm pressure around and down the arm. Start with the shoulder and proceed down to the wrist. As you leave the grip, bring the hands down a little and make another pressure. As a result, blood circulation will increase. Spinal nerve compression is extremely beneficial.

It is done by the palm of the hand. Vibration of the fingers stimulate it. Sleeplessness can be cured by long slow and gentle stroking down the spine and entire back.

Abdominal Massage: This form of massage is beneficial in constipation. It stimulates the peristalsis of the small intestines, tones up the muscles of the abdomen walls and mechanically eliminates the contents of both large and small intestines. Abdominal massage should not be done in general, femoral, inguinal and umbilical hernia, inflammation of the uterus, bladder, ovaries and fallopian tubes, kidney stones, bladder or gall bladder, ulcers of the stomach and intestines, and pregnancy. Abdominal massage should not be done after a heavy meal, but after two hours or so. The bladder should be emptied before the massage.

The patient is made to lie on his back with his knees drawn up. This enable the abdomen wall to relax. The masseur should stand at the right side of the patient and use his finger tips for friction round the umbilical region from right to left. He should likewise alternatively knead the walls and roll with both hands, making deep and firm pressure.

He should knead with the hand and finger tips and keep clear of any wound or tender places. He should later take up massaging of the larger intestines. The manipulation of the large intestine should begin on the right side. Keep it going upwards and across the transverse colon and move right down on the left side to the signoid flexure and rectum. Circular kneading should be done with the help of the three middle fingers. At the same time press into the contents of the abdomen, following the course of the larger colon with a crawling motion. Keep kneading by means of a few circular movements in one spot with the help of finger tips. Keep moving the fingers a little further along. Knead repeatedly.

Use knuckles of the hand to make deep pressure along the large colon, moving the hands along after each pressure. Once the kneading of the abdomen isover, follow up by tapotement with both hands cupped or use the knuckles of the hand. Vibration may also be employed. The patient could also be asked to do some gymnastic exercises for strengthening the walls of the abdomen. Since blood pressure increases during abdominal manipulation, patients with hypertension should avoid abdominal massage. Massage should also be avoided in cases where there has been recent bleeding in the lungs, the stomach or the brain.

Chest Massage: Chest massage is helpful in many ways. It strengthens the chest muscles, increases circulation and tones up the nervous system of chest, heart and lungs. It is especially recommended in weakness of the lungs,palpitation and organic heart disorders. Bust and mammary glands can be developed by proper massage. The patient is made to lie on the back with the arms at the sides. The masseur starts manipulating the chest by means of strokes with both hands on each side of the breast bone. A circular motion is formed by the movement made up and down, moving down the chest. Next the muscle kneading is done by picking up the skin and muscles with both hands. Treatment is given to both sides of the chest likewise. Circular kneading is next done by placing one hand on each side of the breast bone and making the circular motion outward towards the side. Tapotement follows by hacking and slapping.

Massage of Back: The purpose of the massage of the back is to stimulate the nerves and circulation for treating backache, rheumatic afflictions of the back muscles, and for soothing the nervous system. The patient is made to lie down with the arms at the sides.

The masseur effleurages the back from the shoulders downwards using both hands on each side of the spine. Stroking is done from the sacrum upward. Friction follows with each hand at the sides of the spine going down slowly. Next, kneading by muscle picking is done with squeezing. Alternate rapid pushing and pulling movement of the hands sliding down the spine. Circular kneading should also be done.The treatment should end by slapping, hacking and cupping on each side of the spine. Gentle stroking and light kneading of the back is relieving and soothing. Percussion and vibration result into stimulating experience. Vibration of the end of spine benefits the sacral nerves and pelvic organs. It is recommended in constipation, hemorrhoids, weakness and congestion of the bladder and sexual organs.

Benefits of Therapeutic Exercises

After all the technology that has been developed in the last two decades to make people's life as comfortable as possible, health professionals and health conscious people have come to recognize the importance of adding exercise to their daily regimen. People have learned to go back to the basics, to the wisdom of our ancestors, who observed that being active all day long was a powerful medicine for most underlying ailments.

In our modern age, research studies have repeatedly validated the connection between health and therapeutic exercise. This exercise is a physical therapy involving a wide range of activities devised to improve the function of muscles, nerves and organs. Research is one thing, but people tend to learn more from their own experience. For many, it has taken them from making poor health choice, like binge eating and being a couch potato, and finally embracing therapy. It is for this reason that many therapists who suggest therapeutic exercise get help from their own clients and patients in designing the exercise program suitable for them. This way, patients can prevent secondary injury and lessen the chances of getting side-effects from medications and other treatments.

The first thing to realize is that therapeutic exercise program is not for everyone. Women who are pregnant and are having one or more high-risk medical conditions such as vaginal bleeding, preterm rupture of membrane, maternal heart disease, and premature labour should completely avoid it. Precautions need to be taken when their patients have other diseases, such as anemia, extreme fatigue, contractions, musculoskeletal pain and phlebitis, and high risk patients need to be closely monitored by a physician.

Therapeutic exercise program typically consists of a broad range of activities, from simple breathing exercises to high-speed walking on a treadmill. Therapists have long promoted this program to patients because of the multitude of benefits. As a direct result, this exercise generates energy, creates muscle tone, burns calories, lessens constipation and gets rid of depression.

For people who have underlying health conditions, the program is modified to suit the patient's level of endurance, ability, severity of the condition and the stage of recovery.

Therapeutic exercises are used on patients recovering from surgery in order to heal the inflamed tissues. Research shows that just a minimum amount therapeutic exercise yields major protection against post-surgery infections. Low-intensity stretching and mild walking is usually recommended during this period.

People with osteoporosis demonstrate wide variations in their strength levels and tolerance. For patients who are at high risk for pathological fractures due to low bone density, Premier Health Chiropractors recommend low-impact weight bearing exercise. However, caution should be taken while making twisting or explosive movements during the program.

Resistance exercise is another form of therapeutic exercise that plays a major role in curing muscle related pain and inflammation. This type of exercise lowers stress levels and blood pressure readings, resulting in healthier electrocardiograph readings. On the flip side, patients are advised to avoid over working and excessive fatigue causing postures while exercising. For best results, consult Premier Health Chiropractors for details on the best therapeutic exercises for your lifestyle.

Coordination Exercises

The definition of coordination exercises is the ability to execute smooth, accurate, controlled motor responses (optimal interaction of muscle function).

- Coordination is the ability to select the right muscle at the right time with proper intensity to achieve proper action.
- Coordinated movement is characterized by appropriate speed, distance, direction, timing and muscular tension.

It is the process that results in activation of motor units of multiple muscles with simultaneous inhibition of all other muscles in order to carry out a desired activity. The cerebellum is the primary centre in the brain for coordination for movement and the ability to execute smooth accurate motor response.

Components of Coordinated Movement

Coordinated movement is dependent on:

- Volition: Is the ability to initiate, maintain or stop an activity or motion.
- Perception: In tact proprioception and subcortical centres to integrate motor impulses and the sensory feedback. When proprioception is affected it is compensated with visual feedback.
- Engram: A postulated physical or biochemical change in neural tissue that represents a memory. Research proved that high repetitions of precise performance must be performed in order to develop an engram. A 1980 study concluded "Thousands of repetitions are required to begin to form an engram and millions of repetitions are necessary to perfect it. Coordination is developed in proportion to the number of repetitions of an engram practiced just below the maximal level of ability to perform."

Types of Coordination

Motor coordination to complete a task a collaboration of three skills:

1. Fine Motor Skills
   - Require coordinated movement of small muscles (hands, face).
   - Examples: include writing, drawing, buttoning a shirt, blowing bubbles
2. Gross Motor Skills
   - Require coordinated movement of large muscles or groups of muscles (trunk, extremities).
   - Examples: include walking, running, lifting activities.
3. Hand-eye Skills
   - The ability of the visual system to coordinate visual information. Received and then control or direct the hands in the accomplishment of a task.

- Examples: include catching a ball, sewing, computer mouse use.

Causes of Coordination Impairments

Uncoordinated movement or coordination impairment is known medically known as ataxia. There are a number of known causes for ataxia. They range from chronic conditions to sudden onset. However, most conditions will relate to damage or degeneration of the cerebellum.

Toxins can also Cause Ataxia.

These include:

- Alcohol (most common)
- Seizure medications
- Chemotherapy drugs
- Lithium
- Cocaine and heroin
- Sedatives
- Mercury, lead, and other heavy metals
- Toluene and other types of solvents

Examples of Coordination Tests in the Upper Limb In the following tests, you will be looking for signs of Intention tremors and Decomposition of movements or Dysmetria: in the form of hypermetria or hypometria

- Finger-to-nose test - The shoulder is abducted to 90 with the elbow extended, the patient is asked to bring tip of the index finger to the tip of nose. Finger to therapist finger: the patient and the therapist site opposite to each other, the therapist index finger is held in front of the patient, the patient is asked to touch the tip of the index finger to the therapist index finger.
- Finger-to-finger test - Both shoulders are abducted to bring both the elbow extended, the patient is asked to bring both the hand towards the midline and approximate the index finger from opposing hand
- Finger-to-doctor's finger test - the patient alternately touch the tip of the nose and the tip of the therapist's finger with the index finger.
- Adiadokokinesia or dysdiadokokinesia - The patient asked to do rapidly alternating movement e.g. forearm supination and pronation, hand tapping.

- Rebound phenomena - The patient with his elbow fixed, flex it against resistance. When the resistance is suddenly released the patient's forearm flies upward and may hit his face or shoulder.
- Buttoning and unbuttoning test.

Examples of Coordination Tests in the Lower Limb

- Walking along a straight line. Foot close to foot: In case of cerebellar lesion, there is deviation of gait
- Rom-berg test: Ask the patient to stand with heels together. Swaying or loss of balance occurs while his eyes are open or closed.

Coordination Tests for Athletes/ Everyday Sports Person

Many high level tests also exist to help assess and improve an athletes skills and performance e.g. Stick Flip Coordination Test; Wall-Toss Test; Block Transfer; Soda Pop Test; Plate Tapping; Light Board; Test Heel-to-knee test.

General Principles of Coordination Exercises Involve

1. Constant repetition of a few motor activities
2. Use of sensory cues (tactile, visual, proprioceptive) to enhance motor performance
3. Increase of speed of the activity over time
4. Activities are broken down into components that are simple enough to be performed correctly.
5. Assistance is provided when ever necessary.
6. The patient therefore should have a short rest after two or three repetitions, to avoid fatigue.
7. High repetition of precise performance must be performed for the engram to form.
8. When ever a new movement is trained, various inputs are given, like instruction (auditory), sensory stimulation (touch), or positions in which the patient can view the movement (visual stimulation) to enhance motor performance.

Yoga and Yoga Therapy

Working Definitions

Yoga is one of India's oldest and most comprehensive soteriological traditions, which has developed a vast arsenal of physical and mental techniques geared to gain control over the nervous system in order to achieve, at will, conscious and supraconscious states of transcendence.

In order to appreciate the unique contribution of Yoga to our understanding of the human condition, this age-old tradition is best viewed from the kind of broad perspective of the human potential that characterises transpersonal psychology and psychosomatic medicine. Yoga therapy is of modern coinage and represents a first effort to integrate traditional yogic concepts and techniques with Western medical and psychological knowledge.

Whereas traditional Yoga is primarily concerned with personal transcendence on the part of a "normal" or healthy individual, Yoga therapy aims at the holistic treatment of various kinds of psychological or somatic dysfunctions ranging from back problems to emotional distress. Both approaches, however, share an understanding of the human being as an integrated body-mind system, which can function optimally only when there is a state of dynamic balance.

Yoga Past and Present

The beginnings of Yoga can be seen in India's oldest sacred corpus, the Rig-Veda, which was compiled prior to 2000 B.C.E. In this hymnody, composed in archaic Sanskrit, inspired sages expressed their deepest thoughts and intuitions about human life. Yoga achieved its classical form under Patanjali, the compiler of the Yoga-Sûtra, who is assigned to the period from 200 B.C.E. to 200 C.E. He outlined the eight "limbs" of the yogic path: (1) moral discipline (yama), (2) self-restraint (niyama), posture (âsana), breath control (prânâyâma), sensory inhibition (pratyâhâra), concentration (dhâranâ), meditation (dhyâna), and ecstasy (samâdhi). These are intended to lead the practitioner (called yogin if male and yoginî if female) to total transcendence, or liberation. Yogic teachings are also present in Buddhism and Jainism, though in the West the term yoga is most commonly associated with Hinduism.

In contrast to Patanjali's Classical Yoga, the many schools of Post-Classical Yoga are non-dualistic. That is, they pursue their soteriological programme on the basis of the recognition that "All is One." Thus their via negativa leans towards a more life-positive orientation, which is founded in the understanding that if everything is an interconnected and interdependent Whole, there is no need for escape or denial of body, mind, and world.

This orientation achieved its peak in Hatha-Yoga ("Forceful Yoga"). This type of Yoga specialises in exploring the body's potential for the transformative processes of yogic consciousness technology. Understandably, it is this orientation that holds the greatest appeal for contemporary Western students, especially those concerned with the integration of body and mind. Hatha-Yoga has always had a close relationship with India's native naturopathic system called Âyur-Veda ("Life Science"), which is profoundly holistic and for this reason has become fashionable in the West in recent years. A similar osmosis has occurred between Hatha-Yoga and the Siddha naturopathic system of South India, which, however, is as yet little known in Western countries.

The psychosomatic approach of Hatha-Yoga includes many physical purification techniques and a large number of postures that exercise the body in various ways. The last-mentioned feature has been mainly responsible for the great popularity of Hatha-Yoga outside India. Today an estimated six million Americans are practicing postures and other Hatha-Yoga techniques on a more or less regular basis to help restore or maintain their fitness and/or health.

In the West, there are several significant contemporary approaches to Hatha-Yoga, which are based on traditional teachings to varying degrees and also utilise the therapeutic potential of Yoga. The most traditional orientation, which goes by the name of Viniyoga, is found in the school of T. Krishnamacharya and his son T. K. V. Desikachar. It has produced a number of Western Viniyoga teachers, including Gary Kraftsow in Hawaii, who recently authored a significant book on Yoga therapy.

Another well-known system, which has produced over a thousand teachers around the world, is that of B. K. S. Iyengar, a son-in-law and student of T. Krishnamacharya. More than any other teacher, Iyengar has developed Hatha-Yoga for therapeutic purposes and in this context has pioneered the use of props such as wood blocks, benches, bolsters, and straps.

Medical and Psychological Research on Yoga

In the course of its several thousand years of existence, Yoga has accumulated a huge store of experiential data, some of which is contained in the extensive native literature written in Sanskrit and various vernacular languages. Much of the information, however, is still passed on from teacher to disciple by word of mouth, and therefore to learn the subtleties of yogic technology one is obliged to undergo a traditional pupilage even today.

Ever since classical Greece, Westerners have been intrigued by the extraordinary physical and mental abilities of Yoga practitioners. There are numerous anecdotes about yogins being able to stop their pulse and heart beat, to experience no pain when cut or burned, to suffer no injury when ingesting lethal doses of poison, to be buried underground for several days in an airtight box, and not least to remain transfixed in concentration for hours and even days.

Some of these feats have been tested and fully or partially verified in medical laboratories. One of the better known contemporary yogins capable of extraordinary somatic and psychological responses was the late Swami Rama, founder of the Himalayan International Institute in Pennsylvania.

In 1970 he was tested at the Menninger Foundation in Topeka, Kansas, and among other yogic skills demonstrated extensive control over his brain waves. While few Yoga practitioners actually attain this level of mastery, in principle everyone is held to be capable of it. Swami Rama's expertise and humanitarianism attracted many physicians and psychologists, which, in 1989, led to the creation of one of India's best equipped hospitals with 500 beds and a plan for 2,000 more. This hospital, which is meant to be expanded into a medical city, uses Yoga therapy as a complement to conventional medicine.

The earliest medical studies of Yoga were conducted at the Yoga Institute in Santacruz, Bombay. The Institute was founded in 1918 by Shri Yogendra as a research and educational organisation and today is directed by his son Jayadeva Yogendra, Ph.D., who is also the editor of the quarterly magazine Yoga and Total Health, now in its forty-second year of publication. Another well-known Indian Yoga research institution is Kaivalyadhama in Lonavla, which was founded in 1924 by Swami Kuvalayananda, who also launched Yoga-Mimamsa journal.

Over the years, numerous medical studies have been carried out that typically bear out the modest-to-moderate claims made by Yoga authorities. These range from Yoga's beneficial effect on physical flexibility, muscle tone, and stamina to poor eyesight, obesity, indigestion, back pain, hypertension, various respiratory diseases, sinusitis, arthritis, diabetes (I and II), as well as anxiety, nervousness, attention deficit, and memory loss.

In the 1970s, the immense popularity of Transcendental Meditation (TM) introduced to the West by Maharshi Mahesh Yogi led to many studies of this and other forms of meditation. Again, the benefits of regular meditation for physical and mental health have clearly been demonstrated in experiments. The Yoga Research and Education Center in California is currently creating a data base of medical and scientific studies on Yoga, which, when completed, will be made accessible to Yoga teachers and investigators. Some aspects of Yoga-notably meditation-have been fairly thoroughly (and repeatedly) investigated, while others are in need of systematic study. In particular, illness-specific and longitudinal studies are needed toexplore the effects of regular Yoga practice on a person's psychosomatic well-being.

Following are two case histories that illustrate the approach of Yoga therapy.

Two Practical Examples

Morgan, a forty-six-year-old businessman who owned several successful companies, had been referred to me by the trainer of the sports team he was sponsoring and which I was teaching a modified version of Hatha-Yoga. Over the phone he told me that he wanted to learn meditation rather than physical exercises and asked whether I could see him at his home. I told him that my schedule did not allow me to make house calls, especially when long-distance travel was involved, and asked whether he would not be able to come see me instead. I gathered from his cryptic remarks that when he was not in the office, he did not go out much. I insisted that he should come to me for the initial consultation, which he did a few days later.

Morgan was a six-foot-tall lanky figure, slightly stooping, and obviously depressed. I asked him a little bit about his life and medical history, and he admitted to having been on antidepressants on and off for the past several years but currently was not taking anything because he did not like the side effects.

He was told by a friend that meditation could prove beneficial. I confirmed this, but at the same time pointed out to him that meditation is never a quick fix and for it to be helpful must become part of an appropriate lifestyle.

I asked him about his diet, which consisted of restaurant food or snacks at home. He never exercised and had his chauffeur drive him everywhere. He stayed up late, slept little and fitfully, and stayed in bed till noon reading the papers and making phone calls. On the positive side, he did not smoke and drank alcohol only with meals. Morgan seemed reticent to talk about himself, and I had to remind him that although I was not a physician, I needed to know something about him in order to help him. I carefully explored the issue of his depression, and it turned out that he had a long history of failed relationships with women and feared he was becoming impotent. Also, his businesses were more or less running by themselves, and so he had a lot of free time on his hands to brood over his situation, which only made things worse. He had seen a psychiatrist for several months but then grew tired of spilling his guts without ever seeing any change in himself.

I told Morgan quite frankly that before he could benefit from meditation, he would have to do regular physical exercises and breathing techniques to "ground" as well as "energize" himself and thus become able to relax more. He agreed that he had difficulty concentrating and expressed his willingness to try my approach. In turn, I agreed to see him at his home once or twice a week for a while.

On my first visit, I quickly determined Morgan's flexibility, which was poor. I designed a thirty-minute programme for him involving spinal twists in the supine position, easy forward, backward, and lateral bends. I had him do the exercises and helped him find his own optimal form for each. In between each exercise I had him rest for several minutes. I asked his permission to touch him during these relaxations and took the opportunity to help him stabilise his bodily energies by placing my right hand on his solar plexus and then on his heart. His energies responded well, which I conveyed to him. I sensed that he needed all the encouragement I could give him.

We ended the session with a fifteen-minute guided relaxation, which involved first tensing the entire body and then relaxing it limb by limb. When he was adequately relaxed, I asked him to breathe more deeply, filling first his abdomen and then his chest (diaphragmatic breathing). He had difficulty with this, and again I assisted by gently placing my right hand on his solar plexus and guiding the movement of his breath. At the end of the session, I asked him for feedback, and he said that he found the relaxations very good. I encouraged him to practice them every day together with the physical exercises, which he promised he would do. On my second visit, he sheepishly confessed that he had not kept his promise and had no real excuse for this omission either.

I reminded him that he must want to overcome his problems before he could overcome then. Then I very firmly told him that I would not return for further sessions unless he were to practice every day. He seemed surprised at that, but promised to do better. Thereafter he kept his word with only a few exceptions, which I did not hold against him. Over the next several weeks, Morgan's flexibility and capacity for relaxation slowly but steadily increased, and also his energy level seemed to improve. Now and then I got him to talk a little more about his life, though it was difficult for him to open up. Mainly I endeavored to convey to him that we are meaning-creating beings, and that it is largely up to us what meanings we allow to influence our life. I explained that his particular crisis was an opportunity to find or create new meaningsfor himself. Now that his businesses no longer demanded all his energy and attention, he was free to explore new possibilities. At the moment, he felt himself in a vacuum, but looked at differently the same vacuum was an open space for new meanings to emerge. He understood in theory but was frustrated by the fact that he had allowed himself to sink into chronic depression, which now required a lot of remedial work. I had recommended that he see a homeopathic physician for additional help, but he never did; I regarded this as part of his self-sabotaging programme.

Just when I felt we were making some progress, he had to go on an extended business trip. I found out from our mutual friend that during his travels Morgan had completely dropped his Yoga practice, had another disastrous relationship with a woman, and then had promptly succumbed to his usual emotional gloom. He was too depressed and embarrassed to call me after his return. old patterns are difficult to change. Although this case is not a success story, it illustrates well the yogic approach to remedial work. All healing is self-healing, and healers merely assist this process. This is a pivotal message to communicate to clients. Those who are eager to assume responsibility for their own healing inevitably will benefit more deeply and quickly from Yoga.

This was the case with Sally, a fifty-two-year-old woman who had gone through the trials of her husband's bankruptcy followed by an ugly divorce initiated by him. She was suddenly faced with the realisation that, after years of being a housewife, she had to make a new life and career for herself. She came to one of my group sessions twice before she plucked up enough courage to ask me for a private consultation. For years she had been suffering from back problems, which she realised were partly due to prolonged marital strain. Now they were flaring up with a vengeance. I had noticed her discomfort and had her do modified versions of some of the group exercises.

Sally had seen a physician and, apart from chronically contracted muscles in the lower back, there were no structural abnormalities. She had tried a certain style of bodywork but found she was unable to bear the pain of this particular treatment. Yoga, she found, was helping her relieve the discomfort somewhat. She also was aware that she needed to deal with the emotional side of the problem, which was the stored-up anger directed against her husband. Since she understood her difficulties so clearly, I could be very direct with her.

I proposed a two-pronged course of action to Sally. First, she had to let go of the angry "holding pattern," which caused her lower back muscles to be in a chronically contracted state. Second, she had to use the energy freed up by releasing her anger in a creative way. She expressed a great eagerness to do both. I asked her to lie down on her side and then placed my hand on her lower back to let her feel the "holding pattern." Simultaneously, I explained to her that these contracted muscles were her own unloving feelings and that no one but herself was responsible for them and the pain they were causing her. She cried a little, which was a good beginning. I encouraged her to see her life in the larger context of yogic meanings. This included the idea that by projecting anger towards someone, we not only do damage to them, because, according to Yoga, thoughts are forms of energy, but that this action also has inevitable repercussions for ourselves.

I then surprised her by asking her to daily send positive, blessing thoughts to her ex-husband, audibly saying words of forgiveness. She found this very difficult at first and shed some tears, but with some practice she began to feel the transformative power of this exercise and in the end could do it quite naturally. She understood that body and mind go together and that she needed to take care of both. At the same time, I taught her to visualise all muscle tension being released during exhalation and while lying in the supine position with a cushion under her knees to prevent any strain on her lower back.

As she acquired more of a sense of the energy freed up by means of this exercise, I asked her to visualise that energy filling her body with strength and radiance during inhalation. In addition, I designed an individual exercise programme for her, which she could do at home. I also recommended that she take a hot bath prior to exercising so as to loosen her muscles, especially for the stretches, and suggested some vitamin supplements to aid this process. Her physical condition improved surprisingly quickly, mainly because she practiced consistently, intelligently, and with enthusiasm. She also visibly gained in self-confidence, and before long she initiated the necessary steps towards a career in bodywork.

Discussion

As an emerging field, Yoga therapy is still in the process of defining itself both relative to the medical and psychological profession and the Indic Yoga tradition. Throughout its long history, YogaÕs proven vitality has always been integrally connected with the traditional initiatory structure and oral transmission of yogic teachings. In the West, a new approach to Yoga is evolving, which tends to downplay these two traditional elements but which has introduced a battery of new concepts and practices stemming from medicine and psychology.

While this direction is necessary and inevitable, it also exposes Yoga to reductionism, which must be avoided. Specifically, to the extent that Yoga therapy understands itself as little more than physical therapy or breath therapy it will have failed in preserving the holistic paradigm of original Yoga. The challenge confronting Yoga therapists is to remain true to the holistic (psychosomatic and spiritual) content of traditional Yoga while simultaneously serving clients who are suffering from physical and emotional dysfunctions and who may not be prepared to hear that their problems have a spiritual component. To express it differently, Yoga therapists will have to become highly skillful in navigating the potentially hazardous waters between therapy and religion-a challenge they share, for instance, with some psychotherapists.

Yoga has been part of the American cultural kaleidoscope for the past hundred years and is undoubtedly here to stay. Yoga teacher training in the United States is becoming ever more professionalised through the efforts of organisations like the International Association of Yoga Therapists in Mill Valley, California, and International Yoga Studies in Phoenix, Arizona. Training specific to Yoga therapy is also increasingly subjected to higher professional standards, which will serve both Yoga therapists and their clients. The first fruits of these various efforts can be seen in the recent interest by health insurance companies in admitting Yoga and Yoga therapy into their programmes. The future for Yoga and Yoga therapy looks bright.

Hatha Yoga Therapy

Hatha yoga is not only a method of preparing the system for spiritual awakening, it is also a very important science of health. Since ancient times it has been used by yogis and rishis for the relief and elimination of all kinds of diseases, disorders and defects. It is true that the practices require a bit more time and effort on the part of the patient than the conventional therapies. Rut in terms of permanent, positive results, as well as the saving of enormous expenditure on medicines, they are certainly well worth it. What makes this method of treatment so powerful and effective is the fact that it works on the principles of harmony and unification rather than diversity.

The three important principles on which physical and mental therapy is based are as follows:

1. Conferring absolute health to one part or system of the body and thereby influencing the rest of the body.
2. Balancing the positive and negative energy poles.
3. Purifying the body of the three types of wastages.

Mutual Rhythms

If you hang fifteen grandfather clocks with varying pendulum movements together on the same wall, you will notice that after some time all the pendulums become synchronised. This occurs quite naturally according to the law of mutual rhythms and vibrations. In this physical body, the various organs and systems all have to carry out their own functions, but there should be a complete co-ordination between them. If any of the organs or systems of the body are not able to co-ordinate with each other, it means that not one, but all the systems and organs are unbalanced. Thus, in any sickness, whether physical or mental, every system is out of co-ordination.

According to the law of mutual rhythms, all you have to do in order to regain the health of the whole system, is to bring one organ or system to a state of health. Then all the others will naturally follow suit. Ill health of one system creates ill health in the rest of the body. You cannot say that your stomach is bad and everything else is all right. Therefore, if a sick person comes to us with a number of ailments, we generally, give treatment for only one of them and try to get him better on the level of this particular ailment. If you are able to create health in one system of his body, gradually the whole body begins to get better. This is how hatha yoga therapy should be given. Most yoga teachers today, however, do not follow this system. Depending on their knowledge of medical diagnosis, they make a very long list of practices-one for constipation, one for nosebleed, one for something else. They think that by teaching a sick person various hatha yoga techniques for his different ailments, he will get better. Their system is based on the popular concept that various diseases belong to different groups, which does not take into account the interrelationship of all the organs and systems.

to co-ordinate with each other, it means that not one, but all the systems and organs are unbalanced. Thus, in any sickness, whether physical or mental, every system is out of co-ordination.

According to the law of mutual rhythms, all you have to do in order to regain the health of the whole system, is to bring one organ or system to a state of health. Then all the others will naturally follow suit. Ill health of one system creates ill health in the rest of the body. You cannot say that your stomach is bad and everything else is all right. Therefore, if a sick person comes to us with a number of ailments, we generally, give treatment for only one of them and try to get him better on the level of this particular ailment. If you are able to create health in one system of his body, gradually the whole body begins to get better. This is how hatha yoga therapy should be given. Most yoga teachers today, however, do not follow this system. Depending on their knowledge of medical diagnosis, they make a very long list of practices-one for constipation, one for nosebleed, one for something else. They think that by teaching a sick person various hatha yoga techniques for his different ailments, he will get better. Their system is based on the popular concept that various diseases belong to different groups, which does not take into account the interrelationship of all the organs and systems.

Balancing the Energy Poles

Conserving energy in this physical body is another important aspect of health which has been ignored by most of the healing sciences. We have given so much importance to nutrition, but we have missed the real source of energy which is inherent. This energy is something like positive and negative electrical charges pulsating throughout. The correct balance of these plus and minus forms of energy creates good health. Whenever these positive and negative flows are suppressed, blocked, dissipated or poorly distributed, disease inevitably results. The different organs and systems of the body do not merely subsist on food and vitamins. The main source of energy in life is these plus/minus or positive/negative charges. Therefore, the science 'of physical and mental harmony is known as hatha yoga. The meaning of hatha yoga is very clear. The letters 'ha' and, 'tha' are tantric bija mantras, representing the positive and negative poles of energy. Hatha yoga means the union or co-ordination between the positive and negative forces in the physical body.

Elimination of Wastes

Our body functions along very simple lines. Just as a machine produces wastes, likewise our body continuously produces wastes. These wastes are of three types: mucus, gas and acidity. If we cleanse the body internally from time to time, the excesses of these three metabolic products are removed, and their formation is regulated and balanced. Then perfect health can be maintained. It is in this sense that the practices of the six hatha yoga shatkarmas are of very great importance. Gleaning the body of the three types of wastages accumulated in the system is an important aspect of hatha yoga therapy.

Neti: The first shatkarma is the practice of neti, where warm saline water is passed through one nostril and out the other. Neti is also done with a catheter if there is any nasal blockage. Neti should be practised before pranayama in order to clean both the nasal passages. It is used for different types of diseases because when both the nasal passages are regularly cleaned, a scientific healing process takes place.

During respiration, when air enters the nostrils, a message is passed to the brain regarding the ion contents in the air. Then monitoring takes place at the septum of the nose, and the positive and negative ions are separated. Thus for the proper monitoring and separation of ions in the air, it is necessary that the whole nasal passage be cleaned by the practice of neti. We have found that people suffering from epileptic and hysterical fits, breathe through the mouth. Not only at night when they sleep, but even during the day, they unconsciously breathe through the mouth. This is because the mucus membrane at the nasal opening is inflamed. Therefore the air that enters through the nose smells, and the nose is allergic to that smell. When there is inflammation in the mucus membrane, there are certain allergic reactions. For example, the inflamed mucus membrane refuses to accept various odours - it will either sneeze them out, or, if they are forced in, it will cause a cold, headache, or vomiting.

So, those people who have a continuous inflammation in the mucus membrane of the nose, are compelled to breathe through the mouth. When they inhale through the mouth, the bulk of oxygen goes straight to the lungs. The mouth does not have a mechanism to separate the ions into gaseous matter. So what happens is that the lungs create a great stress on the coronary system and also the brain. This in turn becomes a great strain on the sensory channels and the motor cortex, and results in hysteria and both types of epilepsy.

The treatment for these disorders is very simple: stop breathing through the mouth. Mouth breathing is due to the inflamed, sensitive mucus membrane. In order to correct this condition, you have to teach sutra neti, in which a catheter is inserted into the nose and taken out through the mouth. This creates a certain friction at the septum where the monitoring is received, so that the ions can be properly separated. The practice of neti is also very helpful in the relief of migraine, sinusitis, and many other complaints related to the eyes, ears, nose and throat.

Dhauti

Dhauti is a very important system of auto-cleansing which includes three main techniques: (i) kunjal- vomiting, (ii) vastra dhauti- swallowing a strip of cloth, (iii) shankhaprakshalana- drinking saline water and allowing it to pass all through the alimentary canal. Much is known about kunjal, in which you drink saline water and vomit it out.

This is a very important practice for eliminating acidity in gastric complaints. Many diseases are caused by hyperacidity, and this practice of vomiting is an antidote for it. For those who have a bad stomach, or what you call a sour taste from belching up the stomach acids, this is the best practice. Vomiting is very important for improving the digestion and balancing hyperacidity. But if there is hypoacidity, then this practice does not help.

In cases of hypoacidity we use another practice called vyaghra dhauti or tiger wash. Hypoacidity causes chronic dyspepsia or indigestion. Due to lack of acidity, the food is not properly digested. When this type, of indigestion occurs, we wait for three hours after taking food, and then vomit all the remaining contents so that the stomach is clean.

For elimination problems, I have found that the best form of dhauti is shankhaprakshalana. With about 16 glasses (or 4 to 5 litres) of warm saline water, you clean the whole alimentary canal from top to bottom. Within a period of 11/2 hours, you are able to get rid of all the fermenting, decomposed mucus in the intestines. On the intestinal walls there is hard mucus, to which the food sticks fast. As this mucus decomposes, it should be expelled. Unfortunately, however, in our modern system of treatment, when the mucus passes we think that we have a disease, and immediately take some medicine to stop the process. We don't allow this decomposed mucus to be thrown out by nature's obligation. When you practise shankhaprakshalana, the intestines (large and small), are washed clean of this decomposed mucus.

When this mucus is completely expelled, a state of cleanliness and health is created throughout the whole system. You must remember that when the intestines are loaded with decomposed mucus, intestinal peristalsis slows down and the temperature in the colon and the small intestine also falls. When this occurs decomposition and fermentation of food stuff takes place inside the intestines. This means that during the process of assimilation, the body absorbs toxins and the whole body becomes toxicated.

Cleansing of the body through shankhaprakshalana should take place according to the seasons prevailing in the country. When the season changes from hot to cold, there is a corresponding change in the whole body. The heating and cooling system, like a thermostat, changes shifts as the seasons change. At this time shankhaprakshalana should be practised.

Asana and Pranayama

In hatha yoga therapy we have also had excellent results with the practice of asanas and pranayama. The major asanas are very powerful because they influence the endocrine system, which maintains order in the physical body. Imbalance or hyper/hypo conditions can generate any sickness. Coronary disease is a good example. In western countries this disease is increasing day by day, and is known as killer number one. Along with relaxation, we have found the practice of siddhasana beneficial for heart patients.

Siddhasana, the pose in which you press the perineum with one heel and the lower viscera with the other, is not only important as a meditation pose. The pressure of the heels helps to control the outflow of testosterone, the male hormone produced in the scrotum. This hormone is very important because it controls male function and also influences the coronary behaviour. By controlling the outflow of testosterone you can prevent coronary accidents. By suppressing the release of this important hormone, you can automatically control the fluctuation of the blood pressure. Testosterone has an immediate constricting effect on the blood vessels, which in turn, burdens the whole coronary system by raising the pressure. During the practice of siddhasana, however, the outflow of testosterone is inhibited and the blood pressure is able to rebalance itself.

Sirshasana, the headstand pose, is well known for increasing ventilation to the body tissues, especially the brain. Usually ventilation to the brain is very inadequate, but in sirshasana, it is optimal. By the practice of sirshasana, you can completely remove all heaviness from the brain and thoughts. What is not so widely known about sirshasana is that it has a beneficial influence on the behaviour of the heart. During sirshasana the rate of oxygen consumption decreases while the rate of oxygen assimilation increases. This was verified several years ago by a team of Polish researchers. Sirshasana is important in heart disease because when consumption of oxygen is brought down, the heart rate is also brought down. If coronary problems are to be controlled, people will have to be trained to use the minimum amount of oxygen. The practices of sirshasana and kumbhaka are most important for reducing oxygen consumption and training the involuntary muscles of the heart and brain.

The heart is an involuntary muscle, but it is controlled by a centre in the hypothalamus. When a yogi enters into underground samadhi and stops his breath, he does not consume any oxygen, and his heart stops completely. If the heart did not stop completely, it would fill up with impure blood which would damage its tissues and walls. So, in underground samadhi, consumption of oxygen is nil. Even the remote pulsation of energy is absent in the coronary muscles. This state has been known to continue for a number of days, and when the yogi emerges from samadhi, his functions again resume their normal rate.

Meditation

The science of meditation is also part of hatha yoga. It is not merely a way to God, but a way to maintain a balance between the pulsating energies and make them useful for this body. I think that meditation is a game between the two forces, the two energies within us, which are in total conflict with each other. One energy is trying to subordinate the other form of energy. Through the practices of meditation a union is created between these two energies which then become what is called total energy.

Union of Yoga and Science

The psychic and mental diseases which human beings are suffering from are nothing but a state of disharmony in the energy system. In order to alleviate them we will have to take a new look at our body and enlarge the dimension of modern medical science. We will have to redefine the body, the classification of disease and the system of diagnosis. As soon as modern science is able to redefine the body as it is, and correlate the state of the body with the state of mind and the situations of life, then perhaps a happy union can take place between yoga and science. But at the moment we are poles apart; yoga is talking about one thing and science is talking about something else.

Physical and mental therapy is one of the most important achievements of hatha yoga. So far, hatha yoga has succeeded in diseases like asthma, diabetes and blood pressure, where modern science has not. Besides this, hatha yoga has proved very effective in cases of epilepsy, hysteria, rheumatism and many other ailments of chronic and constitutional nature. In fact, we have found that most diseases of chronic and constitutional nature can definitely be reversed through hatha yoga. What is needed at this time, however, is more trained teachers and therapists, and a better quality of training. The hatha yoga teacher has to be an expert of body and mind. At the same time, he or she should not only be a hatha yoga teacher, but a hatha yoga scientist. Much research has to be done on this. This is just a glimpse into how the practices of hatha yoga can create a state of physical and mental health. At the moment, many researches are going on in various countries of Europe, in America, India and South-east Asia to ascertain the effects of the practices on all the organs and systems of the body. Soon we hope that hatha yoga will be accepted as one of the major systems of treatment for physical and mental diseases.

Yoga Therapy in Practice

This chapter outlines the rationale and best practices for helping young people recover from the trauma of sexual abuse using integrative and therapeutic Yoga practices. As a model for such work, we describe a specic programme, Healing Childhood Sexual Abuse with Yoga, currently of-fered by the authors in the Portland, OR area.

The programme includes not only Yoga postures but also guided medita-tion, art projects, mindful eating, and other activities that address a full range of multisensory healing.

The curricu-lum is designed to integrate with non-Yoga therapies the youth are receiving. In our professional experience, Yoga and related mindfulness practices can help restore sexual abuse victims to wholeness and a life of greater joy. We provide recommendations that can be used by clinical therapists, mental health specialists, social workers, Yoga therapists, or anyone who works with young people or adults recovering from sexual abuse. For clarity, the term "Yoga teacher" will be used throughout to distinguish Yoga practitioners from the sexual abuse treatment therapists they collaborate with.

Sexual Abuse In the United States

Sexual abuse is widespread in the United States, and despite recent eorts to destigmatize being a sexual abuse survivor, much remains hidden and underreported.An extensive literature review of U.S. Government sources, as well as retrospective and other clinical studies, reports that one out of four girls and one out of six boys are sexually abused before the age of 18.

Only 10 per cent of these as-saults are committed by strangers; the rest are committed by parents, siblings, foster caregivers, neighbours, or family acquaintances. Two in ve of these children are abused by older or larger children, further increasing the sense of isolation that arises from sexual abuse, and 23 per cent of all incidents of sexual abuse are perpetrated by individuals under the age of 18. The median age for reported abuse is 9 years old, with one in ve cases occurring in children age 8 or younger.

Consequences of Childhood Sexual Abuse

Sexual abuse is a complex trauma that involves many destructive elements, including betrayal of trust, secretive-ness, coercion, threats, unpredictability, long duration, fam-ily disintegration, and feelings of anger, fear, and shame. The long-term consequences of childhood sexual abuse include inappropriate sexual behaviour, poor self-image, troubles with work or schooling, and increased risk of mental health issues and suicide.Because sexual abuse is an extreme violation of an individual's physical, emotional, cognitive, and familial integrity, it contributes to many conditions confronted by adult survivors, including homelessness, addiction, obesity, chronic illness, and depression.

Posttraumatic stress disorder (PTSD) has been reported to be ve times more likely in female survivors of childhood sexual abuse compared to the general female population.Children who have been sexually abused exhibit more post-traumatic fear, anxiety, and concentration problems than do their non-abused peers. Most survivors of child sexual abuse do not meet the full diagnostic criteria for PTSD, but more than 80 per cent are reported to have some post-traumatic symptoms.Overlapping symptomatology between PTSD and the eects of childhood sexual abuse in young girls and women include anxiety, depression, somatic complaints (in particular, greater pelvic and menstrual pain), low self-esteem, learning disabilities, running away, conduct disorders, delinquency, aggressiveness, substance abuse, self-mutilation, suicidal behaviour, inappropriate sexual behaviour, teenage prostitution, and early pregnancy.

Therapeutic Intervention

Given the severe, potentially lifelong consequences of the trauma of sexual abuse, it is critical to seek therapeutic interventions that can help survivors heal from their past abuse. Having seen Yoga's success in our own work with homeless youth, youth in foster care, and youth in other challenging circumstances, we decided to explore whether Yoga could support long-term recovery in survivors of childhood sexual abuse.

Specic research on the applicability of Yoga as a therapeutic intervention for survivors of child sexual abuse is lacking. However, there has been reported success in using Yoga as an intervention for PTSD, anxiety, and depres-sion. For example, in one study, mind-body therapies that included guided imagery, meditation, movement, breathing, drawing, and other elements signicantly decreased posttraumatic stress scores among adolescents presenting postwar PTSD symptoms.A mindfulness intervention that included breathing, meditation, and Yoga has been shown to signicantly decrease anxiety and depression among adults with an anxiety disorder or panic disorder.While these studies, and others like them, support the applicability of mindfulness and Yoga for traumaaected populations, more research is needed to determine the efficiency of similar programmes specically for sexual abuse survivors.

In developing our approach, we also turned to the research examining what types of interventions best support healing from childhood sexual abuse. There is growing evidence that Trauma-

Focused Cognitive Behavioural Therapy (TF-CBT) is an eective treatment for sexually abused children.This treatment model includes eight core com-ponents: education about sexual abuse and PTSD, emotion regulation skills, individualized stress-management skills, an introduction to the cognitive triad (relationships between thoughts, feelings, and behaviours), creating a trauma narrative (a gradual exposure intervention wherein children describe increasingly distressing details of their sexual abuse, to help them integrate the experience), cognitive processing, safety skills and education about healthy sexuality, and a parental treatment component. Randomized, controlled trials for sexually abused children that use models other than TF-CBT are rare.

Yoga Therapy: The Next Wave in Yoga

Soon the formerly athletic LeSure, a 57-year-old social worker from Bellevue, Wash., couldn't walk more than a hundred yards. Two surgeries and lots of painkillers later, LeSure realized that he needed to find the cause of his problem-and do something to prevent it from happening again. He found yoga therapist Robin Rothenberg, who runs The Yoga Barn in Issaquah, Wash. At his first 90-minute private visit, Rothenberg learned LeSure's health history and observed his gait and posture. After determining that habitual off-kilter body mechanics had led to his ruptured disk, she taught him a sequence of yoga poses, breathing exercises and meditation techniques over an eight week course.

LeSure's pain disappeared. Today he's training to walk the Seattle Marathon. "It's astounding to me," LeSure says.

Many people start yoga because of an injury. But the average yoga teacher doesn't have much background in advanced anatomy, or the time to address individual problems in a packed power yoga class.

The Therapist Will See You Now

An emerging field in America, yoga therapy hovers somewhere between a doctor's visit and a stretching class. Yoga therapists work in small groups or private sessions, addressing specific health problems and adapting poses accordingly. A steady stream of interest has become a flood: According to the trade group International Association of Yoga Therapists (IAYT), membership has more than tripled in the last three years, and the number of schools offering training has doubled over the past two years. "Yoga therapy is really just blossoming," says

Larry Payne, Ph.D., a yoga therapist since 1982 and founder of Samata Yoga. "It's the next great thing in yoga." Modern yoga therapy can be traced back to the yoga master T. Krishnamacharya, who produced students that became the West's most influential teachers of therapeutic yoga, including his son TKV Desikachar and BKS Iyengar.

Many have since used yoga for managing high blood pressure, coping with the effects of cancer treatments, or treating symptoms of HIV, depression or anxiety. But lately it's become especially popular for musculoskeletal issues like lower and upper back pain, sciatica, and shoulder, neck and hip pain. Physical therapists use many methods, from targeted stretches to deep tissue massage; exercises with a Theraband, foam noodles, belts, physioballs, bobbleboards, Bosu Balls, or a wall; and heat and/or ice therapy at home. After a physical therapy session, you'll usually leave with a photocopied sheet of exercises.

A yoga therapist works primarily with yoga moves, and clients typically leave with instructions on a custom series of poses that change each week according to the student's progress. Yoga therapy advocates believe that since yoga is a holistic discipline - teaching that the mind, body, and spirit are connected - yoga therapy can go beyond the results that are possible with physical therapy.

"Yoga therapy is very much about the whole person," says Janice Gates, president of the International Association of Yoga Therapists and author of "Yogini." "It is complementary to physical therapy, but we take into account that back pain may be related to an emotional element, or it may be from lifestyle, some pattern that is not serving them, physical movement patterns or other patterns."

What are a Yoga Therapist's Credentials

"Anybody can hang their shingle and say they are a yoga therapist," says Julie Gudmestad, a yoga and physical therapist in Portland, Ore. Indeed, yoga therapy encompasses many different schools, teachers and ideologies. Many yoga therapists are licensed physical therapists or nurses, or have advanced training in Iyengar yoga. Some use the title CYT, certified yoga therapist, after graduating from a yoga therapy teacher training programme such as Integrative Yoga Therapy. Others are yoga teachers who declare themselves yoga therapists.

"Buyer beware," says Gudmestad. "I've seen some strange things done in the name of yoga therapy."

It's this minority that worries some health care professionals. Inexperienced teachers who lack the ability to correctly diagnose a problem are the biggest danger, according to physical therapist Robert Forster in Santa Monica, Calif. "I have patients who say, 'My yoga teacher told me to push through the pain,'" says Forster. "Often that's the worst thing to do." "Everybody should be seen by a medical professional first, without question," says Leslie Bogart, a Santa Monica yoga therapist with a nursing background.

Do the Numbers on Yoga Therapy Add up for you

Yoga itself is being embraced as a health and wellness practice in America: Yoga is offered at 93 per cent of 755 integrative medical centers, which combine western and alternative health care methods, according to Cary Wing, executive director at the Medical Fitness Association in Richmond, Va.

While it's unclear how many of those centers offer yoga therapy specifically, there is evidence that some yoga poses offer effective treatment for one of the most common complaints that lands patients in physical therapists' offices: chronic back pain. In a study reported in the Annals of Internal Medicine in 2005, patients given a sequence of yoga poses by yoga therapist designed by Gary Kraftsow improved more than did patients given a self-care book or sent to exercise class. The National Institute of Health has allocated $1.2 million for a larger follow-up study on yoga therapy's effectiveness for back pain.

Loren Fishman, M.D., director of the Flushing Department of Physical Medicine and Rehabilitation in New York and coauthor of "Relief is in the Stretch: End Back Pain Through Yoga," prescribes downward-facing dog for osteoporosis, twisted triangle pose for piriformis syndrome, and side plank pose for scoliosis.

"It calms people down," Fishman says. "Just being calm is a tremendous asset when you are in pain." Fishman believes yoga and western medicine are naturally well matched - and can help patients avoid unnecessary surgery, medication, and suffering.

Effects of Yogic Techniques

The following effects of Yogic techniques may be attributed towards recovering chronic functional disorders and promoting positive health.

Sedative and Tranquillising Effect: The effects of stresses and strain leading to psychological and behavioural problems are overcome. Some techniques like trataka(still gazing), mantra recitation and meditation induce calming effect on the psycho-physiological system which may be due to an action of the mid-brain, reticular formation and other areas of the brain. Also, Yoga hastens motor recovery in patients having tremors like in Parkinsonism and Multiple sclerosis.

Homoeostatic Effect: All Yogic techniques bring regulatory effect, which means the minute adjustments of the internal environment of the body towards a state of normal and optimal balance. The homoeostatic balance is maintained by the balance of sympathetic and para-sympathetic nervous system as well as by the endocrinal system.

Immune and Analgesic Effect, The body resistance to diseases is increased through an increase in white blood cell, antibodies, gamma globulins and other substances. Kriya, asana and meditation are important aids to strengthen immune system. Also, Yogic techniques increase the pain threshold thus relieving pain of arthritis, cervical spondylosis, low backache, migraine, slip disc, sciatica and other painful conditions.

Yoga Therapy may be effective to these disorders. Musculoskeletal problems (Backache, General body pain, Osteoarthritis, Rheumatoid arthritis), Respiratory Disorders (Bronchial Asthma, Allergic rhinitis),

Cardiovascular Disorders (IHD, Hypertension, Peripheral Vascular Disease), Digestive Disorders (Hyperacidity, Irritable Bowel Syndrome, Constipation), Neurological Disorders (Migraine, Multiple sclerosis),

Psychiatric problems (Neurotic disorders, Schizophrenia, Anxiety), Endocrine Disorders (Diabetes mellitus, Thyroid disorders, Adrenal cortex disorders, Obesity), Geriatric problems: Adjustment disorders, Memory loss, Insomnia), Gynecological Disorder and Obstetric conditions (Menstrual disorder, Menopausal syndrome, Sterility disease, Middle and late pregnancy).

Apart from being a genuine system of spiritual quest firmly rooted in Indian Tradition, Yoga can be a practical tool to Body-Mind integration for the Holistic Healing and Positive Health, which is accessible by and applicable to the majority of people in the society. A systematic attempt to implement Yoga into formal health care system may bring great benefits to general public. For this, health care professionals may have general knowledge of Yoga and the right perspective of its application. General patients may have access to the learning opportunity of Yoga in the formal setting in hospital and public health center.

Chapter 5

Naturopathy Healing Technique

Introduction

Naturopathy, a holistic approach to healthcare, encompasses a range of healing techniques that aim to support the body's innate ability to heal itself and maintain optimal health. Rooted in the principle of treating the whole person - mind, body, and spirit - naturopathic medicine emphasizes the use of natural therapies and lifestyle interventions to address underlying causes of illness and promote overall well-being.

One of the fundamental principles of naturopathy is the belief in the healing power of nature. Naturopathic practitioners utilize a variety of natural therapies, including herbal medicine, nutrition, hydrotherapy, acupuncture, homeopathy, and physical medicine, to stimulate the body's self-healing mechanisms and restore balance.

Herbal medicine, or phytotherapy, involves the use of medicinal plants and botanical extracts to treat a wide range of health conditions. Herbs are chosen for their specific therapeutic properties and may be administered in various forms, such as teas, tinctures, capsules, or topical preparations. Herbal medicine is often used to support digestion, strengthen the immune system, reduce inflammation, and promote detoxification.

Nutrition plays a central role in naturopathic medicine, as diet has a profound impact on overall health and well-being. Naturopathic practitioners assess their clients' dietary habits and nutritional status to identify potential deficiencies or imbalances that may contribute to illness. They may recommend dietary changes, supplementation, or therapeutic diets tailored to individual needs to optimize health and support healing. Hydrotherapy is another common naturopathic healing technique that harnesses the therapeutic properties of water for health promotion and disease prevention. Hydrotherapy treatments may include contrast showers, sitz baths, steam inhalation, and hydrothermal wraps, among others. These treatments are used to improve circulation, support detoxification, relieve pain and inflammation, and promote relaxation.

Acupuncture, an ancient Chinese healing art, is often integrated into naturopathic practice to balance the flow of energy, or qi, within the body. Acupuncture involves the insertion of thin needles into specific points along energy pathways, known as meridians, to stimulate the body's self-healing mechanisms and restore balance. Acupuncture is used to treat a wide range of conditions, including pain, stress, anxiety, digestive disorders, and hormonal imbalances.

Homeopathy is a system of medicine based on the principle of "like cures like," where highly diluted substances are used to stimulate the body's innate healing response. Homeopathic remedies are chosen based on the individual's unique symptoms and constitutional type and are believed to address underlying imbalances on a physical, emotional, and energetic level.

Physical medicine techniques, such as massage therapy, chiropractic adjustments, and therapeutic exercise, may also be employed in naturopathic practice to promote musculoskeletal health, improve flexibility and mobility, and enhance overall vitality.

The naturopathic medicine offers a holistic approach to healing that integrates natural therapies, lifestyle interventions, and preventive measures to support health and well-being. By addressing the root causes of illness and promoting the body's self-healing mechanisms, naturopathic practitioners empower individuals to take an active role in their health and achieve optimal vitality and wellness.

Naturopathy is a natural healing technique using the healing powers of nature. The principle of Naturopathy is that the accumulation of toxins is the root cause of all diseases. Prevention and elimination of toxins is the route to health. Treatments are based on the 5 great elements of nature that have immense healing properties. There is no role of internal medications in the nature cure system.

The Five great elements of nature and the treatments based on them are:

- Earth: Mud baths, Mud packs,

- Water: Hydrotherapeutic methods in the form of Baths, Jets, Douches, Packs, Compresses, Immersions
- Air: Breathing exercises, Outdoor walking, Open air baths
- Fire: Sun baths, Thermoleum baths, Magnetised water, Colour charged oils/ water
- Ether: Fasting therapy.

Other Naturopathic Therapies:

- Yoga
- Oriental healing techniques like Reflexology, Acupressure, Acupuncture and Auriculotherapy
- Food and Nutrition
- Magnetotherapy
- Physiotherapy
- Chromotherapy

This multi disciplinary approach uses the healing power of natural resources like foods, herbs, earth, water, air, sun and magnets to allow the body to heal itself. It helps in degenerative and chronic conditions like asthma and arthritis, gastro-intestinal problems and hypertension.

History of Naturopathy

Naturopaths claim the ancient Greek "Father of Medicine", Hippocrates, as the first advocate of naturopathic medicine, before the term existed.Naturopathy has its roots in the 19th century Nature Cure movement of Europe. In Scotland, Thomas Allinson started advocating his "Hygienic Medicine" in the 1880s, promoting a natural diet and exercise with avoidance of tobacco and overwork.

The term naturopathy was coined in 1895 by John Scheel, and purchased by Benedict Lust, the "father of U.S., naturopathy". Lust had been schooled in hydrotherapy and other natural health practices in Germany by Father Sebastian Kneipp; Kneipp sent Lust to the United States to spread his drugless methods. Lust defined naturopathy as a broad discipline rather than a particular method, and included such techniques as hydrotherapy,herbal medicine, and homeopathy, as well as eliminating overeating, tea, coffee, and alcohol. He described the body in spiritual and vitalistic terms with "absolute reliance upon the cosmic forces of man's nature".

In 1901, Lust founded the American School of Naturopathy in New York. In 1902 the original North American Kneipp Societies were discontinued and renamed "Naturopathic Societies". In September 1919 the Naturopathic Society of America was dissolved and Benedict Lust founded the American Naturopathic Association to supplant it. Naturopaths became licensed under naturopathic or drugless practitioner laws in 25 states in the first three decades of the twentieth century. Naturopathy was adopted by many chiropractors, and several schools offered both Doctor of Naturopathy (ND) and Doctor of Chiropractic (DC) degrees. Estimates of the number of naturopathic schools active in the United States during this period vary from about one to two dozen.

After a period of rapid growth, naturopathy went into decline for several decades after the 1930s. In 1910 the Carnegie Foundation for the Advancement of Teaching published the Flexner Report, which criticized many aspects of medical education, especially quality and lack of scientific rigour.

The advent of penicillin and other "miracle drugs" and the consequent popularity of modern medicine also contributed to naturopathy's decline.

In the 1940s and 1950s, a broadening in scope of practice laws led many chiropractic schools to drop their ND degrees, though many chiropractors continued to practice naturopathy. From 1940 to 1963, the American Medical Association campaigned against heterodox medical systems.

By 1958 practice of naturopathy was licensed in only five states. In 1968 the United States Department of Health, Education, and Welfare issued a report on naturopathy concluding that naturopathy was not grounded in medical science and that naturopathic education was inadequate to prepare graduates to make appropriate diagnosis and provide treatment; the report recommends against expanding Medicare coverage to include naturopathic treatments.

In 1977 an Australian committee of inquiry reached similar conclusions; it did not recommend licensure for naturopaths.

As of 2009, fifteen U.S., states, Puerto Rico, the US Virgin Islands and the District of Columbia licensed naturopathic doctors, and the state of Washington requires insurance companies to offer reimbursement for services provided by naturopathic physicians. South Carolina and Tennessee prohibit the practice of naturopathy.

Beginning in the 1970s, interest waxed in the United States and Canada in conjunction with the holistic health movement.

Salient Features of Naturopathy

The main features of Naturopathy are:

1. All diseases, their causes and treatment are one. Except for traumatic and environmental conditions, the cause of all diseases is one i.e., accumulation of morbid matter in the body. The treatment of all diseases is elimination of morbid matter from the body.
2. The primary cause of disease is accumulation of morbid matter. Bacteria and virus enter and survive in the body only after the accumulation of morbid matter when a favourable atmosphere for their growth is established in body. Hence, the basic cause of disease is morbid matter and bacteria secondary causes.
3. Acute diseases are self-healing efforts of the body. Hence, they are our friends, not the enemy. Chronic diseases are outcome of wrong treatment and suppression of the acute diseases.
4. Nature is the greatest healer. The human body itself has the healing power to prevent itself from disease and regain health if unhealthy.
5. In Nature Cure it is not the disease but the entire body of the patient which is caused and is renewed.
6. Naturopathy Cures Patients suffering from chronic ailments are also treated successfully in comparatively less time by Naturopathy.
7. In Nature Cure the suppressed diseases are brought to surface and are removed permanently.
8. Naturopathy treats all the aspects like physical, mental, social and spiritual at the same time.
9. Naturopathy treats the body as a whole.
10. According to Naturopathy, "Food is only the Medicine", no external medications are used.
11. Performing prayer according to one's spiritual faith is an important part of treatment

Diet Therapy

According to this therapy, the food must be taken in natural form. Fresh seasonal fruits, fresh green leafy vegetables and sprouts are excellent. These diets are broadly classified into three types which are as follows:

1. Eliminative Diet: Liquids-Lemon, Citric juices, Tender Coconut water, Vegetable soups, Butter milk, Wheat Grass juices etc.
2. Soothing Diet: Fruits, Salads, Boiled/Steamed Vegetables, Sprouts, Vegetable chutney etc.
3. Constructive Diet: Wholesome flour, Unpolished rice, little pulses, Sprouts, Curd etc.
4. Being alkaline, these diets help in improving health, purifying the body and rendering it immune to disease. To this end, a proper combination of food is necessary. Our diet should consist of 20 per cent acidic and 80 per cent alkaline food for maintaining health. A balanced food is a must for any individual seeking good health. Food is regarded as Medicine in Naturopathy.

Fasting Therapy

Fasting is primarily the act of willingly abstaining from some or all food, drink, or both, for a period of time. The word id derived from the old English, 'Feastan' means to fast, observe, be strict. In Sanskrit ' Vrath' means 'determination' and 'Upavasa' means 'near to God' A fast may be total or partial concerning that from which one fasts, and may be prolonged or intermittent as to the period of fasting. Fasting is an important treatment modality for health preservation. In fasting, mental preparedness is an essential pre-condition. Prolonged fasting should be done only under the supervision of a competent Naturopath.

The duration of the fast depends upon the age of the patient, the nature of the disease and amount and type of drugs previously used. It is some times advisable to undertake a series of short fasts of two or three days and gradually increase the duration of each succeeding fast by a day or so. No harm will accrue to fasting patient provided they take rest and are under proper professional care. Fasting can be with water, juices or raw vegetable juices.

The best, safest and most effective method is lime juice fasting. During fasting, the body burns up and excretes huge amounts of accumulated wastes. We can help this cleansing process by drinking alkaline juices. Sugars in juices will strengthen the heart, juice fasting is therefore the best form of fasting. All juices should be prepared from fresh fruit immediately before drinking. Canned or frozen juices should not be used. A precautionary measure, which must be observed in all cases of fasting, is the complete emptying of the bowels at the beginning of the fast by enema so that the patient is not bothered by gas or decomposing matter formed from the excrements remaining in the body. Enemas should be used at least every alternate day during the fasting period. The total liquid intake should be approximately six to eight glasses. A lot of energy is spent during the fast in the process of eliminating accumulated poisons and toxic waste materials. It is therefore, of utmost importance that the patient gets as much physical rest and mental relaxation as possible during the fast.

The success of the fast depends largely on how it is broken. The main rules for break in the fast are: do not overeat, eat slowly and chew your food thoroughly and take several days for the gradual change to the normal diet.

Barriers of Healthy Living

In the ancient time man used to live in the midst of nature. As a result he was the master of health, personality, excellence, contentment and pleasure. On the other hand as of today advancement of science and technology as brought forth a heap of option for physical comfort. Nevertheless, there is void with respect to physical and mental health. In this background there is a best possibility of healthy living.

Following are the barriers for healthy living:

- Uncontrolled food habit.
- Liquor consumption and smoking.
- Cardiac disorders.
- Hypertension.
- Diabetes.
- Obesity.
- Stress.
- Insomnia.
- Tension.
- Arthritis and other joint disorders.
- Constipation.
- Distress and disappointment.
- Frustration.

Role of Yoga in Healthy Living

Yoga is a subject of science of high order, which carries in it the mystery of conservation of health and transformation of life. A complete expression of life is possible only through Yoga. Yogasana, pranayam, meditation develops faith in a person, chiefly because it is half a therapy. It is common saying that confidence is half the cure. The concept of Ashtanga Yoga proposed by Mahrashi Patanjali with different aspects have enormous contribution towards healthy living as out lived here:

Yama: Under this include different aspects such as Ahinsa, Satya, Asteya, Bhramcharya and Aparigraha. Through this first step of Ashtanga Yoga one turns to more ideal in his day to day life. With this he discharges his duties towards society in a more orderly manner.

Niyama: The major components under this include Shauch, Santosh, Tapa, Swadhyaya, Ishwarpranidhan. Practice of this aspect of Yoga turns a person, more disciplined and orderly. With this one can overcome the deformities of personal senses. In fact the reformation of personal actions for us is the basic foundation of healthy living.

Asanas: Having achieved the perfection over the guideline of Yama and Niyama only then one must commit for the practice of Yogasanas. Without this the Yoga practices is ineffective. For various Yogasanas body is flexed for an specific posture regularly at a given time for a given purpose. This exerts special effect on different body joints, muscles, heart, digestive system, endocrine glands, lungs and nervous system. This revives the normal functioning of respective organs and body system. At present time special significance to Yogasana is direct relation to healthy living.

Pranayama: Pranayam is a highly sophisticated procedure of Yoga, where by one achieves a total control over the vital force which governs the proper functioning of body's life process. Pranayam helps to tone-up the most vital activities of the body, such as respiratory system, cardio-vascular system. In addition, it strengthens the body immunity which is extremely important for maintaining the quality of life and healthy living.

Pratyahar: The real purpose of this Yoga practice is to drive the body's consciousness inwardly and focus at a pleasant thought or a point of auspicious feeling. In a daily life the practice of such yogic terms helps to achieve a high order of quality life.

Dharna: For the purpose of achieving the spiritual excellence, this type of yogic exercise, called Dharna carries special significance. It is mainly for the reason that Dharna itself means to focus on a solitary point through flow of thought. Continuity of this state is termed as- Dhyan, which is the final objective of Yoga practice for healthy living.

Meditation: Meditation acts as a powerful tonic. It is a mental and nerving tonic as well. The holy vibrations penetrate all the cells of the body and cure the diseases of the body. Those who meditate save doctor's bills. The powerful, soothing waves that arise during meditaion exercise a benign influence on the mind, nerves, organs and the cells of body.

The divine energy freely flows like Tailadhara (flows of oil from one vessel to another) from the feet of the Lord to the different systems of the Sadhakas. Considerable changes take place in the mind, brain and the nervous system by the practice of meditation. New nerve-currents, new vibrations, new avenues, new grooves, new cells, new channels are formed. The whole mind and nervous system are remodeled.

You will develop a new heart, a new view of mind, new sensations, new feeling, new mode of thinking, acting and a view of the universe (as God in manifestation). The fire of meditation annihilates all foulness due to vice. Then suddenly comes knowledge or divine wisdom, which directly leads to final emancipation.

Real peace and Ananda (bliss) manifest only when Sankalpas get extinguished. When you fix the mind on the supreme energy even for five minutes Sattva guna is infused into the mind. Vasanas (impression) are thinned out and the force of sankalpa become less and less. You will feel peace and bliss during the five minutes. You can compare this Ananda from meditation with the transitory sensual pleasures. You will find that this Ananda from meditation is a million times superior to sensual pleasure. Meditate and feel this Ananda. Then you will know its real value. You will get the full Ananda of the divine glory only when you merge deep into silent meditation. When you are on the border land of divinity of God, when you are at threshold of God, when you are in the outer skirts, you will not get the maximum peace and bliss.

Samadhi

Samadhi is provided to super normal healthy person.

Role of Asanas, Pranayam and Meditation in Common Diseases

Anaemia

Pranayama:

- Ujjayi (energy-renewing Pranayama),
- Nadi-Sodhana (altenate breathing).

Asanas:

- Paschimottanasans (stretching the back and legs), Ardhamatsyendrasana (Simplified version of the Yogi Matsyendra Posture),
- Sarvangasana (Shoulder-stand),
- Sirshasana (Head-stand),
- Savasana (Complete Relaxation Posture).

Diet:

- Change over to foods rich in iron and Vitamin-B juice of wheat sprouts(grass), uncooked Juices or soups of leafy vegetables, fresh fruits, germinated corn and beans, pulses etc.

Arthritis

Pranayama:

- Rhythmic breathing,
- Nadi-Sodhana (alternate breathing).

Asanas:

- Trikonasna (triangle posture),
- Padmasana (The lotus Position),
- Salabhasana (The Locust Posture),
- Dhanurasana (The Bow Posture),
- Vakrasana (Spinal Twist),
- Viparitakarani (The Inverted posture),
- Savasana (Complete Relaxation Posture).

Diet:

- Avoid sours and masala food. Eat light vegetable foods. Take alkaline content fruits like sweet lemon and orange, pineapple etc.

Meditation:

- Silent meditation for 20 minutes.

Asthma

Pranayama:

- Rhythmic breathing,
- Nadi-Sodhana (alternate breathing without retention of the breath).

Asanas:

- Vakrasana (Spinal Twist),
- Paschimottanasans (stretching the back and legs),
- Viparitakarani (The Inverted posture),
- Savasana (Complete Relaxation Posture).

Diet:

- Avoid milk and milk product, non- vegetarian food, eat fruits and vegetables in season and cooked rather than raw vegetables.

Meditation:

- Silent Meditation for 15-30 minutes.

Constipation

Pranayama:

- Bhastrika(bellows)

Asanas:

- Uddiyana (Rising of the diapharm),
- Trikonasana(triangle posture),
- Vakrasana (spinal twist),
- Paschimottanasans (stretching the back and legs),
- Sarvangasana (shoulder- stand),
- Supta-Vajrasana (The Supine Pelvic Posture).

Diet:

- Include food with flares and roughage in daily diet. Plenty of raw vegetable, fruits, whole wheat chapaties etc. should be taken.

Diabetes

Pranayama:

- Rhythmic breathing,
- Nadi-Sodhana (alternate breathing without retention of the breath).

Asanas:

- Uddiyana (Rising of the diapharm),
- Paschimottanasans (stretching the back and legs),
- Ardhamatsyendrasana (Simplified version of the Yogi Matsyendra Posture),

- Sarvangasana (shoulderstand),
- Savasana (Complete Relaxation Posture).

Diet:

- Avoid starchy food, eat more fibbers and protein content food, restrictions should be followed.

Exhaustion

Pranayama:

- Rhythmic breathing,
- Nadi-Sodhana (alternate breathing without retention of the breath).

Asanas:

- Halasana (The Plough posture),
- Vakrasana (spinal twist),
- Paschimottanasans (stretching the back and legs),
- Sarvangasana(shoulder- stand),
- Matasyasana (The fish posture),
- Sirshasana (Head- stand),
- Savasana(Complete Relaxation Posture)

Haemorroids

Pranayama:

- Rhythmic breathing,
- that revitalises the nervous system.

Asanas:

- Uddiyana (Rising of the diapharm),
- Viparitakarni (The Inverted Posture),
- Sarvangasana(shoulder-stand),
- Matsyasanas (The fish posture),
- Shirsasana (Head-stand),
- Savasana (Complete Relaxation Posture).

Diet:

- Only light easily digestable food with plenty of fiborous materials should be taken.

Headaches

Pranayama:

- Rhythmic breathing,
- Nadi-Sodhana (alternate breathing).

Asanas:

- Viparitakarani (The Inverted posture),
- Savasana (Complete Relaxation Posture).

Diet:

- Easily digestable food.

Heart Trouble

Pranayama:

- Rhythmic breathing,
- Nadi-Sodhana (alternate breathing).

Asanas:

- Depending on the case Uddiyana (Rising of the Diapharm),
- Trikonasana (Triangle Posture),
- Sirshasana (Head-stand),
- Savasna (Complete Relaxation Posture).

Diet:

- Avoid foods containing fats and cholesterol. Eat more ***vegetable and fruits. Take light vegetarian meals.***

Meditation:

- Silent meditation for 20-30 minutes.

High Blood Pressure

Pranayama:

- Rhythmic breathing,
- nadi-sodhna (alternate breathing, without retention of the breath).

Asanas:

- Padmasana (the lotus position),
- viparitakarani (the inverted posture),
- savasana (complete relaxation posture).

Diet:

- Consume less salt and fat. Eat 10 vegetables more.

Meditation:

- Silent meditation for 20 minutes.

Indigestion

Pranayama:

- Bhastrika (Bellows),
- Nadi-Sodhana (alternate breathing).

Asanas:

- Uddiyana (Raising of diapharm),
- Bhujangasana (The Cobra Position),
- Salabhasana (The Posture),
- Salabhasana (The Locust Posture),
- Dhanurasana (The Bow Posture)
- Trikonasana (Triangle Posture),
- Pachimottanasana (Stretching the back and legs),
- Sarvangasana (Shoulder-stand),
- Savasana (Complete Relaxation Posture).

Diet:

- Include food with flares and roughage in daily diet. Plenty of raw vegetable, fruit whole-wheat chapaties etc. should be take.

Naturopathic Physicians and Traditional Naturopaths

There are two groups in the United States calling themselves "naturopaths." The term as originally coined by Scheel and popularized by Lust was to apply to those receiving an education in the basic medical sciences with an emphasis on natural therapies:

Naturopathic Physicians

Naturopathic physicians in the United States are independent providers with training in conventional medical sciences, diagnosis, and treatment, as well as natural therapeutics with licenses or registration granted by an individual state's Naturopathic Board of Medical Examiners.

They graduate from four-year nationally accredited naturopathic medical graduate schools.

Naturopathic physicians' training with respect to modalities is different from traditional naturopaths, with a focus on nutrition, botanical medicine, homeopathy, hydrotherapy, joint manipulation, manipulative therapy, pharmacology, and minor surgery.

Some naturopathic physicians have additional training in the following: natural childbirth, acupuncture, and Chinese medicine. These subspecialties often involve additional years of study. Naturopathic physicians are required to attend continuing education yearly in order to maintain and renew their license. Naturopathic physicians bridge both conventional and non-conventional treatment, and work in cooperation with both conventional and alternative practitioners to provide patients with complete medical care. Naturopathic physicians are able to identify and prescribe appropriate treatment, including referral to conventional medical doctors.

Naturopathic physicians are licensed in various states in the United States and in Canadian provinces. For licensure, candidates must have a Doctor of Naturopathic Medicine (abbreviated as N.D. or less commonly N.M.D.) or Doctor of Naturopathy (abbreviated as N.D.) from an accredited institution in the U.S. or Canada and pass licensing board examinations.

The abbreviation N.D. can also denote the professional title and status Naturopathic Doctorthat is conferred by the licensing body in the state or province. In contrast, the "degree" Doctor of Natural Medicine (abbreviated D.N.M.) does not qualify for licensure as a naturopathic physician and carries no regulatory status in the U.S. or Canada.

Traditional Naturopaths

Vis medicatrix naturae, or the healing power of nature, is the central tenet of Traditional Naturopathy. The view is that bacteria and viruses, which are always present, seldom cause problems in a healthy body.

According to naturopathic practice, disease occurs when toxins that have accumulated internally-often due to incorrect lifestyle, a poor diet, and improper care of the body-weaken a person.

While conventional medical treatments may rid the body of symptoms, these treatments alone do not bring about true healing. Rather than trying to attack specific symptoms and diseases, Traditional Naturopathy offers a holistic approach to the individual that supports the body in finding its way back to homeostasis.

Traditional Naturopathy is not a medical practice. While prescribing drugs and pharmaceuticals, performing surgery, and other invasive procedures clearly have their place in the hands of properly trained medical doctors, these practices are outside the scope of Traditional Naturopathy and are at odds with its fundamental principles.

Instead, Traditional Naturopaths focus on educating clients to lead healthier lives and on the use of naturopathic modalities such as light, water, herbs, healthy foods, and exercise to cleanse and strengthen the body and support its natural healing process.

Traditional Naturopaths receive training from correspondence schools, or they receive their training from other practitioners. None of the schools that award degrees to Traditional Naturopaths are accredited by the U.S. Department of Education.

Traditional Naturopaths are individuals who are not regulated by a licensing board.

Contention and Confusion between the two Factions

In the United States, both naturopathic physicians and traditional naturopaths use the degree designation of N.D. (Doctor of Naturopathic Medicine), leading to considerable confusion about the scope of practice, education, and training of a naturopathic practitioner. (In the United Kingdom, N.D. stands for Diploma in Naturopathy.)

There is great contention between the two factions as their political agendas are in opposition to each other: Naturopathic physicians, whose national professional organization is the American Association of Naturopathic Physicians, strive to secure licensure in all 50 states, whereas traditional naturopaths, whose professional organization is the American Naturopathic Medical Association, oppose licensure and often block licensing attempts.

Science and naturopathy: There is widespread support for the application of an evidence-based medicine framework to assess health outcomes, and that systematic reviews with strict protocols are essential. There are reports of evidence-based medicine trials published for naturopathy (Bastyr 2007). Organizations such as the Cochrane Collaboration and Bandolier publish such reviews.

Some modalities used in naturopathy are widely regarded as pseudoscience. Medical doctors often cite the large differences between naturopathic practitioners and the lack of scientific documentation as to the safety and efficacy of their practices in order to justify limiting naturopathic scope. Advocates claim that naturopathic practitioners find it difficult to obtain financing for research due to the lack of prior research in many areas. Proponents state that this is slowly changing as naturopathic physicians develop research programs to help build up a foundation for evidence-based treatment.

Conventional medicine is required to undergo rigorous testing; drug trials often last for a decade. A criticism of alternative therapies is that they are not subject to detailed safety assessment.

Retrospective analysis of various herbal agents have found many to be of little therapeutic value and others to be harmful. This can be tied to the fact that "natural" does not necessarily correspond to being beneficial or even benign. Also of concern is the ambiguity of the word "natural" and poor agreement as to its meaning.

While the above addresses a primary challenge to the validation process for "natural" remedies, perhaps of greater concern among critics is the lack of regulation of manufacturer claims in advertising. Common labeling practices suggest that herbal extracts are devoid of "drugs" or "chemicals." Claims of this type are patently false as every component of any plant extract is a chemical by definition.

Likewise, claims as to the relative absence of toxicity in herbal extracts, when compared to conventional pharmaceutical preparations, are tainted by incongruent regulations for reporting of side effects. The manufacturers of conventional pharmaceutical agents are legally bound to record and report any perceived negative experiences during large-scale clinical trials, though there may be no actual link between the tested drug and the perceived side effect.

To wit, it is often the case that drugs are labeled with side effects such as headache, constipation, diarrhea, or sleep disturbance. These "side effects" are required to be listed even if they are found with no more regularity than they are in a placebo control group or within the general populace for that matter. Conversely, herbal manufacturers are not required to carry out such clinical studies nor to report any known adverse effects, even if said effects have been directly linked to ingestion of the herbal preparation in question. While these advertising techniques do not negate the potential for some beneficial uses of various herbal agents, and they do not necessarily reflect upon the validity of naturopathic medicine as a field of study, critics suggest that they do serve to beguile the public through the employment of nothing more than legally permissible semantics and selective reporting. Naturopathic modalities may be controversial (e.g., homeopathy), or have proven effectiveness only for very specific conditions (e.g., acupuncture, aromatherapy). Some naturopaths may use these modalities as panaceas or to improve the patient's quality of life.

Earth - Mud Therapy

Of the five elements of nature, mud represents Earth and has tremendous impact on the maintenance of health and prevention of diseases. Minerals and trace elements present in the mud are known for its renowned effects and healing properties.

Mud also has the remarkable property of holding moisture for a long time, which has a cooling effect on the part of the body applied.

- Helps improve circulation and relax the muscles
- Improves the digestive activity and sets right the metabolism
- Local application helps relieve inflammations, swellings and reduces pain
- Excellent in skin conditions without open lesions
- Helps bring down blood pressure
- Nourishes the skin
- Conditions the hair
- Specific kind of application relieves the stiffness of joints

Mud Packs

Frequent application of mud helps in improving the complexion of the skin by getting rid of spots and patches, which appear in various skin disorders. Mud baths are also generally recommended for all skin diseases, including psoriasis, leucoderma and urticaria and other allergic conditions of the skin.

Body Wraps: Using special Natural Muds high in natural minerals and salts the pack is applied on the entire body except the head.

Dead Sea Mud Body Wrap: The mud from the Dead Sea is highly saturated with natural salts and minerals like calcium chloride, iron and sulphates. These minerals are known for their renowned effects and healing properties.

- It cleanses, exfoliates, draws out toxins, hydrates and improves the flow of nutrients to the skin surface

Moor Mud Body Wrap: This mud is from the boggy lake and marshland in Austria, which is home to a rich inheritance of plants and herbs, some of which are unique It contains about 300 medicinal herbs, lipids, enzymes, essential oils, minerals and vitamins.

- Good for acne, eczema, psoriasis and other skin disorders
- A natural anti-inflammatory
- Good for rheumatism and arthritic conditions
- Helps break down cellulite by stimulating the circulation and lymphatic system

Great Salt Lake Mud Body Wrap: The whole body is covered with this mud which is composed of pure natural clay and a trace elements and minerals blend product from the Great Salt Lake.

- Restores and revitalises the skin for a healthy appearance
- Excellent for psoriasis, eczema, acne and other skin irritants

Hungarian Wellness Mud Body Wrap

- Improves the skin cells metabolism and gently soothes irritation
- Provides firmness and strength and deeply penetrates the tissues to help clear stored toxins

Water - Hydrotherapy

This uses the therapeutic properties of water. This medium was made use in therapeutics hundreds of years ago. Water has great healing properties and exhibits different properties at different temperatures. The temperature of the water for any treatment depends on the effect desired. Kellogg is considered to be the Father of Hydrotherapy. Water is used internally and externally in all its forms- steam, liquid or ice, to cleanse and restore health. It is used in the form of Baths, Jets/Douches, Packs, Compresses and Immersions to name a few.

Drinking a specific amount of water also has therapeutic effects:

- Helps maintain hydration of the body
- Helps in proper secretion of body fluids and maintenance of Ph.
- Aids digestion and prevents constipation
- Improves skin condition and nourishes it
- Maintains the flexibility of joints
- Helps in detoxification

Hydro Washes: This helps cleanse and detoxify even the internal cavities of the face.

Hydro Baths

Arm and Foot Bath

- Relieves localised pain and inflammations
- Relieves congestive headaches
- Relieves the spasms of the bronchioles and facilitates easy breathing as in asthma and bronchitis
- Excellent for relieving the numbness and tingling in the extremities as in diabetes mellitus

Hip Bath

- Stimulates the circulation towards the pelvic and digestive organs relieves constipation, flatulence and indigestion
- Helps set right the menstrual disorders like dysmenorrhoea, menorrhagia, leucorrhoea
- Helps strengthen the hips and lumbar sacral spine and the coccyx and relieves pain if any
- Beneficial in relieving haemorrhoids

Spinal Bath/Anti-Stress Bath

- Stimulates the spinal nerves
- Relaxes the paraspinal muscles
- Helps maintain the blood pressure
- Helps in regulating the moods like anxiety or depression
- Relaxes irritable nerves

Steam Bath

- Exposing the entire body with the exception of the head to a superheated atmosphere helps in many ways. Steam inhalation helps decongest the respiratory tract
- Medicated ayurvedic or herbal steam helps rejuvenate the body
- Helps open up the skin pores
- Helps remove the toxins of the skin through sweating
- Helps the skin maintain its natural moisture and softness

Naturopath on Treating Depression

Symptoms of Depression

Depression is a mood disorder where the individual feels sad or irritable, or experiences a general lack of enthusiasm in normal daily activities.

In severe cases, depression may lead to suicidal thoughts. Depression often comes and goes, but for some the overwhelming feeling of sadness persists and treatment is necessary. This type of depression, also known as dysthymia, can last years to a lifetime.

Alternative Therapies for Depression

If depression is suspected, the first thing to do is to consult a physician or psychotherapist to try and determine an underlying cause. Occasionally depression is related to the change of seasons, when a lack of natural sunlight causes a change in mood referred to as seasonal affective disorder (SAD). Other symptoms of SAD may include lack of energy, fatigue, sweet cravings and weight gain. Some individuals with SAD may respond to traditional antidepressant medication. Others may respond with exposure to light via natural sunlight (whenever available), specialty light boxes, or full spectrum lighting. Conventional treatment of depression typically includes a combination of psychotherapy and prescription medication intended to bring neurotransmitters (serotonin, norepinephrine, dopamine) into balance. Adverse effects from such medications are not uncommon, and side effects may include insomnia, dry mouth, blurred vision, drowsiness, dizziness, sexual dysfunction, and weight gain or loss.

Some studies have linked smoking to depression, so a smoking cessation programme would be recommended for depressed patients who smoke. Complementary therapies include a combination of lifestyle and dietary recommendations.

Exercise Therapy

Daily exercise increases the body's natural production of endorphins, which naturally improve the mood. Endorphins are more apt to be released during long, moderate to high-intensity aerobic workouts. Exercises that are more apt to produce endorphins include running, swimming, cross-country skiing, long distance rowing, bicycling, aerobics, or playing a sport such as basketball, soccer, or football. Exercising outdoors is preferred, so that the individual can take in fresh air and sunlight.

Nutritional Therapy

There are key nutrients in the diet that can help improve your mood. If these nutrients are lacking, depression may be a result. Like most things in life, moderation is the key. The body needs carbohydrates to manufacture serotonin, but excess intake of carbohydrates and simple sugars can lower serotonin levels and be factors in symptoms of depression. Turkey, salmon, and dairy products can help elevate levels of serotonin. Caffeine and alcohol have powerful effects on the central nervous system and should be avoided by those suffering from depression. Food allergies can also have a powerful effect on the brain, and individuals with depression should avoid foods known to trigger sensitivities/allergies.

It is a good idea to keep a log of your daily food intake along with your mood. Do this for at least two weeks, and note any patterns or foods that may correlate with feelings of sadness, lack of focus or desire, or fatigue. Frequent small meals that include protein, whole grain carbohydrate and essential fat throughout the day (every 2 to 3 hours) will help maintain balanced blood sugar. High or low blood sugar (hyper- or hypoglycemia) can mimic symptoms of depression. Enjoy foods rich in calcium, magnesium and B vitamins like whole grains, organic dairy products, nuts, seeds, green leafy vegetables. These will help to maintain proper nutrient balance and help prevent depression.

Supplements

Natural supplements to consider for treating depression include St. John's wort, SAMe, 5-HTP, and a high quality multiple vitamin and mineral combination. Check with a qualified medical professional first.

- St. John's wort is probably the most widely studied herbal medicine for the treatment of mild to moderate depression. In systematic reviews of the medical literature, St. John's wort therapy for mild to moderate depression demonstrated significant advantage compared to placebo. It has fewer reported side effects compared to conventional prescription medication. Standard dosing begins at 300 milligrams three times daily.
- S-Adenosyl Methionine (SAMe) is an amino acid that influences emotions and moods. Although more research is needed, SAMe has been shown to be an effective alternative treatment for mild depression with fewer side effects than conventional prescription medications.

- 5-Hydroxytryptophan (5-HTP) is metabolized from tryptophan, and needed for the body to produce serotonin. While 5-HTP is found naturally in very small amounts in foods such as turkey and dairy products, the supplement form exerts a more powerful effect on the body. 5-HTP is potentially an alternative to SSRI medications. Standard dosing typically starts at 50 milligrams twice daily and again further research is warranted to substantiate initial claims. A multiple vitamin/mineral will help prevent most nutritional insufficiencies. B vitamins, for example, are essential for neurotransmitter production.

Other Alternative Therapies for Treating Depression

Additional alternative therapies to consider for depression include aromatherapy, acupuncture, homeopathy, yoga, and music therapy.

- Aromatherapy (essential oil therapy) may help in mild forms of depression. It may ease mental tension, fatigue, help with insomnia, and elevate the mood. Essential oils can be added to massage oils, bath water, put in a diffuser, or diluted and applied to the skin. Ylang ylang, clary sage, basil, jasmine, and rose have all been used to help ease depressive symptoms.
- Although there are reports of depressed individuals benefiting from acupuncture, evidence for the use of acupuncture to treat persons with depression is lacking. Clinical trials yield mixed results, and further research is necessary. The same is true for homeopathy.
- Yoga has shown initial promise in helping alleviate mild symptoms of depression. Soft music and visualization therapy have also shown initial positive outcomes in individuals with depression. It has been especially useful in hospital and in-patient settings and in patients suffering from serious illness.

Naturopathic Considerations for Treating Depression

The sun is coming out and the temperatures are warming up! This should be the time of year where we relax, play outdoors, travel, feel light and happy... right? Not always. Although you are likely exposed to more sunlight and creating more vitamin D, which has a mood-boosting effect, if you are feeling down and out you are not alone. Common symptoms of depression include persistent sadness, crying, fatigue, lethargy, body aches and pains, irritability, loss of interest in things that you previously enjoyed, and isolating yourself from friends and family. These symptoms can strike any time of year.

In the summer months, however, we tend to overextend ourselves and get less sleep. This in and of itself can create an environment where you don't feel great. Add to this the increase in travel and other activities that throw you off schedule and it means you likely aren't sticking to the diet choices that you know keep you on track. But even when you are getting enough sleep and your diet is great, you may still feel sluggish and sad. There are several reasons this might be and that may be worth exploring with a naturopathic physician.

Dietary: What and how you eat can truly affect your mood. It's important to regulate your mood by keeping your blood sugar stable. For instance, people often notice feeling more anxious if they skip meals. Eating regularly is an easy way to stabilise your mood. The foods that help do that are proteins like eggs, nuts, beans, dairy, lean meats, and fish. Make sure you eat carbohydrates like breads, pastas, and sweets in moderation and always in combination with proteins so your blood sugar is not as affected. Individual food reactions can also play a role in mood changes. There are several easy ways of identifying problem foods, one of which is the elimination diet. In this diet, you take out the most common reactive foods: gluten, dairy, eggs, sugar, soy, citrus, nightshade vegetables and alcohol for a period of 2-4 weeks and note changes in mood. Another way to identify potential food problems is through blood testing for IgG antibodies that can be produced up to 3 days after you eat a problem food. There are several labs that offer these tests, which give a more personalised and inclusive guideline on specific foods to avoid.

Nutrient Deficiencies: Even though it's lighter out, many folks still have vitamin D deficiency because they aren't actually getting skin exposure. It's important to have your levels of vitamin D tested to identify this deficiency and to help target the appropriate daily dose for you. Other nutrients that may have an effect on mood are iron and B-vitamins, which can be easily screened via a blood test. Of course, there are numerous other vitamins and minerals which the body needs to make hormones and neurotransmitters, which keep us balanced and feeling good. These can also be identified through lab testing and easily supplemented.

Hormone Imbalances: There are certain times in life where hormonal changes can make people feel depressed. Puberty, pregnancy, PMS and menopause are just a few. Imbalances can often be diagnosed and treated based on symptoms in these cases, although lab testing does exist if needed. Thyroid deficiencies and adrenal hormone imbalances are common and really make people feel lousy.

These can come with or even be the cause of the other hormone symptoms mentioned, making it more complicated to figure out the cause. Again, there are easy lab tests that can be done to help get to the root of the issue. Fortunately, treating hormone imbalances does not necessarily mean taking hormones! There are many natural therapies that work well on this system-including vitamins, minerals, and herbal therapies to name a few.

Neurotransmitter Deficiencies: When most people think of treatments for depression, what comes to mind are antidepressant medications. These target specific neurotransmitters in the central nervous system-most commonly, serotonin. Using lifestyle, diet and nutrient therapies, it is possible to effect these neurotransmitters without medications, and in certain situations even wean off of antidepressant medications. There are easy tests that can be done to evaluate neurotransmitter levels when patients are not responding to a given therapy or have a more complicated situation.

If you aren't feeling like yourself lately there are several factors to consider. Consult your naturopathic physician to begin exploring together why this may be and get you started on a plan to feel your best.

Naturopathic Medicine

Living things have an innate ability to heal themselves. Our vital force promotes self-cleansing, self-repair, and therefore self-healing. This process can be achieved by focusing on the immune, hormonal, nervous, and detoxification/elimination systems of the body. Once these systems are in balance, restored health is a probability. Naturopathic doctors treat their patients holistically, taking into consideration the individual's biochemistry, biomechanics, and emotional predispositions. The body's self-healing ability can be better understood if one takes into account the fact that homeostasis, or biological balance, is the main characteristic of any healthy system.

A good example is fever. When the body is invaded by a pathogen (a substance capable of producing illness or disease), the body will usually respond by producing a fever to fight the invader. If the body is properly supported through nutrition and rest, the fever will turn up the immune system and permit the recovery of health.

Other examples are the immune system, hormonal system, nervous system, and detoxification/elimination pathways, which all work as a unit to ensure our survival. If given the proper support, care, and the chance to function freely without suppression, they can bring the system back to a state of balance or "ease" (as opposed to "dis-ease").

There are no panaceas or magic bullets. Each individual has his or her own unique set of symptoms and reactions which will, in turn, dictate the approach the Naturopathic doctor takes to treat them. This is why each person seeking help from a Naturopathic doctor will receive an individualised treatment protocol. Naturopathic medicine is practiced either as a primary system of medical care, or as a complementary adjunct to conventional medical treatment. The goal of Naturopathic Medicine is to develop optimal wellness for each patient, and to teach the principles of ideal health. Although Naturopathic doctors are educated and trained to treat acute and chronic disease, prevention is the ultimate goal. This is based on the Naturopathic philosophy of wellness enhancement -- not disease management.

Types of Treatments do Naturopathic Doctors Offer

Clinical Nutrition: The dynamic relationship between disease and nutrition is well known. Many conditions can be improved through changes in diet alone, and others respond well to proper supplementation of specific nutrients. In most cases of disease or wellness, nutritional counseling and support are a major component of Naturopathic treatments.

Botanical Medicine (Phytotherapy): Botanical medicine, or phytotherapy, was a cornerstone of traditional medicine long before the development of synthetic pharmaceuticals. Most of today's drugs were derived from medicinal plants. Modern scientific investigations have substantiated many of the early uses of medical plants, and have increasingly found ways to use them in treating modern diseases. The World Health Organisation has encouraged programmes in herbal medicine, especially in developing countries, as a means of providing affordable primary health care and of creating agricultural markets for those economies. Herbs are characterised by their low toxicity and lack of accumulation in the body. When appropriately selected, botanical medicines offer powerful, safe, and effective approach to healing, with few side effects.

Homeopathy: Homeopathy is a holistic form of treatment that has been integrated into naturopathic medicine. Virtually all homeopathic medicines are produced from natural sources-plants, animals and minerals. The success of homeopathic treatment has been recognised in many countries around the world including France, Germany, India, Latin America, the United Kingdom, Australia, and North America. Traditional Chinese and herbal medicine are often confused with homeopathy, but in fact, they are all different systems of holistic medicine. Homeopathy was standardised in 18th century Germany by Samuel Hahnemann, MD. This chemist and physician discovered that when quinine, an effective treatment for malaria, was taken by a healthy individual, it produced symptoms similar to those found in people stricken with malaria. This was noticed with other medicines, too. That is to say, he noticed that: "Substances that are specific for certain illnesses, cure or aid the body because they actually cause similar symptoms to the disease process they are being employed to treat."

This in turn stimulates the patient's vital force to help resolve the disease. The true mechanism behind this phenomenon is as unknown today as it was then. This process is referred to as the Principle of Similars. It is important to note that homeopathy is not based on the same principle as immunisation, which uses substances that cause the same disease, not similar symptoms. Immunisation is based on isopathy -- giving a substance known to cause the exact disease in question. Also, immunisation has an immunological bases to it; that is, the production of T-memory cells. The mechanism of action of homeopathy is unknown at this time. There are several models that try to explain it, but none are sufficient. In short, homeopathic medicines have no relationship to the disease in question, but rather the symptoms in question. The skilled practitioner finds a substance that causes similar symptoms to that of the patient's, physical or emotional. This therapy is non-toxic and can be safely be used with pregnant women, infants, and children.

Hahnemann also noted that after treatment, many of his patients' conditions worsened for a short period of time before improving. He termed this phenomenon aggravation. Through systematic experimentation, Hahnemann learned that this process could be avoided by diluting the medicines. When used in a homeopathic context; that is, when the substance in high doses causes similar symptoms to that of the disease in question, the diluted medicines were surprisingly more effective than full-strength medicines. This led Hahnemann to further experiment with dilutions until he learned that surprisingly small amounts of the active ingredient in a remedy resulted in treatments free from side effects but also increased their effect. This phenomenon he called the Principle of Infinitesimal Dose.

The Difference between a Naturopath and a Homeopath

In brief, homeopaths use only the homeopathic approach, whereas Naturopaths train in several forms of diagnosis and treatment, one of which is homeopathy. Training in homeopathy varies from a several-hundred-hour correspondence course to a three-year course for which candidates need not be university graduates. In contrast, Naturopaths must complete a minimum of three years of university training prior to beginning their four-year residential medical school training in Naturopathic Medicine.

Traditional Chinese Medicine

Tongue and pulse diagnosis, Chinese herbs, nutrition, and acupuncture comprise the ancient practices of Traditional Chinese Medicine (TCM). Although this medical system dates back some 3,000 years, it was only introduced to North America at the turn of the century. TCM has even more recently become a respected alternative therapy in the West during the last decade. A TCM diagnosis is holistic in nature.

The practitioner trained in Traditional Chinese Medicine will take into consideration all the aspects of the individual, including special observation of the tongue and the wrist pulses. These two areas (among others), according to TCM, tell the practitioner about certain characteristics of the person regarding their overall constitution. These findings tell the practitioner what treatment is needed. Acupuncture involves the insertion of fine needles through the skin and tissue at specific points on the body. There is no injection of any substances, and the treatment itself causes minimal discomfort.

Acupuncture has been found to be effective in treating a variety of painful disorders, both acute and chronic. The World Health Organisation in 1979 drew up the following provisional list of disorders that lend themselves to acupuncture treatment.

The list is based on clinical experience and not necessarily controlled clinical research:

- Digestive disorders such as gastritis, hyperacidity, spastic bowl, constipation, and diarrhea.
- Respiratory disorders such as sinusitis, bronchitis, asthma.

- Neurological and muscular disorders such as headaches, neck and back pain, neuralgia, frozen shoulder, tennis elbow, sciatica, and arthritis.
- Urinary, menstrual, and reproductive disorders.
- Addiction and substance abuse.
- Sleep disorders such as insomnia and sleep apnea.

According to TCM, acupuncture works due to its effect on the essential substance that makes up the human body and enables it to sustain life activities and functions. This "substance," for a lack of a better word, is known as Chi or Qi (pronounced "chee"). Western biomedical research has learned that acupuncture works in certain situations by stimulating the body to produce endorphins, a morphine-like chemical that helps block pathways that relay pain messages. The result is relief from pain, general relaxation, and restoring the body's own internal regulatory system.

Naturopathic Manipulation (Bodywork): Often in conjunction with other treatments, bodywork uses a variety of systematic movements to help heal musculoskeletal and neurological conditions. Manipulation of bone alignment is used, similar to both osteopathic and chiropractic adjustments. One technique in particular, "strain/counter-strain," is very gentle and effective, especially for pain and injuries of the neck and upper back.

Lifestyle Counseling and Modification: The cornerstones of Naturopathic philosophy are prevention and responsibility for one's own health. Naturopathic treatments often are based on assessing risk factors connected to the patient's lifestyle, diet, and environment. Each of these factors is taken under consideration when developing a treatment plan with a client. The goal is to remove obstacles to the patient's own state of optimal health. What Can I Expect During My First Visit To A Naturopathic Doctor Once the patient's history has been taken, the Naturopath may do a screening physical, which is a standard physical examination supplemented by in-depth questions, and may seek laboratory testing or diagnostic imaging of the complaint. After the intake and physical are completed, the Naturopath will discuss the treatment plan or protocol with the patient.

If needed, the patient will be referred for laboratory or other diagnostic tests, or to their medical doctor for further consultation. Follow-up visits are scheduled from one to four weeks after treatment has begun. If a chronic illness is being addressed, the patient can expect to undergo at least one month of treatment for every year of illness.

Conditions Can Naturopathic Medicine Treat

There is a wide range of conditions that Naturopathic doctors treat, either alone or in combination with other complementary or usual medical treatments. These include:

- Acute conditions such as headaches, sore throats, ear infections, intestinal upsets, colds and flu, etc.
- Chronic illnesses such as migraines, musculoskeletal pain, gastrointestinal, gynecological, arthritis, heart disease, etc.
- Inherent tendencies before they become a serious illness or degenerative disease.
- Mental and emotional problems to reduce the effects of recent stresses and long-term patterns of anger, depression, or anxiety.
- Physical injury and trauma, including possible referral to appropriate specialists.

Women and Naturopathy

Naturopathy, or naturopathic medicine, is a form of alternative medicine based on a belief in vitalism, which posits that a special energy called vital energy or vital force guides bodily processes such as metabolism, reproduction, growth, and adaptation. Naturopathy favors a holistic approach with non-invasive treatment and, similar to conventional medicine, encourages minimal use of surgery and drugs. The term "naturopathy" is derived from Greek and Latin, and literally translates as "nature disease". Modern naturopathy grew out of the Natural Cure movement of Europe.

The term was coined in 1895 by John Scheel and popularized by Benedict Lust, the "father of U.S. naturopathy". Beginning in the 1970s, there was a revival of interest in the United States and Canada in conjunction with the holistic health movement. Today, naturopathy is primarily practiced in the United States and Canada. The scope of practice varies widely between jurisdictions, and naturopaths in unregulated jurisdictions may use the Naturopathic Doctor designation or other titles regardless of level of education.

Naturopathic practitioners are split into two groups, traditional naturopaths and naturopathic physicians. Naturopathic physicians employ the principles of naturopathy within the context of conventional medical practices. Naturopathy comprises many different treatment modalities of varying degrees of acceptance by the conventional medical community; these treatments range from standard evidence-based treatments, to homeopathy and other pseudoscientific practices. Some of the ideology and methodological underpinnings of naturopathy are in conflict with the paradigm of evidence-based medicine (EBM). Many naturopaths have opposed vaccination based in part on the early views that shaped the profession. According to the American Cancer Society, "scientific evidence does not support claims that naturopathic medicine can cure cancer or any other disease, since virtually no studies on naturopathy as a whole have been published".

Concepts of Naturopathy

Naturopathy focuses on naturally occurring substances, minimally invasive methods, and encouragement of natural healing. Naturopaths generally favor an intuitive and vitalistic conception of the body, and complete rejection of biomedicine and modern science is common. Prevention through stress reduction and a healthy diet and lifestyle is emphasized, and pharmaceutical drugs, ionizing radiation, and surgery are generally minimized. The tenet of naturopathic practice is self-described by six core values. Multiple versions exist in the form of the naturopathic doctor's oath, various mission statements published by schools or professional associations, and ethical conduct guidelines published by regulatory bodies:

- First, do no harm; provide the most effective health care available with the least risk to patients at all times (primum non nocere).
- Recognize, respect and promote the self-healing power of nature inherent in each individual human being. (Vis medicatrix naturae, a form of vitalism).
- Identify and remove the causes of illness, rather than eliminate or suppress symptoms (Tolle Causam).
- Educate, inspire rational hope and encourage self-responsibility for health (Doctor as Teacher).
- Treat each person by considering all individual health factors and influences. (Treat the Whole Person).
- Emphasize the condition of health to promote well-being and to prevent diseases for the individual, each community and our world. (Health Promotion, the Best Prevention)

Practice

Naturopaths use a wide variety of treatment modalities, focusing on natural self-healing rather than any specific method. Some methods rely on immaterial "vital energy fields", the existence of which has not been proven, and there is concern that naturopathy as a field tends towards isolation from general scientific discourse. The effectiveness of naturopathy as a whole system has not been systematically evaluated, and efficacy of individual methods used varies.

A consultation typically begins with a lengthy patient interview focusing on lifestyle, medical history, emotional tone, and physical features, as well as physical examination. The traditional naturopath focuses on lifestyle changes and approaches that support the body's innate healing potential. Traditional naturopaths do not undertake to diagnose or treat diseases but concentrate on whole body wellness and facilitating the body healing itself. Practitioners of naturopathic medicine hold themselves to be primary care providers and in addition to various natural approaches seek to prescribe prescription drugs, perform minor surgery and apply other conventional medical approaches to their practice.

Naturopaths do not necessarily recommend vaccines and antibiotics, and may provide inappropriate alternative remedies even in cases where evidence-based medicine has been shown effective. "All forms of naturopathic education include concepts incompatible with basic science, and do not necessarily prepare a practitioner to make appropriate diagnosis or referrals."

Methods: The particular modalities used by an individual naturopath varies with training and scope of practice. The demonstrated efficacy and scientific rationale also varies. These include: Acupuncture, applied kinesiology, botanical medicine, brainwave entrainment, chelation therapy for atherosclerosis, colonic enemas, color therapy, cranial osteopathy, hair analysis, homeopathy, iridology, live blood analysis, nature cures-i.e. a range of therapies based upon exposure to natural elements such as sunshine, fresh air, heat, or cold, nutrition (examples include vegetarian and wholefood diet, fasting, and abstention from alcohol and sugar,-ozone therapy, physical medicine (e.g., naturopathic, osseous, and soft tissue manipulative therapy, sports medicine, exercise, and hydrotherapy), Psychological counseling (e.g., meditation, relaxation, and other methods of stress management), public health measures and hygiene, reflexology, rolfing, and traditional Chinese medicine. A 2004 survey determined the most commonly prescribed naturopathic therapeutics in Washington State and Connecticut were botanical medicines, vitamins, minerals, homeopathy, and allergy treatments.

Vaccination: Many forms of alternative medicine, including naturopathy, homeopathy, and chiropractic are based on beliefs opposed to vaccination and have practitioners who voice their opposition. This includes non-medically trained naturopaths. The reasons for this negative vaccination view are complicated and rest, at least in part, on the early views which shape the foundation of these professions. A survey of a cross section of students of a major complementary and alternative medicine college in Canada reported that students in the later years of the program opposed vaccination more strongly than newer students.

A University of Washington study investigated insurance claim histories for alternative medicine use in relation to the receipt of vaccinations against preventable illnesses, grouped into children aged 1-2 years and 1-17 years. Both groups were significantly less likely to receive a number of their vaccinations if they visited a naturopath. The study found a significant association between visits to naturopaths with a reduced receipt of pediatric vaccinations and with increased infection by vaccine-preventable illnesses.

Evidence Basis: Naturopathy lacks an adequate scientific basis under the methodology of evidence-based medicine (EBM). Members of the medical community show a critical or rejecting view of naturopathy. Traditional naturopathic practitioners surveyed in Australia perceive EBM as an ideologic assault on their beliefs in vitalistic and holistic principles. They advocate the integrity of natural medicine practice. Traditional natural medicine practitioners surveyed in Australia could have problems in understanding and applying the concept of EBM. If naturopathy offers verifiable results for specific conditions, greater scientific knowledge of the mechanisms of those naturopathic protocols could result in improved therapy models. Some naturopathic physicians have begun to contribute to research and adapt modern scientific principles into clinical practice. There are growing collaborative efforts between naturopaths and medical doctors to evaluate the safety and efficacy of naturopathic medicine in prevention and management of a broad range of common ailments, and to decide whether accessibility of naturopathic services will enhance patient health in a cost-effective way. Naturopathy is criticized for its reliance on and its association with unproven, disproven, and other controversial alternative medical treatments, and for its vitalistic underpinnings. As with any medical care, there is a risk of misdiagnosis; this risk may be lower depending on level of training. Certain naturopathic treatments offered by traditional naturopaths, such as homeopathy, rolfing, and iridology, are widely considered pseudoscience or quackery. "Natural" methods and chemicals are not necessarily safer or more effective than "artificial" or "synthetic" ones; any treatment capable of eliciting an effect may also have deleterious side effects.

Stephen Barrett of Quackwatch and the National Council Against Health Fraud has stated that Naturopathy is "simplistic and that its practices are riddled with quackery". "Non-scientific health care practitioners, including naturopaths, use unscientific methods and deception on a public who, lacking in-depth health care knowledge, must rely upon the assurance of providers. Quackery not only harms people, it undermines the ability to conduct scientific research and should be opposed by scientists", says William T. Jarvis. K. C. Atwood writes, in the journal Medscape General Medicine, "Naturopathic physicians now claim to be primary care physicians proficient in the practice of both "conventional" and "natural" medicine.

Their training, however, amounts to a small fraction of that of medical doctors who practice primary care. An examination of their literature, moreover, reveals that it is replete with pseudoscientific, ineffective, unethical, and potentially dangerous practices". In another article, Atwood writes that "Physicians who consider naturopaths to be their colleagues thus find themselves in opposition to one of the fundamental ethical precepts of modern medicine. If naturopaths are not to be judged "nonscientific practitioners", the term has no useful meaning. An article by a physician exposing quackery, moreover, does not identify its author as "biased", but simply as fulfilling one of his ethical obligations as a physician. According to Arnold S. Relman, the Textbook of Natural Medicine is inadequate as a teaching tool, as it omits to mention or treat in detail many common ailments, improperly emphasizes treatments "not likely to be effective" over those that are, and promotes unproven herbal remedies at the expense of pharmaceuticals. He concludes that "the risks to many sick patients seeking care from the average naturopathic practitioner would far outweigh any possible benefits".

Specific Health Conditions of Women

Women have special health needs that change with age. Naturopathy is a system of medicine that can help women to improve and manage their health through every stage of the lifecycle. A woman experiences significant phases of hormonal change from adolescence, through pregnancy and motherhood and into menopause and older age. At each of these phases, her hormones require support from the rest of her body to function optimally, promoting hormonal balance and reducing the susceptibility to illness or disease.

The specific health problems of women are:

- Menstrual cycle irregularities
- Painful or heavy periods
- Premenstrual symptoms/syndrome
- Stress, emotional instability, depression and anxiety
- Skin problems
- Abnormal pap smears or cervical dysplasia
- Fertility concerns
- Preconception concerns
- Postnatal support
- Breastfeeding support
- Endometriosis
- Polycystic ovaries
- Uterine fibroids
- Menopausal symptoms
- Digestive problems and weight management
- Fitness and cardiovascular health
- Musculoskeletal pain or injuries
- Diabetes and blood sugar regulation
- High cholesterol
- Osteoporosis

A woman's health is the barometer of her environment. It is moulded and shaped according to her evolution in the womb and the social, cultural and ecological environment of her childhood. It is created out of her relationships, her joys and traumas. It is grounded in the quality of her nutrition and the purity of the air and water around her.

The Hormonal Life Cycle

Adolescents: Young women have significantly different nutritional needs and may experience different symptoms of hormonal imbalance than a woman in her 30's or 50's. Ensuring an adolescent's nutritional needs are met and hormonal balance is optimised helps with problems such as period pain, skin, weight or mood changes whilst also ensuring healthy bones for later life.

Young women: A woman in her 20's or 30's may need help with stabilising hormones, optimising fertility and preparing for pregnancy. There may be areas she has struggled with for a long time, including period pain, weight issues, changing diet and nutritional needs or emotional problems.It is also a time when women become more aware of hereditary factors that could potentially affect their health in later life (or their children's health) including bone density, diabetes, cardiovascular disease and obesity. Addressing the lifestyle factors that contribute to these conditions is a step toward greater longevity and better quality of life now and in older age. The health of a woman in her 40's influences her experience of menopause in her late 40's or 50's.

Older women: Natural medicine is also appropriate for older women. Menopause signals a new phase of changes for women and many 'common' symptoms can be successfully managed using natural remedies. Women may also start to "feel their age" with the beginning of niggling problems that may worsen as they age if left untreated. Arthritis, libido, energy levels, emotional stability, memory/concentration and weight changes are common areas of change among older women and can be supported with the help of naturopathic and nutritional medicine.

Chapter 6

The Healing Potential of Meditation, Yoga, and Well-being

Introduction

In today's fast-paced world, the pursuit of holistic health and well-being has become increasingly paramount. Amidst the hustle and bustle of daily life, individuals seek refuge in practices that not only nurture the body but also cultivate inner peace and balance. Among these, meditation and yoga stand out as ancient yet timeless methodologies that offer profound healing benefits, fostering a harmonious union of mind, body, and spirit.

At the heart of both meditation and yoga lies the principle of mindfulness - the art of being present in the moment with awareness and acceptance. Through meditation, individuals cultivate a state of inner stillness and clarity, allowing them to observe their thoughts and emotions without judgment. This practice not only reduces stress and anxiety but also enhances emotional resilience and fosters a deep sense of inner peace.

Similarly, yoga, with its blend of physical postures, breathwork, and meditation, serves as a holistic system for promoting health and well-being. The practice of yoga not only increases flexibility, strength, and balance but also calms the mind and uplifts the spirit. By synchronizing movement with breath, practitioners enter a state of flow, where body and mind become attuned, and stress melts away.

Both meditation and yoga have been scientifically proven to offer a myriad of health benefits, from reducing blood pressure and improving cardiovascular health to boosting immune function and alleviating symptoms of depression and anxiety. Moreover, these practices have been shown to enhance cognitive function, promote better sleep, and increase overall quality of life.

In addition to meditation and yoga, the concept of well-being encompasses various lifestyle factors that contribute to optimal health and vitality. This includes proper nutrition, regular exercise, adequate rest, and meaningful social connections. By nurturing these aspects of life, individuals can create a foundation for holistic well-being that supports their physical, mental, and emotional health.

Furthermore, the integration of complementary healing modalities such as acupuncture, massage therapy, and naturopathy can further enhance the healing potential of meditation and yoga. These practices work synergistically to address imbalances in the body, restore energy flow, and promote overall vitality.

In essence, the healing potential of meditation, yoga, and well-being extends far beyond the physical realm to encompass the totality of human experience. By cultivating mindfulness, embracing movement, and nurturing holistic health practices, individuals can unlock the innate capacity for healing and transformation that resides within each of us. As we journey on the path towards greater health and well-being, may we continue to explore and embrace these ancient wisdom traditions, finding solace, strength, and inspiration along the way.

"In meditation, healing can happen. When the mind is calm, alert and totally contented, then it is like a laser beam - it is very powerful and healing can happen." - Sri Sri Ravi Shankar

Only a healthy bud can blossom. In the same way, only a healthy being can succeed.

So, What is it to be Healthy

To attain a perfect state of health, one has to remain mentally calm, steady and emotionally stable. 'Swasthya' means health. It also means being in one's self. Swasthya or health is not just confined to the body and the mind but it is also connected with the consciousness. The clearer the consciousness is, the more well-being is gained.

Meditation Increases Prana (Life Energy)

Prana (the vital life energy) is the very basis of health and well being, for both body and mind. You can gain prana through meditation.

When your body is alive with more prana, you feel alert, energetic, and full of good humor. A lack of prana results in lethargy, dullness and poor enthusiasm.

Dealing with Illness - Through Meditation

It is said that the root of an illness is in the mind/consciousness. So, by attending to the mind, clearing it of any disturbances, the recovery speeds up. Illnesses can develop from:

- Violation of natural law: such as over-eating
- Imposed by nature: such as common cold, an epidemic
- Release of past impressions or Karma

Nature itself provides a cure for these illnesses. Health and illness are a part of physical nature. By practicing meditation, the stresses, worries, anxieties drop off and gives rise to a positive state of mind, which has a positive impact on the physical body, brain and nervous system, then illnesses change.

Health and illness are a part of physical nature. You should not worry too much about it. When you worry about illness, you are giving more power to the illness. You are a combination of health and illness. When you keep that in mind and have a positive state of mind, then illnesses change.

- Heal the mind - through meditation
- Meditation prevents stresses from entering the body system and also releases accumulated stress.Health,happiness and a positive state of Being wells up
- The practice of meditation brings a coolness to the brain, it's like servicing the whole body-mind complex

Clear Emotional Pollution - With Meditation

A time may come in the future, when people will be fined for being depressed, because they are creating emotional pollution! The words that you hear from people around you, affect your state of mind. They either give you peace and joy, or create disturbance (such as jealously, anger, frustration or sadness). You're affected because the mind is not in its Self; it is not centered. Meditation is the key to control 'emotional pollution'.

Blossom with Meditation

Meditation can bring about a spiritual transformation. As you learn more about life, the mystery of the whole Creation unfolds. Then the questions that arise in the mind are - What is the meaning of Life? What is its purpose? What is this world, what is love, what is knowledge...

Once these questions arise in you, know that you are very fortunate. These questions need to be understood; you cannot find the answers in books. You have to live through them and witness the transformation. That is perfect health; you are transformed from within. And the bud becomes a totally blossomed flower.

Heal the World through Meditation

Meditation purifies the environment. Meditation and Sudarshan Kriya have transformed aggression and violence in people - to compassion, love and care. For example, notice how you feel when you enter a room where someone is really angry ? It leaves you feeling the same!

Similarly, when there is a harmonious or a happy activity, you feel good. You may wonder why. Feelings are not isolated in one's body - they are all around.

It is in the whole environment, because the mind is subtler than the five elements (earth, water, fire, air, ether). If there is a fire somewhere, the heat is not just in the fire, it is also radiating throughout the place.

Note: If you are unhappy or depressed, you are not the only one who is feeling it; you are spreading it to the whole environment.

In the current global situation of conflicts and disease, it's important to meditates a little every day. Through meditation, you can nullify the negative vibrations in the environment, thereby creating a more harmonious environment.

The Healing Breath & Meditation

A jewel in The Art of Living is the healing breath, known as the Sudarshan Kriya.

This unique breathing practice is a potent energizer:

- Every cell becomes fully oxygenated and flooded with new life
- It flushes out negative emotions from the body
- It releases tensions, frustrations and anger
- It clears anxiety, depression and lethargy
- It gives relief to both the mind and body

After the practice, one is left calm and centered with a clearer mind. A sense of joy in the moment prevails, and you're able to smile from your heart.

'Do the Healing Breath and meditate. These practices completely transform you, and kindle the love deep inside.'

Understanding the Relationship between Health and Yoga

According to the World Health Organization (WHO) the state of Health is defined as a state of complete physical, mental, and social well being and not merely an absence of disease or infirmity. WHO also suggests a fourth dimension- spiritual Health. It is clear from this definition that health and ill-health are not two discrete entities as commonly understood but health should be conceived as a continuous function indicating the state of well being. " The region of ill-health" represents what normally we designate as 'Sickness' Below this, man acts instinctively and is akin to an animal man. Coming to the first quadrant, the region of 'Normal Alan' the state of normal health is indicated. As one moves along the line further up, he becomes healthier featured by the dormant faculties expressing more vividly in man. This is shown as the region of Super Man, the next region after the human spectrum.

In this state, the limitations of normal man namely the strong urges of thirst, hunger, fear and sex are reduced greatly and are fully under control. In the concept of Sri Aurobindo 17 the new faculties of deeper perceptions of the world beyond the five senses emerge in this phase of super human existence. Further growth leads man to unfold even deeper layers of consciousness and widen the spectrum of his knowledge to move towards divinity or perfection.

In this march towards perfection, Yoga is a systematic conscious process for accelerating the growth of a human being from his animal level to normalcy, then to super human level and ultimately to divinity. It is a systematic methodology for an all round personality development- physical, mental, intellectual, emotional and spiritual components-of man. Thus, Yoga in its general methodology for the growth of man to divine heights. includes techniques useful for therapeutic applications in making man healthier.

The Five Sheaths of Our Existence

Notwithstanding the sincere and subtle, (atomic level) researches, the attempts to understand life as an offshoot of matter, a conglomeration of a complex configuration of atoms and molecules (called DNA & RNA), are leading man to regions of greater complexity. *The decades of subtler and expensive research have yielded much less fruit than expected.

However, better understanding of life appear to be forthcoming with efforts directed in fields of modern psychologyand Parapsychology. The forerunner of many of these efforts could be traced back to the work of Kirlian. Controversies apart, Kirlian photography triggered the interest of a large number of scientists and technologists all over the world. Investigations into the unknown regions of human existence started unravelling the mysteries of 'life'. Parapsychology Institutes have grown in number. Scientists have started reconsidering their hypothesis that 'life' also is an emergence from matter. They recognize some existence beyond the physical body. The scientific study of the Human Aura by Tart 15, the professor of psychology at the University of California at Davis, USA, delineates the following sheaths of human aura:

1. The physical aura
2. The psychological aura
3. The psychical aura &
4. The projected aura.

In relating the experience of the psychics the term's human aura, Etheric double, Astral body, Thought-forms etc have been studied. Nirmala has summarised the various systems about the layers of consciousness as depicted in Indian philosophical and Yogic texts.

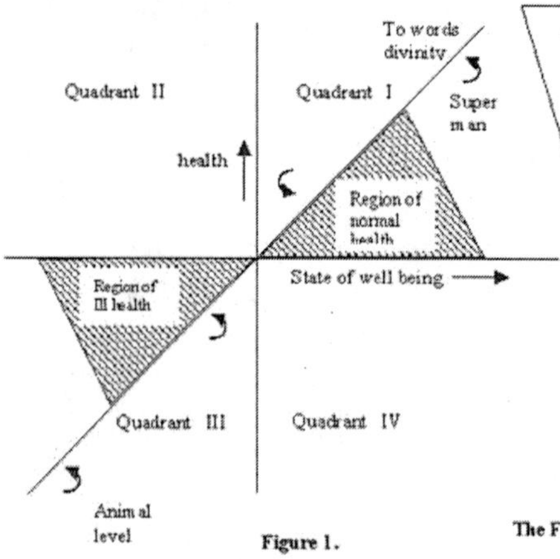

Figure 1.
Concept of Health

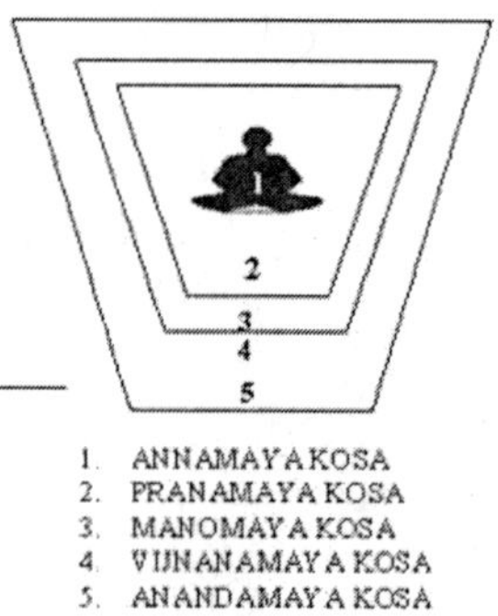

Figure 2.
The Five Sheaths (Kosas) of our existence

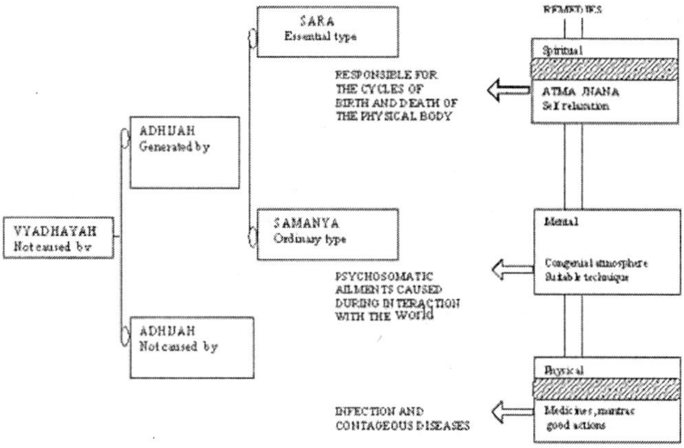

Figure 3.
A Schematic Diagram of our Ailments (See Appendix 1)

In the tradition of Yoga and Upanisats there are five sheaths of existence of Man. The first and the grossest - the physical frame which we are all so familiar is called ANNAMAYA KOSA. The second subtler sheath is the 'PRANAMAYA K0SA' featured by the predominance of Prana, the life principle. Through the invisible channels called NADIS in this sheath flow the PRANA.

The next sheaths in the order of subtlety are:

1. Manomaya Kosa
2. Vignanamaya Kosa
3. Anandamaya Kosa

Anandamaya Kosa as the inner most and the subtlest. As the sheaths become subtler, the freedom of operation in the living beings increases, the bondage decreases and the bliss associated with it also increases. While in Manomaya Kosa the creative power predominates, in Vignanamaya Kosa it is the power to discern and act in tune with it discriminate. Bliss is embodied in Anandamaya Kosa, the highest stage of evolution in the manifested existence. It is the subtlest among the 5 sheaths of existence.

In his journey towards the Ultimate, Man crosses these sheaths of existence one by one. Through analysis, called 'Panca Kosa Viveka' (Knowing through experience his 5 sheaths of existence) 18 and the associated practices called "Tapas" man transforms himself by gradually getting relieved from the bondages and constrictions of each sheath. This is one of the methods of reaching the ultimate goat enumerated and described in the Upanisats.

Basic Concepts of Yoga

Although the tradition of yoga is 5,000 years old, it is mainly attributed to the Sage Patanjali as the father of yoga, who transcribed the book, The Yoga Sutra, over 2,000 years ago. This sacred Sanskrit text is a compilation of 196 aphorisms in four chapters which outlines the Eight Limbs of Yoga offering wisdom and guidelines for living a meaningful and purposeful life. The origin of yoga itself precedes the Yoga Sutra and is attributed to Lord Shiva as the first yogi (adi yogi) and Parvati, his wife, as the first student.

The union of Shiva (consciousness and wisdom) and Parvati (creative energy shakti) symbolizes the completion of the whole through the fusion of the male and the female energies. It is also symbolic of the balance that the practice of yoga creates within ourselves. To this day, The Yoga Sutra and The Bhagavad Gita, another sacred Hindu scripture gives deep insight on yoga, are capable of transforming one's personality, and are sources of inspiration to countless self-help books published around the world.

The United Nation's designation of June 21st as the International Day of Yoga in 2015 is a testament to the global popularity of yoga as the path to attain good health and happiness. Modern science has provided ample evidence to validate the benefits of yoga and thus perpetuated the yoga movement across cultural and religious barriers. The Western medical world has come to acknowledge the effectiveness of yoga on managing various physical, mental and emotional illnesses to improve quality of our life.

Modern Medicine and Yoga

Although modern medicine and yoga are complementary to each other for the wellbeing of the society but there are some differences in their approach. The difference between Western medicine and traditional yogic methods lie in the distinction of understanding the meaning of health. In the English language, the word health is defined as "the state of being free from illness or injury." However, the Sanskrit word, swastha, means "to be established within oneself". Therefore, according to the Western definition, a person is healthy as long as he or she is not ill or injured. It is purely a physical and negative definition, not taking into consideration the imbalances in a person, which might be causing the ailment. In contrast, the concept of swastha highlights the root of a problem and never isolates the symptoms from the entire person. Simply put, Western medicine is based on suppressing the symptoms of the disease with the use of external intervention or drugs, whereas the practice of yoga unifies the body, mind and spirit to create an internal balance, which is healing in itself. Yogic approach is holistic and includes every aspect.

Yoga as a Discipline

Yoga begins with the practitioner taking a resolve to dedicate him or herself to the discipline. A daily hour practice in the morning of asana, pranayama and meditation will slowly change the personality.

In the evening, a quiet reflection of our actions of that day also increases our awareness to live consciously. The very first stanza of The Yoga Sutra (1:1) states, "AthaYoganushasanam." "Atha" means now, "anu" is atom and "shasanam" means to govern, signifying our responsibility to govern subtle (every) part of our own body, down to the atomic level. This is the quintessential difference between yoga and Western medicine. Yoga develops self discipline to live with mindfulness to prevent outer or inner illness and face the challenges of the society with confidence.

Yoga teaches us to take charge of our entire being where as modern medicine delegates the responsibility to doctors and drugs. Yoga empowers us to create a union and balance within ourselves which allows prana, the universal life force and energy, to flow in our bodies for our physical and mental wellbeing. There are times where we need to rely on modern medicine. In such a case, smooth flow of prana would even enhance the effectiveness of the medication, which results in rapid healing.

Patanjali defined yoga as "Yogachittavrittinirodhah," which means "Yoga is the removal of the fluctuations of the mind." "Chitta" is mind or consciousness, "vrittis" are thought impulses and "nirodah" is removal. In other words, cleaning the mind of emotions and thoughts is yoga. Through meditation we can still the mind and get to know who we really are. As we transform and balance our personality, our koshas (the sheaths), we also change on a cellular level, which positively influence our blood and energy flow.

In other words, yoga is cleaning the mind from emotions and thoughts.

It is a scientific fact that our cells change every seven years and our bodies are renewed. On average, it takes approximately 23 to 60 seconds for blood to make a complete circuit in our bodies. When prana through blood reach each and every cell then it creates natural balance in whole system. Yoga says that imbalance or illness in our personality is due to imbalance or disruption or lack of flow of prana. Through physical practice we try to encourage blood and prana to reach everywhere by creating space and pranayama used as a carrier and coordinator between body, mind and emotion. When the blood circulation is too fast, we unnecessarily exhaust ourselves and age faster. Yoga slows down the process through controlling the breath and relaxing the mind and the body. Only in a relaxed state healing takes place. No modern exercise can relax us in the way yoga can. Modern medicine tries to replicate this state of relaxation by prescribing sleeping pills to patients. In contrast, yoga allows us to create a healing state of mind and body ourselves. Yoga requires discipline in order to achieve a stilled equanimity within ourselves so that we may know who we are, the purpose of our lives and to face life's challenges. Many students misunderstand yoga as only a physical practice of asanas. Such false knowledge is the responsibility of the teacher. The practice of asana is only a warm up for the main practice of breathing because it is the pranayama that can bring the deep relaxation to the body and mind. It is important for the student to seek a good teacher who is capable of teaching yoga in its totality and should be able to diagnose any imbalances in the student's koshas.

Through our practice of yoga, we strive to sharpen our awareness, which is distributed 70-75% to our bodies, 20-25% to our minds, 4% to our emotions and only 1% to our divine, higher self. These precious, but fleeting moments of awareness in union with the divine within ourselves, is the source of creativity and godliness. There is no "god" but the divine resides in godly actions. Through the practice of yoga, we try to govern the subtle qualities of ourselves to spread godliness. Spending hours on the yoga mat but displaying inconsiderate or hurtful actions to others defeats the entire purpose of this lifestyle. Yoga is an experiential study through self-introspection.

We can start the discipline from the body by having different movements then to breath management then to the mind management with the integrated and holistic approach to evolve as a better human being. It transforms us and as we benefit from the changes, we must become goodwill ambassadors of yoga so that others may also benefit.

Wellness and Restoration

When you suffer from a disease, you must realize that you have broken certain fundamental laws of nature. Even if you have inherited the disease from your family, still the major responsibility lies with you, because by breaking the laws of nature you have destroyed the immune system. You should understand that your disease indicates a breach of discipline.

Therefore, side by side with medical treatment, you must try to discover and understand where you have made an error in your relationship with nature. There are many diseases where you need not go for medical treatment, and there are certain diseases where medical treatment is absolutely indispensable, but in most diseases, side by side with medical treatment, you will have to become aware of and understand the mistake in your physical, mental and emotional personality.

This physical body is very mysterious. It is much more than we have understood. It has powerful secretions inherent in it, which definitely affect the metabolic, catabolic and anabolic processes without your knowledge. Breach of discipline in any realm can put the natural system completely out of order.

Laws about diet, thinking, responses and reactions, stress and strain have to be well understood. When a disease comes, then a spiritual discipline in the form of yoga and meditation comes in. Many times when we suffer from a disease, we are hopelessly worried about it. In order to find a cure for the sickness, we run from pillar to post and have no faith at all in ourselves. When we have no faith in ourselves, then the disease is aggravated even more.

Role of the Mind

The mind plays a very important part at all stages of your life. A disease may have been caused due to mental defects, and when the disease takes place you are worried about it. Then again, the mind plays the part of an aggravator, and you do not know what to do, so you are confused. Then the mind plays the part of a complicator. At all stages it is a generator, an aggravator and a complicator. Even if the disease is purely biological and physiological in origin, still the role of the mind is important. Therefore, you should try to treat the patient first.

Methods of Healing

Medical science has great limitations because doctors only treat the disease. Of course, it gives some sort of relief, but the patient remains sick. One sickness is gone, and another sickness is in waiting. Therefore, spiritual healing comes into the picture.

In India, there are spiritual healers in every village, and they are very humble people. They heal through mantra, through touch, through group sessions, and by exploding emotions.

However, apart from these spiritual healing systems, there is another one, which is the practice of yoga in day-to-day life. It has been found even by scientists today that when you meditate, great changes take place in your body. Pratyahara, dharana or dhyana, concentration and meditation practices, are not merely psychological or purely spiritual. Body and mind are in total interaction with each other. What happens to the body happens to the mind and vice versa. Therefore, you should try to become your own healer.

Prana

When you can awaken your mental and spiritual force, then you can start independent spiritual healing. However, at the same time, there are other methods of spiritual healing. Some people are endowed with special magnetic or electro-magnetic radiation. You can study this force by studying the Kirlian photographic system, which has shown that every individual body has an aura. This aura belongs to everybody, but some people have the special magnetic force of prana.

This pranic force can be radiated, transmitted and transferred into another person's body. In the tantric system, we call these sciences prana vidya. There are many forms of prana vidya and their purpose is to increase the quantum of pranic force in your body. When there is plenty of pranic force, your resistance increases. As a result of this resistance, your body can exercise what we call the powers of immunity. Nature has created this physical body with many kinds of defences.

Due to nature's strong defence and immune systems, diseases do not happen all of a sudden. These systems of resistance or immunity are always backed by prana or the life force. When there is a disease in your body, you should realize that it has been developing for a long time. -Chateau Theyrargue, France, 19 July 1984

Is Spiritual Healing Effective and Lasting

Every form of healing is effective, but not lasting, because it is only healing the symptoms of sickness, not the person who is sick. The mind, emotions, thinking and philosophy of the patient should be healed. The process of spiritual healing improves the condition for some time, but if there is no change in the person's attitude and reactions, after some time, the person falls sick again.

Law of Karma

When you are trying to heal a sick person, you must understand the reason for the sickness. Karma is the first law in science and life. Karma related to eating, sleeping and thinking is responsible for sickness.

The karmic process of the individual must be corrected and reorganized. If you are not reorganizing the karmic process, you are only trying to suppress the law of nature and scrap the disease. Therefore, there is sickness after sickness.

The purpose of disease is not suffering, but the expulsion of the toxins of karma. With diarrhoea, an abscess or fever toxins are expelled, and you must undergo the sickness because it is the process by which nature is trying to force the expulsion of toxins. You did not allow nature to release the poisons before but were withholding the process. Therefore, nature is finally trying to push the process by force.

Any kind of sickness, whether it is insomnia, schizophrenia or a physical disease, should be treated without obstructing the laws of nature. Nature is an all powerful and omnipresent force which controls the entire universe by certain inexorable laws.

Prakriti

Nature, known as prakriti, is a very organized system. According to samkhya and tantra, prakriti, is of two types: para prakriti, the transcendental, and apara prakriti, the material nature. The material nature is of eight types: the five tattwas, the elements, and chitta, the mind,buddhi, the intelligence, andahamkara, the ego principle. This is called ashtadha prakriti, the eightfold prakriti. The eight queens of Krishna, the ashtha rani, symbolize these eight forms of nature. However, the transcendental prakriti controls the invisible laws of the entire cosmos.

Healers

For the last twenty years I have been talking to spiritual healers in the West. Often they become terribly sick because the purpose of disease is suppressed. Many spiritual healers have chronic and incurable diseases that medical science, acupuncture or homeopathy fail to heal. They also have another difficulty. When they treat a patient suffering from rheumatism, in the end, they have the rheumatism themselves. They don't know how it happened because they don't know the laws of nature. Nobody knows.

Ramdas

Samarth Ramdas had a very high fever, but he had an important consultation with his disciple, the king, Shivaji. Therefore, he transferred his fever to his tiger skin. When the king came, they had their consultation and the king found the tiger skin was shivering. Ramdas said, "Shivaji, do not worry, it is my fever.

There is a process of evolution in the body and mind, and karmas must be undergone in order to evolve. Spiritual healing is a good science. It will help people, but it is not the ultimate healing of suffering. It is a relief at the time of agony, yet the whole structure of mind, body and spirit must be reorganized. -Bombay, India, 3 November 1981

How can Memory be Improved

The memory centres in the brain undoubtedly do degenerate. The degeneration is caused by strong toxins, like alcohol, narcotics or sedatives. Even if we do not take alcohol, smoke or take sedatives, there is ample in our day-to-day food habits. Food produces alcohol, and some amount is definitely necessary for the body but not in excess. When people are suffering from cerebral or paralytic stroke, they lose their memory. This means that we should avoid clotting in the blood vessels and high blood pressure. This is the physiological sign of memory loss.

There is also a psychological aspect to memory. When your mind is distracted and overcrowded, you miss many details. One yoga practice is known as antar mouna, inner silence, in which you sit down quietly and do not concentrate on anything, but just observe all the thoughts that come into your mind. Many times you are able to think of what happened to you during your childhood. Depending on the particular frequency at which your brain is functioning, you sometimes remember the immediate past and then suddenly jump to your childhood. Sometimes you begin to remember such insignificant things which you did not even notice when they happened. This is a practice which has to be done day in and day out assiduously.

All memories are recorded in the brain, but the capacity for reproduction is very inadequate. Therefore, when you want to know about maintaining memory, you are actually talking about the capacity for reproduction.

When people are on their deathbed, they remember so many events of their lives, even to the tiniest detail. The most insignificant things are remembered. Just before death, the memory becomes brilliant and sharp. It means that everybody has the memory intact and it is only the capacity for reproduction that has to be maintained. For retention and reproduction of memory the best and most effective practice is pranayama. -Helsinki, Finland, July 1981

How can Obesity be Eliminated

People have time and money for everything but not for the life-saving system of yoga. It is not only food that is the cause of obesity. The cause is a process of thinking. This process of thinking eliminates certain processes of digestion in the system. There are various yoga practices that could be prescribed for eliminating obesity. One important practice for jolly fat people is tadagi mudra, the puta ed abdomen technique.

Practitioners should stretch out both legs and just hold the toes. The knees and elbows should be straight, and the head not bent towards the knees. In this particular posture, you breathe out through the mouth and then push your belly a little inside. Then breathe in through the nose, expand the abdomen, wait for a while and then blow the breath out. Contract the abdomen and breathe in through the nose. Repeat this as many times as you can.

When it is not possible to hold the toes, then hold the ankles. If that is also not possible, then tie two handkerchiefs to the two toes and hold the other ends of the handkerchiefs. In about a week's time you will find that your hands are becoming longer and the legs shorter!

Another practice is ushtrasana, the camel pose. Not everybody can do it, especially fat jolly people. Instead, they should stand straight, hold their hips and slowly move the palms down the legs over a period of time. Gradually, they will also be able to move into puta vajrasana, the sleeping thunderbolt pose. These are two more exercises for obesity

Lastly, people who are suffering from obesity also have fat bank balances. They should try to correct that through yoga, because obesity in the bank is not good for the mind. It is said in the Bible that, "It is easier for a camel to pass through the eye of a needle than for a rich person to enter the kingdom of heaven." It is one of the most important pieces of advice. It does not mean that you should not become rich, but it is important that you improve your legacy. There are millions of people to whom you can distribute your wealth. -Las Palmas, Spain, 23 September 1980

Self-Healing

Self-healing refers to the process of recovery (generally from psychological disturbances, trauma, etc.), motivated by and directed by the patient, guided often only by instinct. Such a process encounters mixed fortunes due to its amateur nature, although self-motivation is a major asset. The value of self-healing lies in its ability to be tailored to the unique experience and requirements of the individual. The process can be helped and accelerated with introspection techniques such as Meditation.

Self Healing as a Way to Overcome Racial Trauma

Historically, communities of Color in the United States and around the World have attempted to use different modes (i.e. scholarship, art, and community gathering) to create self-healing as a way to combat the daily trauma of living in a racialized society.

The Different Meanings of Self-Healing

Self-healing is the ultimate phase of Gestalt Therapy.

Self-healing may refer to automatic, homeostatic processes of the body that are controlled by physiological mechanisms inherent in the organism. Disorders of the spirit and the absence of faith can be self-healed.

In a figurative sense, self-healing properties can be ascribed to systems or processes, which by nature or design tend to correct any disturbances brought into them. Such as the regeneration of the skin after a cut or scrape, or of an entire limb. The injured party (the living body) repairs the damaged part by itself.

Beyond the innate restorative capacities of the physical body, there are many factors of psychological nature that can influence self-healing. Hippocrates, considered by many to be the father of medical treatment, observed: "The physician must be ready, not only to do his duty himself, but also to secure the co-operation of the patient, of the attendants and of externals." - Hippocrates.

Self-healing may also be achieved through deliberately applied psychological mechanisms. These approaches may improve the psychological and physical conditions of a person. Research confirms that this can be achieved through numerous mechanisms, including relaxation, breathing exercises, fitness exercises, imagery, Meditation, Yoga, qigong, t'ai chi, biofeedback, and various forms of psychotherapy, among other approaches.

Varieties of mechanisms for self-healing have been proposed, including:

1. Decreases in stress hormones that may impair physiological functions when there is chronic stress.
2. Decreases in muscle tension, which can worsen or produce pains in muscles, tendons and joints when there is chronic muscle tension due to stress.
3. Improved sleep that can be achieved through relaxation, which improves physiological functions.
4. Improvements in emotional tensions, depression, anger and other emotions that can otherwise impair social relationships and functioning in the workplace, leading to vicious circles of increased psychological symptoms.

Another phrase that often includes self-healing is self-help. In 2013 Kathryn Schulz examined it as "an $11 billion industry". Twelve-step programs support individuals recovering from dysfunctional families and addictive/compulsive behaviors.

Self-Responsibility in Health

Self-responsibility and self-empowerment are important concepts in the Medical Yoga model. The idea that we can contribute to the recovery of our health and vitality is both empowering and possible with these Yoga practices. There are many things we can learn to do to recover and maintain the health of our body. Although it is important to follow the medical guidelines given by your doctor and other healthcare providers, it is equally important that you assume some responsibility for assisting in the health of your body and mind. For example, using common sense and moderation in your eating and alcohol intake is one area that will promote a higher state of health. Equally so, movement exercises, relaxation, and getting enough rest are also very important. Assuming responsibility and being proactive in your lifestyle choices helps in the final outcome of your health status.

What we are aiming for in the practice of Medical Yoga is to assist in activating the innate self-healing capability that is part of our biology. The human body has an incredible ability to repair and heal itself. There are times, however, when we push the body too far in one direction or another and it starts to break down and respond in a dis-eased manner. A good analogy of pushing the body too far is to think about salt-water taffy. If you pull taffy apart, nothing happens for a short period of time. However, as you continue to pull, the taffy becomes more and more thin and less resistant and strong. Eventually the taffy will snap. The body acts the same way. It will accommodate our stress levels, lack of sleep, poor diet, etc. for a period of time, but then it, too, will start to eventually breakdown and tear. This is the point at which disease can begin to manifest in the body. It is also at this point that we shouldn't rely only on the doctor's intervention in terms of surgery and medications for healing. We can also assist and contribute to our health status by using the tools of Medical Yoga. Making healthy lifestyle changes, utilizing relaxation strategies, and managing our stress will give our body a chance at recovering and healing.

The Body's Fuel

The body is similar to an automobile in terms of the care and maintenance it needs. When we fuel our car we don't put watered-down gasoline or a mixture of sugar and gas in the gas tank. This obviously will affect how the car runs. Similarly if we chronically feed our body foods high in saturated fat, white flour, or sugar or have chronically high stress, our body will not run efficiently and will eventually start to breakdown.

Our body fuels and rejuvenates itself through several mechanisms, some of which include sleeping, breathing, and eating. We need all three of these types of fuel in order to keep the body and mind well-maintained and functioning. If we aren't feeding it the proper fuel, i.e., healthy foods, water, and air, the body won't run efficiently. Equally so, if we don't reduce stress and get enough rest and exercise, hormones continue to flood the body with a stress response that causes various problems and invites dis-ease to manifest. Similarly, if our breathing is constantly agitated or short and jerky we aren't providing the body with proper amounts of fuel (oxygen) to be able to function well.

The proper care and functioning of the body and mind may require some thinking about what kind of fuel you need to give yourself to bring your body and mind back to a state of ease, health, and vitality. We sometimes fall into old habits that really don't serve us very well. We may be choosing foods or stress levels that are contributing to fatigue, depression, anxiety, lack of vitality, or other problems that eventually lead to higher and higher levels of dis-ease (and eventually disease) in the system. The Medical Yoga program aims to bring about a balance in your physiology and psychology. The practices of Yoga help to promote a sense of peace, calmness, vitality and health in the entire system.

What Caused the Symptoms

In order to better understand the idea of introducing health back into the system, it is important to also understand that the removal of symptoms is only half the answer to health. We must also recognize what caused the symptoms to appear in the first place. If we just remove the symptoms of dis-ease or disease and haven't removed the cause of the symptoms, we are placing ourselves at risk for the symptoms to reappear.

This is similar to having someone vigorously mop up the floor when the sink is overflowing with water, yet failing to pull the plug to let the water drain out of the sink. Mopping up the floor is only one part of the solution. We also have to determine what caused the water to overflow in the first place. Not pulling the plug out when the water is continuously running would obviously cause problems. Therefore, the other part of the solution is to unplug the sink so it doesn't run over anymore. Just mopping up the floor (removing the symptoms) won't stop the problem from reoccurring.

In order to really heal the body and mind, we need to go back far enough in the causal chain of events to determine the origin and causes of the problem and not just remove the symptoms. In order to effectively do this, we have to be willing to examine our lifestyle choices, our thoughts, attitudes, and our emotional blueprints to see which of these areas might be impacting negatively on our health and where we might need to revise our choices. Not all disease manifestation is due to lifestyle choices, but we have to be willing to honestly examine this area and make changes where needed so that we can empower ourselves and impact positively on our health. We have to be willing to take responsibility and change the places in our lives that are causing problems. Assisting in our health and contributing to our recovery can be interesting, fun, and definitely empowering.

Healing vs. Curing

As we move toward higher levels of health and vitality in the body and mind, it is important to understand the difference between healing and curing. In the field of Yoga and mind-body medicine, healing is seen as a process of recovery that takes place on the physical, emotional, mental and spiritual levels and results in a person having a sense of balance, completeness, and harmony in the self and in the environment. Curing, on the other hand, is viewed as an externally applied medical intervention that removes all evidence of a diagnosed disease. Although both of these concepts are important, there may be times when a cure has occurred but that healing has not necessarily taken place. Conversely, healing may be evident in the person and the system, but a cure may not be possible. Both healing and curing are important concepts to embrace and, ideally, having both occur in the system would be the best outcome.

Health, Healing, and Yoga

Yoga is very comprehensive and includes a great variety of approaches. Before you go off hiking in the countryside, you need to take a quick look at the map or risk getting lost. Likewise, before you start experimenting with Yoga, you want to know what it is and how it works. That's how you can ensure that your practice of Yoga is both enjoyable and safe.

The source of your health and happiness lies within you. Outside agents like physicians, therapists, or remedies can help you through major crises, but you yourself are primarily responsible for your own health and happiness. The following sections show you how Yoga helps you mobilize the inner strength to live responsibly and wisely. What is health? Most people answer this question by saying that health is the opposite of illness, but health is more than the absence of disease - it's a positive state of being. Health is wholeness. To be healthy means not only to possess a well-functioning body and a sane mind but also to vibrate with life, to be vitally connected with your social and physical environment. To be healthy also means to be happy.

For centuries, the traditional time for Yoga practice has been sunrise and sunset, which are thought to be especially auspicious. These days, busy lifestyles can toss out lots of obstacles to your best intentions, so be pragmatic and arrange your Yoga practice at your convenience. Just keep in mind that statistically, you have a 30 percent greater chance of accomplishing a fitness goal if you practice in the morning. More important than holding tight to a pre-set time is just making sure that you work Yoga into your schedule somewhere - and stick with it. Practicing at roughly the same time during the day can help you create a positive habit, which may make it easier to maintain your routine.

To get a sense of the nature of enlightenment, sit in a warm room as still as possible, with your hands in your lap. Now sense your skin all over; it's your body's boundary separating you from the air surrounding you. As you become more aware of your body's sensations, pay special attention to the connection between your skin and the air.

After a while, you realize that no sharp boundary really exists between your skin and the outside air. In your imagination, you can extend yourself further and further beyond your skin into the surrounding space. Where do you end, and where does the space begin? This experience can give you a sense of the all-comprising expansiveness of enlightenment, which knows no boundaries.

Because life is constant movement, you shouldn't expect health to be static. Today health is increasingly difficult to achieve because the environment has become highly toxic. Perfect health is a mirage. In the course of your life, you can expect inevitable fluctuations in your state of health; even cutting your finger with a knife temporarily upsets the balance. Your body reacts to the cut by mobilizing all the necessary biochemical forces to heal itself. Regular Yoga practice can create optimal conditions for self-healing. You achieve a baseline of health, with an improved immune system that enables you to stay healthy longer and heal faster.

Yoga is about healing rather than curing. Like a really good physician, Yoga takes deeper causes into account instead of slapping a bandage on surface symptoms. These causes are more often than not found in the mind - in the way you live and how you think. That's why Yoga masters recommend self-understanding. Most people tend to be passive in health matters.

They wait until something goes wrong and then rely on a pill or a physician to fix the problem. Yoga encourages you to take the initiative in preventing illness and restoring or maintaining your health. Taking control of your health has nothing to do with self-doctoring (which can be dangerous); it's simply a matter of taking responsibility for your health. A good physician can tell you that a patient's active participation in the process greatly facilitates healing. For example, you may take various kinds of medication to deal with a gastric ulcer, but unless you learn to eat well, sleep adequately, avoid stress, and take life more easily, you're bound to have a recurrence before long. You must change your lifestyle to realize any deep-seated healing.

How the healing power of meditation works

"In meditation, healing can happen. When the mind is calm, alert and totally contented, then it is like a laser beam - it is very powerful and healing can happen." ~ Gurudev Sri Sri Ravi Shankar

Just like how only a healthy bud can blossom, similarly, only when we are healthy can we blossom to our full potential. To attain a perfect state of health, one has to be mentally calm, steady and emotionally stable. 'Swasthya' means health. It also means being in one's self. Swasthya or health is not just confined to the body and the mind but is also connected with consciousness. The clearer one's consciousness, the more one's sense of well-being increases.

Listed below are 6 ways how meditation has the power to heal:

1. Meditation increases prana (life energy): Prana (life energy) is the basis of health and well-being for both, the body and mind. You can gain prana through meditation. When your body is alive with more prana, you feel alert, energetic, and full of life. Lack of prana results in lethargy, dullness, and low enthusiasm levels.
2. Meditation heals illness

- Heal the mind through meditation.
- Meditation prevents stresses from entering the body system.
- It releases accumulated stress.
- It helps improve health, ups the happiness quotient and sustains a positive state of mind.
- The practice of meditation makes you peaceful.
- Meditation is like the servicing of the body-mind complex.

It is said the root of an illness is in the mind/consciousness. So, by attending to the mind, clearing it of any disturbances, the recovery speeds up. Illnesses can develop from:

- violation of natural law: for example, overeating
- imposed by nature: for example, common cold, or an epidemic
- release of past impressions or karma.

Nature itself provides a cure for these illnesses. Health and illness are a part of physical nature. The practice of meditation helps to let go of stress, worries, and anxieties. This results in a positive state of mind, which in turn has a positive impact on the physical body, brain, and nervous system. Consequently, the illness decreases.

One of the secret understanding of illness is that when you worry about illness, you give more power to it. You must remember that you are a combination of health and illness. When you know this and have a positive state of mind, then illnesses gradually disappear.

3. Clears emotional problems : A time may come in the future when people will be fined for being depressed because they are creating emotional pollution! The words that you hear from people around you affect your state of mind. They either give you peace and joy or create negative emotions, such as jealousy, anger, frustration or sadness. You are affected because the mind is not centered. Meditation is a key to clear away the emotional issues. Experience a state of deep rest and clarity of mind with 'Transforming Emotions', an online guided meditation by Gurudev Sri Sri Ravi Shankar.
4. Blossom from within: Meditation can bring about a spiritual transformation. As you learn more about life, the mystery of the whole creation unfolds. Then the questions that arise in the mind are - what is the meaning of life, what is its purpose, what is this world, what is love, what is knowledge Once these questions arise in you, know that you are fortunate. These questions need to be understood, you cannot find the answers in books. You have to live through them and witness the transformation. When you are transformed from within is the sign of a perfect health.
5. Heal the world : Meditation purifies the environment. Meditation and Sudarshan Kriya have transformed the aggression and violence to compassion, love, and care in a cross-section of people. When you enter a place where someone is angry, the energy of that place is not pleasing. Similarly, when there is a harmonious or a happy activity, then that place has a different vibe. This happens because feelings Feelings are not isolated in one's body they are all around. It is in the whole environment because the mind is subtler than the five elements (earth, water, fire, air, ether). If there is a fire somewhere, the heat is not just in the fire, it is also radiating throughout the place. Similarly, if you are unhappy or depressed, you are not the only one who is feeling it, you are also spreading it to in your surrounding. In the current global situation of conflicts and disease, it's important to meditate for a short while every day. Through meditation, you can nullify the negative vibrations in the environment, thereby

creating a more harmonious environment.

6. Heals chakras : The Sudarshan Kriya & meditation

The cornerstone of The Art of Living programs is the healing breath, known as the Sudarshan Kriya. This unique breathing practice is a potent energizer, with following benefits:

- every cell becomes fully oxygenated and flooded with new life
- flushes out negative emotions from the body
- releases tensions, frustrations and anger
- clears anxiety, depression, and lethargy
- gives relief to both the mind and body.

With regular practice, one becomes calm and centered with a clearer mind. A sense of joy in the moment prevails and one is able to smile from the heart.

Benefits of meditation are innumerable and each and every human must tap into their inner being for a more enriched living.

Heal Your Body with Yoga

There's a good reason you feel like goddess when you walk out of yoga class, and it's not because you finally got your money's worth out of your gym. It's because yoga and similar mind-quieting methods have the potential to work as well as many medications at treating what ails you. "We now have compelling scientific proof that the mind can heal the body," says Herbert Benson, M.D., director emeritus of the Benson-Henry Institute for Mind Body Medicine at Massachusetts General Hospital and author of Relaxation Revolution. The latest promises:

Your Body Dials Down Stress

Dr. Benson's research has found that mind/body practices-meditation, yoga, tai chi, deep breathing, visualization-all elicit the relaxation response, quelling the release of stress hormones cortisol and adrenaline. Your heart slows, blood pressure falls and digestion eases.

Your Immunity Soars

The relaxation response causes cells to release micropuffs of nitric oxide, a gas that dilates blood vessels and stabilizes the immune system, Dr. Benson reported in Medical Science Monitor. Mind/body methods worked as well as drugs designed to do the same thing, without the side effects.

Your Brain Grows

As you get older, your brain begins to shrink. But in a study in NeuroReport, researchers discovered that the prefrontal cortex and the anterior right insula, areas linked to attention and sensory processing, were thicker and more robust in those who meditate.

"It's like exercise for the brain, making it stronger," says Rick Hanson, Ph.D., a neuropsychologist in San Rafael, California, and author of Buddha's Brain.

Your Genes Change

Here's the real slap-your-forehead news: In a study in PLoS ONE, Dr. Benson compared the genes of 38 people, half of whom meditated regularly and half of whom never did. Controlling for other factors, he found that genes associated with stress-related illness behaved differently in the two groups.

"These genes control not only stress but also premature aging and inflammation," he says. It seems meditators' genes were essentially telling their body to stress less and age more slowly.

Your Relaxation Rx

Which mind/body treatments have the most rock-solid science backing them up? Brent Bauer, M.D., director of the Complementary and Integrative Medicine Program at the Mayo Clinic in Rochester, Minnesota, provides the big picture.

For...	Try...
Back pain	Yoga
High cholesterol	Qigong
Depression	Music therapy, qigong, yoga
Eating disorders	Meditation, yoga
Fertility	Visualization, yoga
Heart health	Deep breathing, qigong, yoga
Immunity	Breathing, chants, meditation, qigong
Insomnia	Acupuncture, visualization, yoga
Joint pain	Music therapy, qigong, yoga
Migraines	Acupuncture, yoga

The #1 Health Habit You're Not Doing... Yet

Only 13 percent of SELF readers meditate regularly, but two thirds of you say you'd be willing to give it a try.

What's holding you back? Avoid your biggest roadblocks to inner peace and find your way om.

Roadblock 1: "I don't know how."

29 percent of you merely need instruction, so here goes: Pick something simple and recurring to focus on, a mantra. "It could be your breath, a prayer or a saying, like, 'May this be a good day,'" says Hanson, who teaches meditation. Then repeat it in your head as long as you can, up to 20 minutes. "If you get distracted, that's OK," he says. Gently refocus until the mantra has recaptured your attention.

Roadblock 2: "I have no time."

Stop everything to do nothing? No can do, say 18 percent of you. Luckily, you may get benefits from meditating for as little as five minutes. If even that's a stretch, you can reduce stress simply by doing daily chores more mindfully.

"Staying steadily, attentively present with everyday tasks such as doing the dishes or brushing your teeth can be a calming, informal kind of meditation," Hanson says.

Roadblock 3: "I can't sit still."

Patience is the issue for 36 percent of you. Instead of fostering a quiet mind, meditation sets off a mental ticker tape of to-do and should-have-done lists. If you're a fidgety or anxious type, try a walking meditation, Hanson says.

As you stroll, focus on the sensation of breathing or on your footfalls. Walking not active enough? Yoga, tai chi and jogging can all elicit the relaxation response.

Breathing Lessons

There may be no quicker way to trigger the magical relaxation response (and all the good genetic changes that come with it) than by controlling your breath.

Not only will deep breathing lower your blood pressure, but recent research shows sucking wind, as it were, can also increase antioxidant levels in your blood, helping protect you from oxidative stress and all the dastardly conditions associated with it, including heart disease, hypertension, Alzheimer's disease and plain ol' aging.

It's sort of silly to think you'd need instructions on how to breathe, but trust us and try this exercise from Dr. Bauer, who is also the author of the Mayo Clinic Book of Alternative Medicine. Do it twice a day, and you'll feel better.

1. With eyes closed and shoulders relaxed, inhale through your nose for six counts. Expand your belly, not your chest.
2. Try to hold your breath for four counts.
3. Exhale through your mouth for a count of six. Repeat the sequence three to five times.

It's Not All in Your Head

But a heck of a lot of it is. Tap into the amazing power of placebo.

Wait. Yoga Can Help Cure That?

Those Sun Salutations, Downward Dogs and Chaturangas are your ticket to much more than sexy curves and a lean body. Choose the right method and you can pose your way out of...

Back Pain

What we know: People who attended only one 90-minute yoga class a week for 16 weeks reduced their back pain by two thirds and their pain medication usage by 88 percent, according to one study in the aptly named journal Pain.

How it works: One of many theories-Pressing into the floor activates your pressure receptors, blocking the neural pathways that signal pain, suggests Tiffany Field, Ph.D., director of the Touch Research Institute at the University of Miami.

Which type to try: Skip the hard-core yoga and emphasize meditation and stretching. "Tight muscles can be a factor in pain, and calming your nervous system will help relax them," says Timothy McCall, M.D., author of Yoga as Medicine.

Migraines

What we know: Still more proof of yoga's power to alleviate ouches. Migraine sufferers who took up the habit for three months reported fewer and less intense headaches, a 2007 study in the journal Headache shows.

How it works: For starters, yoga reduces cortisol by relaxing you. "Nasty stress hormones only aggravate pain," Field says. Yoga also promotes better sleep, and the more soundly you snooze, the fewer pain chemicals your brain secretes.

Which type to try: As with treating back pain, pick a calming practice, Dr. McCall advises. Zenning out in a long Savasana (Corpse pose) at the end of class will help. So will focusing on exhalations. If it feels good, make each twice as long as your inhalations.

Depression

What we know: People on antidepressants who added thrice-weekly yoga for two months said they felt less depressed, anxious and angry, University of California Los Angeles research notes. In 65 percent, their depression went into remission.

How it works: Your hormones are at work here, too. "Yoga helps your body produce serotonin, a natural antidepressant, and helps lower cortisol levels, which are elevated in people with depression," Field says.

Which type to try: If you're in a slump (but still fairly fit), energizing poses such as Sun Salutations may lift you out of it. "There's a misconception that yoga is only about relaxation," Dr. McCall says. "Some practices can stimulate you."

Eating Disorders

What we know: Could a yogi heal your eating issues? In a recent study of 50 adolescent girls with eating disorders, scientists found that an hour of yoga a week for eight weeks reduced subjects' symptoms and their overall preoccupation with food.

How it works: Anxiety and depression pop up more often in people with eating problems, says study coauthor Amber Frye-Johnson, a research scientist at Abbott Northwestern Hospital in Minneapolis. Yoga fans have lower rates of both.

Chanting with the Stars (and More la-la Moves)

Mel B.

Treatment Reiki for Stress

What she says: The former Spice Girl says Reiki-in which a healer lightly touches you, supposedly transferring energy-helped her cope during the delivery of her youngest daughter, now 3. "Sometimes you can create lots of panic and problems," she told British OK! "I think [Reiki] helped me relax."

Treatment Acupuncture for the Promotion of Fertility

What she says: Carey took up needling after a miscarriage in 2008. Happily, her first child is due this spring. "People who know me would be, like, 'You scheduled acupuncture at a certain time every day?'" she told Access Hollywood.

Courtney Love

Treatment Chanting for Anxiety and Depression

What she says: Love has been known to spend two to three hours a day chanting repetitive prayers created by ancient yogis. "It kills anxiety and depression dead," she told The Telegraph.

What science says: Dooo it. Dooo it. Chanting confers all the benefits of meditation and helps blood flow in two parts of the brain that regulate stress, Nuclear Medicine Communications reports. But no need to emulate Courtney (please!).

A mere 12 minutes a day improves memory, energy and mood, says Dharma Singh Khalsa, M.D., medical director of the Alzheimer's Research and Prevention Foundation, in Tucson, Arizona.

Uma Thurman

Treatment Gemstone Therapy for Fatigue

What she says: Thurman has reportedly donned an orange carnelian necklace to boost vitality. The idea is that gemstones embody energy that encourages cells to heal.

What science says: "Can we say from a scientific standpoint that a gem can help your body? No," says Dr. Bauer of the Mayo Clinic. "That said, if you want to hang an amethyst in front of your breakfast bowl, I can't argue too much. It's pretty."

Get Your qi on

More than half of you say you've never heard of qigong. But the ancient Eastern practice, also known as Chinese yoga, can ease a long list of ailments, including heart disease, bone loss, high cholesterol and type two diabetes.

Lifting Hands

Stand tall with your feet hip-width apart, knees slightly bent, hands hanging down in front of thighs.

Inhale and lift both hands to chest level, leading with the wrists (as shown).

Then exhale and bring hands back to thighs, "painting the wall" with fingertips. Repeat for two minutes.

The Healing Power of Sound

From humming to drumming to Tibetan singing bowls - recent research suggests that the influences of certain rhythms, sounds and vibrations can help us resist and recover from a wide variety of ailments.

Sound can set a mood. The soundtrack in aerobics class gets us moving, for example, while the one in yoga promotes quiet concentration. Sound also has a powerful effect on how we feel throughout the day. Our bodies and minds react differently to the unrelenting noise of a jackhammer than to a trickle of water in a creek.

In other words, some sounds simply make us feel better than others. Whether our conscious minds are paying attention or not, our bodies take their cues from these sounds and rhythms, knowing when to get energized and when to slow down.

Now, a growing body of research suggests that when used in a directed way, sound can also help us reduce stress, create a deep sense of well-being and even promote healing. From playing Bach in the nursery to yogic chanting in the oncologist's office, sound therapy is gaining popularity as both a preventative medicine and as a complement to more-traditional treatments. Good for both the mind and the body, it has been shown to help lift depression, clear sinuses and help cancer patients recover more quickly from chemotherapy.

Good Vibrations

The idea that sound affects the health of the mind and body is not new. Chanting and mantra recitation have been part of Hindu spirituality and the healing power of yoga for thousands of years. Given the recent interest in mind-body medicine, it's not surprising that this ancient tradition is experiencing a modern-day renaissance.

So what, exactly, is it

Using the human voice and objects that resonate to stimulate healing (think tuning forks and singing bowls), sound therapy is one of a growing number of subtle-energy therapies that make up the field of vibrational medicine. According to the law of physics, everything vibrates: the chair you're sitting in, the food you eat, the rocks and trees.

"Whether or not we hear it, everything has a sound, a vibration all its own," writes Joshua Leeds in The Power of Sound (Healing Arts

Press, 2001). That sound is called resonance, the frequency at which an object naturally vibrates. Each part of our bodies has its own natural resonance, and vibrational medicine is based on the idea that disease is a result of those natural resonances getting out of tune - whether due to stress, illness or environmental factors.

As opposed to the highly focused and fast vibrations used in ultrasound (a technology already employed in hospitals to break up kidney stones and check on the health of fetuses, for example), sound therapy works more gently - but just as powerfully - to return the body's own vibrations to their natural states.

Getting in Tune

But does it work? Yes, say sound therapists, who have successfully treated everything from stress to Parkinson's disease to hormonal problems. Jonathan Goldman, director of the Sound Healers Association in Boulder, Colo., has seen tuning forks alleviate many maladies, including headaches and misaligned vertebrae. Diáne Mandle, a certified sound healer in Encinitas, Calif., uses Tibetan singing bowls to bring her clients' bodies back in tune.

The Future of Healing

Sound therapy, many experts say, is at the cutting edge of healing. And soon, they insist, like yoga and meditation, it will enter the mainstream.

The truth is, you're probably already using sound therapy in your life. Several years ago, three out of four people who responded to a Prevention magazine health survey said that they listen to music to ease tension and stress. Of those, 82 percent reported that it brought them significant relief.

So even if you're not interested in investing in a fancy tuning fork or a singing bowl, sound healing is still available to you. The next time you need a little pick-me-up or mellow-me-out, hum a little tune, or, better yet, go for a walk and enjoy nature's own healing harmonies.

Yoga for Weight Reduction

Does yoga help in weight management? Most definitely. There are a number of factors involved. Firstly, some of the asanas stimulate sluggish glands to increase their hormonal secretions. The thyroid gland, especially, has a big effect on our weight because it affects body metabolism. There are several asanas, such as the shoulder stand and the fish posture, which are specific for the thyroid gland. Fat metabolism is also increased, so fat is converted to muscle and energy. This means that, as well as losing fat, you will have better muscle tone and a higher vitality level.

Secondly, yoga deep breathing increases the oxygen intake to the body cells, including the fat cells. This causes increased oxidation or burning up of fat cells.). Yogic exercises induce more continuous and deeper breathing which gradually burns, sometimes forcefully, many of the calories already ingested.

Thirdly, yogic practices that reduce anxiety tend to reduce anxious eating. When under nervous strain we tend to gulp our food without attaining much genuine satisfaction. We end up in eating more. If, on the other hand, we approach our meals with greater calmness of mood, whether produced by habits which have calmed our life or by yoga (like a pause for prayer before a meal), we tend to be less likely to overeat in a frantic effort to quiet our midday anxieties.

Lastly, yogic aids may be employed between meals whenever one becomes tempted to search for a snack. One may deliberately turn to yoga, rather than to the icebox or snack bar, when he feels the need for a lift or relief from restless nervousness. Practicing yoga may make you aware of your weight problem that may also act as a deterrent from overeating.

If you are not overweight, your weight will remain about the same. If you are underweight, you will gain weight. The weight you gain will be healthy firm tissue, not fat. That is, yoga will tend to produce the ideal weight for you. This is due to yoga's effect of 'normalizing' glandular activity.

"Would you like to lose weight without resorting to the miseries of dieting? Well, try the miseries of Yoga exercises instead. One staunch advocate is Metropolitan Opera star Robert Merrill, who has been practicing these exercises for two years, and keeps trying to win converts. In those two years he has lost twenty pounds and now he's down to a trim, rhythmic-breathing one hundred and sixty, even though he continues to eat like a lumber jack. 'At one time we went on a lot of diets but just couldn't lose any weight,' he said. 'Then along came Yoga and look at me now.' He punched his hard flat stomach and started breathing through one nostril. And to further demonstrate what it's all about, he did a little flip and stood on his head. After that he showed the lotus position, legs scissored under the body. Was he still breathing through one nostril? Yes, the other one. 'If people weren't so lazy they wouldn't have to worry about diets,' he said."

For those whose eating habits, whether at meals or between meals, are believed to be due to feelings of weakness rather than anxieties, most yogic postures and breathing exercises are designed to increase one's strength. Hence, they may relieve feelings of weakness more effectively than additional eating. The exercises themselves, although consuming some energy, also store up energy which, when combined with oxidizing breathing, provide energy that is ready for use rather than for storage.

Yoga and Mental Health

Those practicing yoga experiences a number of factors that results in a profound effect on their mental health. These can be classified under:

1. reduction of tension and
2. restoration of pliability.
3. "personal" and
4. "social."

Reduction of Tension

Many people who practice yoga speak of "freeing the mind from mental disturbances," "calming the spirit," or "steadying the mind." Reduction of nervousness, irritability and confusion, depression and mental fatigue are some of the benefits experienced. One experiences a relief from the pressure of his "compulsions." His nervousness, especially any jitteriness, should subside or disappear.

The extent to which these benefits may be expected will depend in part upon whether or not one can approach and participate in them willingly and wholeheartedly; for one who tries to practice postures with anxiety cripples his chances for very much benefit.

Restoration of Pliability

"The positive side of the benefits from a full round of yogic exercises may be described as renewal of mental agility. Both mood and capacity for alertness, attentiveness and willingness to tackle problems revive. One may not be able to rekindle boundless enthusiasm late in a working day; early morning, or even noonday, efforts to recharge mental energies can revive a full measure of willingness. Traditional phrases, such as restored "spiritual vitality," intend to convey the complex idea of mental spryness, agreeableness, resiliency, and feelings of confidence and self-sufficiency. Some even testify to attaining feelings of buoyancy and euphoria; these then provide a background or mood of well-being and assurance such that one naturally more fully enjoys both his ability and the worthiness of being more tolerant and generous."

Archie Bahm, 'Executive Yoga'

Avoidance of Fear

Yoga is said to result in the reduction of a variety of mental ills. These may range all the way from vague feelings of frustration, persecution, insecurity, on the one hand, to acute and specific types of insanity, on the other.

Yoga is not a cure all for all conditions. But its attack upon, and diminution of, some basic mental ills may indeed be just enough to pay dividends that grow in magnitude.

If, through use of yogic techniques, we can merely halt and reverse some mental cancer, some compulsive complex that keeps us chained to unrelenting, omnipresent and gradually increasing anxiety, we may reset a course which will bring us around to a healthier adjustment. We are all at times insane. We are all, in some degree, insane. Overwhelming waves of tension and stress, which may catch us in periods of physical and mental exhaustion, can produce a spiritual explosion which leaves us so helpless that we are at a loss to know how it all came about.

By recurrent, regular efforts to reduce tension through yogic exercises, we may stay and finally reverse our tendencies toward insanity.

Most of us succumbs to fears and anxieties - some valid and some purely imaginary. For example, as one gets older, he begins to fear that his life has not been sufficiently worth while, that he has fallen short of his goals, that he has failed to attain his proper ambition, that he has lost out in the race to keep up with the Joneses or in his attempt to measure up "in the sight of God"-however he happens to conceive his shortcoming.

Thus, when Ramacharaka, in his 'Hindu-Yogi Science of Breath', says one may, by controlled breathing, "practically do away with fear and worry and the baser emotions," he refers to the growing ability of a devoted practitioner to diminish the power which both momentary and permanent fears have over us. One seeks to develop habits of resistance to the disturbing effects of excitement, ambition, antagonism and frustration.

The long-range goal of yoga is not just momentary relaxation, but the living of a relaxed life.

Acceptance of Faith in Life

The goal of yoga is confident living. Its aim is to replace pessimism and its varieties such as cynicism with a "Yea-saying" appreciation of life, not only on any given day, but as a gracious, wonderful whole. When you achieve the yogic spirit, then you can say with the Stoics, "I accept the universe."

If you cannot accept all of it, because some problems remain unavoidably troublesome, then you will accept the troubles which you have as (1) yours and (2) enough for you, without wishing you had still more troubles.

Poise, serenity, contentedness, patience, assurance-all of these are positive mental values attainable by anyone who has achieved a willingness to be at peace with himself and the world. The confidence desired is not just enough to do the day's work but enough to live one's whole life and one can do his day's work more confidently if he has already predisposed himself to living his life with trustful serenity.

Thus a person seeks through yoga not merely momentary mental agility, but an agile life; not just momentary pliability, but a continuingly pliable existence; not just momentary relief from disturbance, but a permanently peaceful perspective.

Although not everyone who undertakes to experiment with yoga can expect to achieve or maintain the goal described by Shri Yogendra, Yoga: Personal Hygiene, as "exuberant and exultant health, he should notice the sun more often when it shines. Swami Sivananda pictures the goal as "ecstatic joy" (Yoga Asanas).

Dechanet, a Roman Catholic monk who was led into yoga by his Catholic predecessors, gives a vivid account of how he uses yogic techniques as aids to worship. He describes a "euphoria that pervades the story of my experiment. We wish to make it clear that this euphoria is real and lasting and spreads through the various levels of my daily life, physical, Psychical and spiritual" (Christian Yoga). Even though few of us will achieve anything like perpetual exuberance, ecstatic joy or euphoria, attainment of a more trusting outlook on life provides a spiritual soil from which spiritual roses have a better chance to grow. The pragmatic experimentalist will say: "Try it and see."

Social Values

a. Yoga may reduce your annoyance with others and others' annoyance with you. If you become less irritable, you tend to irritate others less and tend to be less irritated by what others do when they present themselves as problems to you. Your obdurate, demanding, insistent, morose attitudes can make you hard to get along with. Diminution of these should make you less difficult to deal with. The social effects-upon your colleagues and clients, superiors and inferiors, to say nothing of family, public officers and service specialists-could be overwhelming.

b. You tend to be easier to get along with and you tend to find others easier to get along with.

Or, if your personal improvement grows beyond mere contentment, to exuberant appreciation, you may find both more people liking you and you liking more people. You become more adaptable, reliable, steady, alert, responsive, ever-ready, patient, gentle and humane.

When this happens, you become recognized as a more desirable person to deal with.

If you develop a buoyant spirit, you will find that buoyancy is catching.

Others, seeing you as cheery, tend to respond in kind, reacting more cheerily to you.

Your rewards increase.

The effects of yoga upon character as noted by Dechanet in Christian Yoga.

"Yoga also produces a more active, willing and generous disposition. It quickens the life of faith, of love of God and our neighbor. It quickens our sense of duty and responsibility as men and, above all, as Christians". "It follows that Hatha Yoga influences character to the good. One man, after some weeks of practice, admits he no longer knows himself, and everyone notices a change in his bearing and reaction. He is gentler, more understanding. He faces experience calmly. He is content; the pinpricks of life affect him less or not at all. He is in command of his own will and goes about his studies without fear and anxiety.

His whole personality has been altered and he himself feels it steadying and opening out; from this there arises an almost permanent condition of euphoria, of 'contentedness' ". "You will feel that gentleness and sympathy come more readily. You will not feel like venting your spleen on others as frequently as before, and if it should occur, you will regret it all the more.

You will make a kind of pact of non-violence with yourself. You will still have fits of impatience often enough, and even of anger. But something will be telling you that this is not only bad but even useless, and that it really is not worth the trouble to fly out and get beside yourself for nothing. 'A great need for sincerity -will bring you to detest, more than others do, not only lying but all forms of duplicity and dissimulation. You will sense the more keenly whatever is not genuine, and even what is merely conventional in speeches and words, and also in attitudes that men think they can take up in order to edify, but more often they take up lest they should lose face"

Yoga and Beauty

Beauty of figure, graceful carriage, melodious voice, glowing face and charming smile have all been mentioned as possible rewards of yogic practice.

Swami Sivananda says that "By practicing the Asanas regularly, men and women will acquire a figure which will enhance their beauty and that suppleness which gives them charm and elegance in every movement," and "be endowed with a peculiar glow in his face and eyes and a peculiar charm in his smile" (Yogic Home Exercises).

Clara Spring, expressing an American woman's point of view, reminds us that "A number of world-famous beauty courses contain certain exercises based on Yoga" (Yoga for Today).

Yoga and Sex

Yoga's view of sex is the same as of every other issue - moderation. Yoga considers sex to be a natural function, very beneficial in a loving relationship and, of course, essential for the continuation of the human race.

Yogis warn against overindulgence in sex since they consider this will deplete the life force. They state that the sexual secretions contain very concentrated life force and nutrients, since they contain the seeds of life. Depletion of life force results in a reduced vitality level and reduced resistance to disease. It also retards progress from the practice of yoga. A whole field of yoga called Tandric Yoga or Kundalini Yoga is concerned with harnessing the sexual power. Yoga enables one to get into meaningful relationships and enjoy the process, at the same time provides a path to use the powerful energy involved in sex.

The yogis consider that normal sexual function occurs when the reproductive system is in a state of optimum health. They have found that the most effective way of attaining this optimum health state is by doing yoga asanas and breathing exercises.

Those who are physiologically weak and partially or wholly impotent may restore potency as they regain their physical health. Steadier practice of milder yogic exercises may yield results when more vigorous bodybuilding workouts end in undue exhaustion. Those who approach sexual matters nervously rather than relaxedly may profit from previous relaxing yogic exercises.

Marriage counselors suggest that a relaxed condition is one of the essentials for a harmonious sex relationship because when hurried and strained it leaves the couple (the woman especially) dissatisfied and irritated, adversely affecting her entire well being. Indra Devi, author of many books on yoga, remarked that "The wives of several of my students have often told me that since their husbands had taken up Yoga exercises, their marital relationships had undergone remarkable changes."

It's true that advanced yogis practice celibacy. They need every ounce of their life force for their quest for cosmic consciousness. They also know that the realization of their goal produces eternal bliss, besides which the brief pleasure of sex pales into insignificance. Their minds have progressed so far that they are not prepared to settle for a watered-down version of happiness.

Yoga and Pride

Pride, and especially anxiety about pride, is something which hatha yoga seeks to diminish or eliminate. We are not advocating pride, but some will choose to consider pride a value anyway. To one who has been dejected because he cannot do his work properly when he becomes tired, irritable, or haggard, any degree of refreshment may be accompanied by additional degrees of self-respect. Furthermore, one who has benefited from yoga may be moved to help his friends who are obviously in need; he may instruct others and be rewarded with appreciation due a gracious teacher.

But if one succeeds in achieving skill which provides health and self-confidence, one may justly raise his self-esteem simply by observing himself living the improved results as an achieved fact.

Yoga and Knowledge

Readers of treatises on yoga soon become familiar with a recurrent refrain. Yogic theory and practice lead to increased self-knowledge. Although many of these treatises extend the meaning of yoga beyond hatha yoga the values of self-knowledge indicated are intended to include those derivable from using breathing and posture exercises for attaining and maintaining health, physical and mental, and relaxation. The knowledge is not merely that of the practical kind relating to techniques, but especially of a spiritual sort pertaining to grasping something about the nature of the self at rest.

Knowing the self at rest, at peace, as a being rather than merely as an agent or doer, is a genuine kind of knowledge which usually gets lost in the rush of activities and push of desires. The value of discovering one's self and of enjoying one's self as it is, rather than as it is going to be, is indeed a value as well as a kind of knowledge.

Yoga and Wealth

About the last thing one should expect from yoga is wealth. Yet, when certain facts are pointed out, it becomes obvious that here is a value not to be overlooked.

First of all, as Swami Sivananda argues, "Health is wealth.... If you do not possess good health you cannot prosper in any walk of life" (Yogic Home Exercises). As we can see from the factors listed under Physical Health and Mental Health, yoga does affect our ability to deal with the problems in our businesses and professions. Many factors affecting our day-to-day and long-range; capacities for achieving business and professional goals may be influenced by yogic endeavors. One can hardly calculate results, but still can easily sense the significance of improved health for business success.

Not only may one acquire more financially from good health, but he need spend less upon measures to alleviate illness. By reducing anxiety and desirousness, yoga tends to diminish our desires and the expenditures we make trying to satisfy those desires. A person who achieves peace with himself, even if only part of the time, has less motive for spending money to win the bàttle for satisfaction of his cravings. Yoga is less expensive than most other methods of attaining and maintaining health and relaxation.

Yoga for Insomnia

Yoga will benefit your sleep in three ways:

1. The quality of your steep will improve because of yoga's beneficial effect on the nervous system, and in particular the brain. This results from certain yoga asanas increasing the blood supply to the steep center in the brain, which has the effect of normalizing the steep cycle.
2. You will need less sleep because of the improved quality of your sleep, and because yoga increases the elimination of toxins from the body. On average, for every minute you put into yoga you will need one minute less sleep. This makes yoga an excellent time investment.
3. You will fall asleep in a shorter time. This is mainly because the body and mind are more relaxed.

Yoga will make you fall asleep sooner and improve the quality of your sleep so that you need less. You will have a more restful sleep because of the relaxing aspect of yoga and the subsequent relieving of stress, tension and fatigue.

The Healing Power of Yoga and Health

Like yoga, the osteopathic approach to wellness focuses on your body's natural tendency toward health and self-healing.

"The purpose of yoga is to create strength, awareness and harmony in both the mind and body," explains Natalie Nevins, DO, a board-certified osteopathic family physician and certified Kundalini Yoga instructor in Hollywood, California.

While there are more than 100 different types, or schools, of yoga, most sessions typically include breathing exercises, meditation, and postures (sometimes called asana or poses) that stretch and flex various muscle groups. "As an osteopathic physician, I focus a lot of my efforts on preventive medicine and practices, and the body's natural ability to heal itself," says Dr. Nevins. "Yoga is a great tool for staying healthy because it is based on similar principles." Yoga can help improve balance, strengthen muscles, prevent injuries and calm the mind.

Physical Benefits

"The relaxation techniques incorporated in yoga can lessen chronic pain, such as lower back pain, arthritis, headaches and carpal tunnel syndrome," explains Dr. Nevins. "Yoga can also lower blood pressure and reduce insomnia."

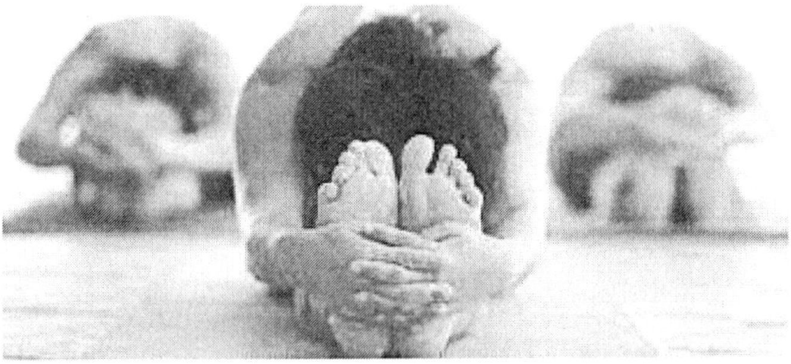

Other physical benefits of yoga include:

- Increased flexibility
- Increased muscle strength and tone
- Improved respiration, energy and vitality
- Maintaining a balanced metabolism
- Weight reduction
- Cardio and circulatory health
- Improved athletic performance
- Protection from injury

Mental Benefits

Aside from the physical benefits, one of the greatest benefits of yoga is how it helps a person manage stress, which is known to have devastating effects on the body and mind. "Stress can reveal itself in many ways, including back or neck pain, sleeping problems, headaches, drug abuse, and an inability to concentrate," says Dr. Nevins. "Yoga can be very effective in developing coping skills and reaching a more positive outlook on life."

"Regular yoga increases body awareness and relieves chronic stress patterns."

Yoga's incorporation of meditation and breathing can help improve a person's mental well-being. "Regular yoga practice creates mental clarity and calmness; increases body awareness; relieves chronic stress patterns; relaxes the mind; centers attention; and sharpens concentration," says Dr. Nevins. Increasing awareness of body and self can be particularly beneficial, she adds, because they can help with early detection of physical problems and allow for early preventive action.

Beginners Welcome

The multitude of yoga styles and levels makes it a great activity for people of all ages and body types. "Whether you're a couch potato or a professional athlete, size and fitness levels do not matter because there are modifications for every yoga pose and beginner classes in every style," says Dr. Nevins. "The idea is to explore your limits, not strive for pretzel-like perfection. It is a great way to get in tune with your body and your inner self."

Healing with Yoga: Poses to Heal from the Inside Out

We know yoga is a great physical practice-it tones the body, encourages flexibility and promotes relaxation. But it's also an extremely powerful emotional practice.

We tend to hold emotions and past traumas in our bodies. Any heartaches, heartbreaks or trials we've experienced, but haven't felt deeply, can easily make their home within our bodies.

Yoga is a very useful tool to help clear out these toxic energies and find true healing, from the inside out.

Long Holds: Learning to Feel

When we hold asanas (poses) for long periods of time, feelings start to bubble up within us. Especially as we turn our focus inward, we become more aware of what is going on within.

Holding poses for a long time activates our feelings and emotions. We begin to tune in and really feel whatever is coming up.

As we continue our practice, we'll notice specific poses hold more tension than others. Those are likely to be the same ones that will help us feel and heal the most.

This deep hip opener is a great place to start. We carry a lot of tension in our hips and Frog pose is quick to let us know.

This pose can become very uncomfortable.

Grounding: Mind-body Connection

Establishing a strong mind-body connection is one of the first steps to healing past traumas. In order to heal, we must learn how to look inward.

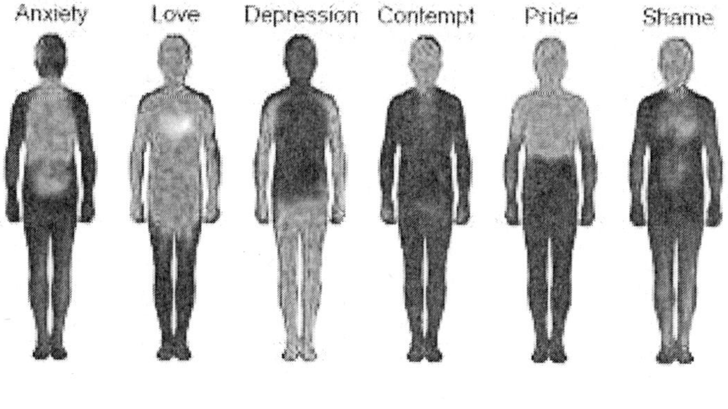

Yoga helps us do this because it gives us a safe place to explore the sensations in our bodies. As we get more practiced at noticing what's going on within, we begin to notice more emotions arise.

Grounding poses help us form a powerful mind-body connection because we are both in our bodies but supported by the earth at the same time. They give us space to feel and be held simultaneously.

Supta Baddha Konasana is a good place to ground while completely relaxing into the mat. Place one hand over your heart and one hand over your belly to keep your attention on your breath and in the present moment.

Figure: *Supta Baddha Konasana*

Surrender: Emotional Release

Sometimes all we really need to heal is to let go. Unfortunately, letting go has become somewhat of a cliché in yoga bubbles.

However, letting go doesn't necessarily mean releasing pain or anger, sometimes it means surrendering to it; letting go to it.

Oftentimes, we resist the feelings that don't feel 'good.' But in actuality, feelings are neither good nor bad. They just are. And feeling them isn't what's painful. It's our resistance to feeling that causes us pain.

So sometimes, we simply need to surrender to our feelings to heal them fully.

Pigeon pose is a fantastic place to let go. Because our hips carry so many emotions, when we open them deeply we often have no choice but to surrender.

If you find yourself crying in Pigeon a lot, that's completely normal. In holding this pose for a long period, we break through those walls we've built up around past traumas and often release them through crying. This is very healing.

Figure: *Eka Pada Rajakapotasana*

Heart Openers: Vulnerability

Have you ever experienced a 'light bulb moment' in a yoga class? Like you suddenly realized why you've been feeling specific way for so long. Yoga helps us dig deep and get very vulnerable. Vulnerability is essential to our healing. When we can't be vulnerable, we start to shut people out. We build walls around our hearts as a form of 'protection' when all we're really doing is harming ourselves.

We must be able to open our hearts in order to find self-love, healing and ultimately, to love others fully. Heart opening poses help us do just that. By physically opening our hearts, we send a signal to our inner heart to open up as well. Wheel is a deep heart opener that helps us break down those walls and learn to open up our hearts.

Figure: *Urdhva Dhanurasana*

This is a great pose because we're opening our hearts but we have our hands and feet on the floor at the same time keeping us grounded.

Balance: Respond Vs. React

So often, when we get angry, we react rather than respond. Reactions turn into regrets. We snap and don't take a moment to think, or even breathe, before we speak and end up hurting someone else or ourselves.

Yoga creates a space for us to learn how to respond to tense or unfortunate situations with equanimity. Responding to these situations instead of reacting usually results in a more calm-minded and kind interaction. And, we'll most likely walk away from it feeling better than if we'd reacted.

Pose: Natarajasana (Dancer pose)

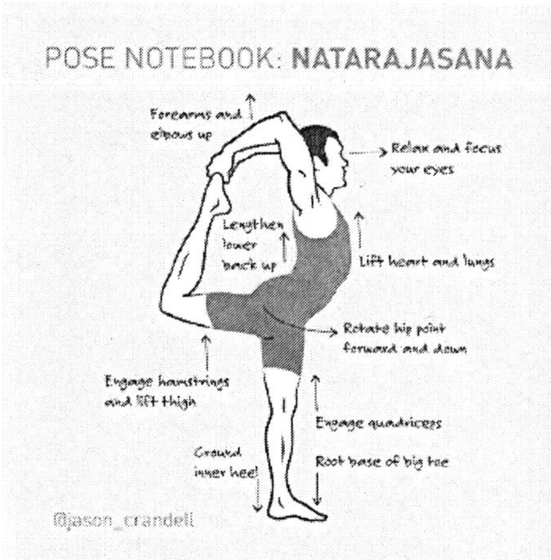

Figure: *Natarajasana*

Ahimsa: Non-Violence

Ahimsa translates from Sanskrit to, 'non-violence.' It is inspired by the concept that all living things are sacred, and therefore, should not be harmed.

This applies to you, too. We talk a lot about being kind to others, but sometimes we forget about ourselves. Just as we should treat other with kindness and compassion, we need to treat ourselves the same way.

A lot of us tend to be very hard on ourselves. Whether it's the way we look, how smart we are or our general standing in life. Think back on how you talk to yourself when you make a mistake. Would you speak to your best friend in the same way? Yoga teaches us to be gentle with ourselves. We're taught to take rest when we need it and to listen to our bodies. When we learn how to do this both on and off the mat, we become more in tune to our feelings and emotions, and we understand that we must be kind to ourselves in order to heal and find self-love.

Often, all it takes is going back to basics. Child's pose serves many purposes, one of which is as a place of rest.

Figure: *Balasana*

Take Child's pose in class anytime your body is telling you to slow down. You can even take it on your own, anytime you're feeling overwhelmed and need to take a few moments to nurture yourself.

Self-Empowerment: Courage

Finally, in order to heal past traumas, we must bring our inner power to life. This is not aggressive or controlling power, this is empowerment. It's confidence, courage, truth; it's a willingness to show up in your life.

Chapter 7

Exploring the Concept of Marma Points in Ayurveda and Yoga

Introduction

In the ancient sciences of Ayurveda and Yoga, the concept of Marma points serves as a focal point for understanding the intricate relationship between the body, mind, and consciousness. Marma points are vital energy centers located at specific anatomical sites, where the subtle flow of Prana, or life force energy, converges and intersects. These points are not merely physical landmarks but are imbued with profound spiritual and therapeutic significance, serving as gateways to deeper levels of awareness and healing.

Ayurvedic texts, such as the Sushruta Samhita and the Charaka Samhita, extensively document the location, properties, and therapeutic applications of Marma points. According to Ayurveda, there are 107 major Marma points distributed throughout the body, each with its unique attributes and functions.

These points are classified based on their anatomical location and the type of tissue they influence, encompassing vital organs, joints, nerves, and subtle energy pathways.

In Ayurveda, Marma points are considered to be the seats of consciousness, linking the physical body with the subtle energy body. They are believed to be portals through which Prana flows, regulating the functions of the body and mind. Stimulating or balancing these points can have profound effects on one's physical health, mental well-being, and spiritual evolution.

Similarly, in the practice of Yoga, Marma points hold significance as key junctures where the flow of Prana can be redirected and harmonized through the practice of asanas, pranayama, and meditation. By focusing awareness on these points during Yoga practice, practitioners can deepen their connection to the subtle aspects of their being, facilitating the free flow of energy and enhancing the benefits of their practice.

The therapeutic applications of Marma points are vast and diverse, encompassing both preventive and curative measures. In Ayurvedic medicine, Marma therapy involves the gentle manipulation of these points through massage, acupressure, or herbal applications to restore balance and alleviate various health conditions. By stimulating specific Marma points, practitioners can address imbalances in the doshas (bioenergetic forces), clear energy blockages, and promote the body's natural healing mechanisms.

Furthermore, Marma points play a crucial role in the management of pain and trauma, as they are intimately connected to the nervous system and the body's innate ability to self-regulate. By targeting specific Marma points, therapists can alleviate pain, reduce inflammation, and promote relaxation, offering a holistic approach to pain management that integrates the physical, mental, and emotional dimensions of healing.

The concept of Marma points encapsulates the profound interconnectedness of body, mind, and spirit within the holistic frameworks of Ayurveda and Yoga. By understanding and working with these vital energy centers, individuals can access deeper levels of healing, transformation, and self-awareness, ultimately aligning with the innate intelligence of the body and the wisdom of the ancient sages.

Marma Point

Marma points are acupuncture points that are used for various healing purposes.

Marma means 'a point that can kill,' and there are some marma points used specifically in martial arts.

Marma massage is an essential massage therapy in Ayurveda. The essential points of the body are known as marmas. The meaning of marma is hidden or secret. It ensures relaxation of mind, body, and spirit.

Ayurveda believes that various pains are caused by blocking of the flow of air through the air vessels in the body. Rubbing makes the bodily airs expand, and the movements of massage generate heat. Circulation of Vayu in the siras removes tension and reduces pain. A good massage can help in having a broader and a natural breathing structure. Marma therapy is the energy healing therapy of Ayurveda; which utilises 107 points of the body and our consciousness. These marma points then play a vital role in releasing the pain through the vessels in the body through various massage techniques and therapies.

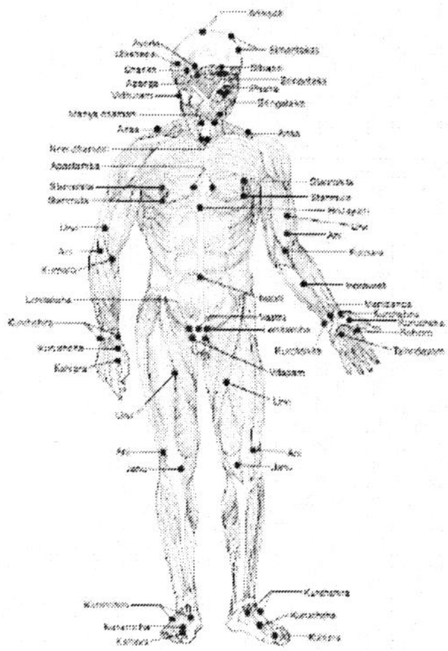

There are approximately 108 energy points in a human body, and they appear at different crossings of different joints, ligaments, bones, veins, nerves and other energy points. These points are vulnerable in nature, and they have different responses to the various methods. The various energy channels that are found within the body are incredibly crucial. However, of those 108 marmas, 12 points are significantly vital due to their impact on the physical and mental strength of our body. The remaining 96 are stock characters that are better paired with the initial 12 points. These 12 energy centers are located between the center of the perineal floor and the crown of the head which also includes the 7 chakras.

History of Marma Points

Marma therapy is the utilization of 107 points in the body which are judged to be access points to body, mind, and cognizance. Marma allows a person to determine the flow of life through both the authorities for the faith of rendering health and peace of mind.

It is the new point system of healing in the body. It has inspired the evolution of Chinese acupuncture and Kung fu. Its roots are South

India within a martial arts custom known as Kalaripayattu. It was utilized to secure kingdoms during times when expertise in face-to-face battle was the mark of an exceptional fighter. These biblical heroes understood complex power, and they used their knowledge to damage or kill an enemy. The 107 Marma points are sections concerning their impact on the energy of the body. The word Marma is derived from a Sanskrit word which implies to kill. While warriors understood these things to protect territory, it was the job of the practitioners to utilize these same points for healing.

The master had the understanding both of how to induce pain as well as how to utilize the information and experience of healing. An essential policy of Marma healing is pretty simple where a strong punch can cause pain, a soft nudge can cause healing. This is the most significant principle of Marma massage. It converts into a compelling tool for determining the healing of every known ailment. While Marma therapy is not well established or followed except by a few practitioners in India, its practice is becoming more popular in the United States. Thus, it is an amazing learning and growth experience that connects people with their inner traits.

Marma Points Chart

There are a lot of marma points in our body, marma points can be found on our tissues, tendons, muscles, tendons, bones, nerves, and joint. There are also points in some of our body or organ systems like the circulatory and glandular. There are one hundren and eight marma points in our body and out of that number there are twelve that was considered essential and vital, while the ninety-six remaining other marma points has secondary use in sustaining the function of the first twelve. Right utilization of the marma points will improve the functions of Nadis or channels that is responsible in moving the life force in our body. All in all, there are 8 channels that can be found in are body.

Upon proper practice, an individual will be able to close a certain marma point at their own will. Gaining voluntary control over your marma points will increase the inner power in the midst of our bodies called Shakti.

Introduction of Marma Points

What is a Marma Point

We have all heard of Marma Points and recently it is gaining popularity all over the world.

Marmas are ayurvedic acupressure points. Marma means secret, hidden. Marmas are points on the body that can give life and death.

These marma points carry the vital "life force energy". When these marma points are pressed, they work through the subtle energy channels called "nadis" to bring healing and energy to the body, mind and consciousness. Even though Marma means to cause harm or death. Quite interestingly, on the other hand, it can bring life force and give energy.

Marma Points Chart - Back of Legs

Marma Point Name	Function / Purpose
Sphij	Enhances circulation in the lower extremities and entire leg
Urvi (posterior)	Benefits bladder, colon and kidneys, it is functionally related to kidneys and bladder
Janu (posterior)	Benefits the knees and relieves knee pain, tenderness, swelling and weakness
Indrabasta	Promotes circulation of the lower leg and relaxes the muscle
Gulpha (lateral)	Benefits the ankles, ankle pain, edema, swelling due to arthritis
Gulpha (medial)	Regulates kidney function and water filtration
Anupada	Benefits the heels, pain in the heel or foot

Front of Legs

Marma Points Chart - Front of Legs

Marma Point Name	Function / Purpose
Lohitaksha	Promotes circulation in the lower extremities
Urvi (anterior)	Benefits bladder, colon and kidneys, it is functionally related to kidneys and bladder
Janu (anterior)	Benefits the knees and relieves knee pain, tenderness, swelling and weakness
Charana (lateral)	Promotes circulation to the lower leg and responsible for movement of the knee
Charana (medial)	Similar to Janu, tenderness, tingling, numbness, swelling and weakness
Indrabasta (medial)	Balances emotional disturbances and stabilizes the mind
Pada Charan	Benefits the ankles, ankle pain, edema, swelling due to arthritis
Pada Kshipra	Relieves headache instantaneously as it is connected to the brain

Side Leg

Marma Points Chart - Side Leg

Marma Point Name	Function / Purpose
Urva (1)	Helps in relieving hip pain, knee pain
Urva (2)	Enhances lubrication of the joint, relieves dryness and inflammation
Charana (lateral)	Promotes circulation to the lower leg and responsible for movement of the knee
Gulpha (lateral)	Benefits the ankles, ankle pain, edema, swelling due to arthiritis

Neck

Marma Points Chart - Neck

Marma Point Name	Function / Purpose
Manyamula	Enhances cerebral blood circulation
Vidhuram	Relieves headache related to Cervical Spondylosis
Krikatika	Helps in pinched nerve, tingling and numbness
Griva 1	Relieves neck pain and stiffness. Connected to thoracic duct and vocal cord
Griva 2 & 3	Connected to thyroid and controls their function
Griva 4	Connected to colon and small intestine and relieve toxins in the colon
Manyamani	Relieves neck pain and stiffness

Face

Marma Points Chart - Face

Marma Point Name	Function / Purpose
Nasa Madhya	Relieves nasal conditions like sinus, nose bleeds, snoring
Bhruh Antara, Madhya and Agra	Relieves stress and calms mind. Pressing on these points stimulates tears
Shankha	Strongly pacifies Pitta – High acidity, gastritis, peptic ulcer, duodenal ulcer
Apanga	Benefits the eye and improves vision
Chakshu	Benefits the eyes and nose, regulates the fluid in the eye
Chibuka	Regulates salivary secretions, improves digestion by kindling appetite.
Kaninaka	Controls the fluid inside the eyeballs

Historically Marma or the 'vital' points were studied to gain a better understanding of the body and how this can translate on the battlefield, as well as in the field of medicine. The word itself denotes an area that is 'vulnerable'. In the Vedic times, this became instrumental in developing the art of war and how one could strike these vulnerable points and cause the opponent immense harm, and in some cases, cause instant death.

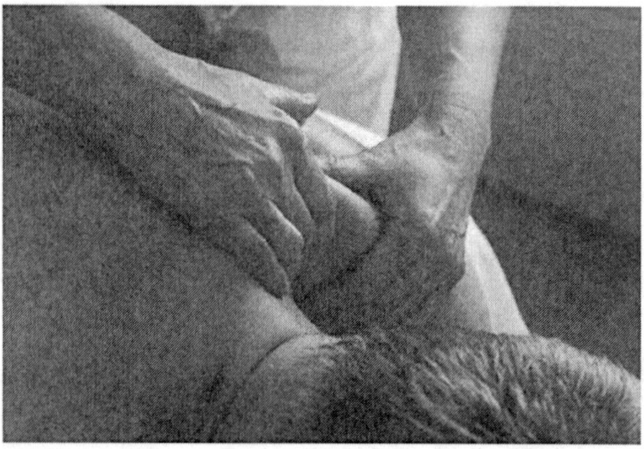

Interestingly, practitioners of the Kalaripayattu art form are taught these 'vital points', not only to wield during a battle but also post-practice, as a form of therapy. These vital points occur at specific intersections where joints, veins, muscles, tendons, tissues, and ligaments cross paths with each other. These areas offer one the opportunity to hurt or heal and that is why understanding Marma gives us insight into the 'vulnerable' spaces within the body.

The 108 Marma Points Chart

The 108 Marma Points Chart is a map of vital points across the body and shows exactly how each point is meant to revive or rejuvenate a specific organ, function, or process within itself. Being connected to the various processes within the body, how one breathes, how one uses muscles, etc. is also essential to understanding the way to access these points more accurately. Therefore many practitioners of yoga, martial arts, and dance take an interest in studying the chart... So that they may bring together a more holistic understanding of every aspect of how one's being is connected, and influenced by one another. It also encourages the use of the nature of life. Life is vulnerable and within that vulnerability lies a certain strength and power as well. The chart allows one to realize which area of the body is connected to the others and how to encourage a 'communication' system between these areas.

According to the Marma Chart, there are 108 points - 107 on the physical body and one in the mind. Each point corresponds to a specific vayu (function of prana), dosha (constitutional type), dhatu (bodily tissue), and srota (physical channel). The health of the body is determined by how freely 'prana' flows from the 'nadis' through these points. Any disruption to this flow causes impairment to one's health. These points range in size from one to six inches in diameter. The points were mapped out in detail centuries ago in the Sushruta Samhita, a classic Ayurvedic text.

Major points correspond to the seven chakras, or energy centers of the body, while minor points radiate out along the torso and limbs. The points cover both the front and back body, including 22 on the lower extremities, 22 on the arms, 12 on the chest and stomach, 14 on the back, and 37 on the head and neck. The mind is considered the 108th marma. Traditionally, the points are grouped into 3 categories... Those on the legs and feet are Sanakha Marma; On the trunk, Madhayamanga Marma; and on the neck and head, Jatrurdhara Marma.

Can the 108 Marma Points Chart Help in Healing

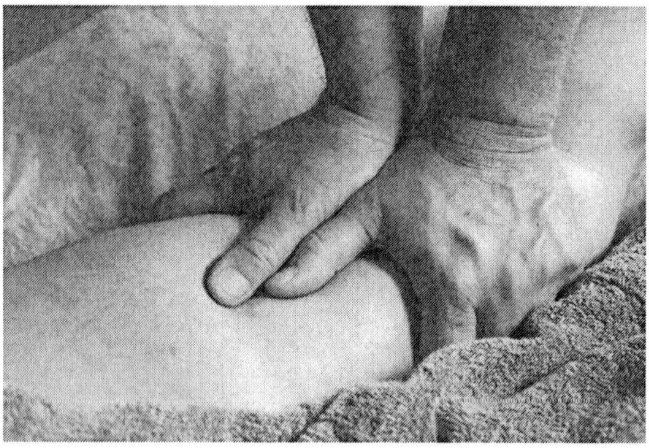

There are several factors that can inhibit the free flow of energy through the body. From lack of sleep, poor diet, lack of exercise, emotional stress, and disconnect from the natural environment. One must not underestimate the effect our modern lives have on our inner state. We feed our environments as much as they feed us back. If you notice a certain stagnation in the regular functioning of the body, it would be good to see if any of the above factors make up your daily routine.

Marma therapy works to clear stagnation in the vital energy points and thus increase vitality within the corresponding body parts. Because marma techniques work at the level of raw prana (prana that has not yet been differentiated into its various functions within the human body); its ability to facilitate physical, mental, emotional, and spiritual healing is immense.

Ayurvedic physician and author Dr. Vasant Lad suggests that flushing energy within the marma points can activate the body's inner pharmacy, shifting one's biochemistry and causing the unfolding of radical, alchemical changes. It's the subtle layers of our being that hold the greatest power and potential. So how we treat those layers will determine the response from the depths of the body. Marma Point Therapy requires a specific firmness and gentleness - a precise, soft dance, between the giver and the receiver. Energy is of a subtle nature. It requires communication in a similar manner. Here, the intent is greater than force or pressure.

The Relevance of Intent in Marma

Our intent must remain at the forefront of this process. One who practices Marma Therapy needs to remain in tune with the intent to move gently, as much as the receiver of the therapy must remain in tune with being open and vulnerable. This will facilitate the right kind of subtle communication and allow the channels to communicate back to the body and the points as well.

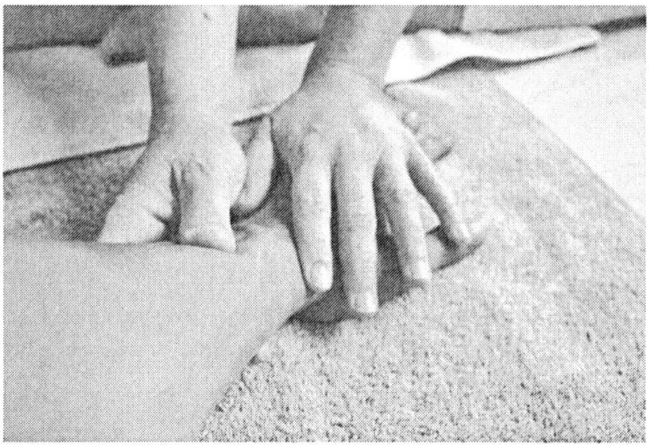

Having said that, if one is afflicted with heart disease, cancer, varicose veins, a high fever, ruptured discs, a skin disease, or if one is pregnant, it is advised that they contact their doctor prior to submitting to the Marma Point treatment. While this Ayurvedic form of therapy is rooted in the deep ancient wisdom of the body, it is essential that the nuances of one's predicament be made aware through clear communication and dialogue with the therapist so they may proceed accordingly.

The Healing Ability of Ayurvedic Energy Centers

For centuries, practitioners have meticulously mapped the human body, establishing connections between various limbs, organs, immune responses, and even emotions with distinct energy points.

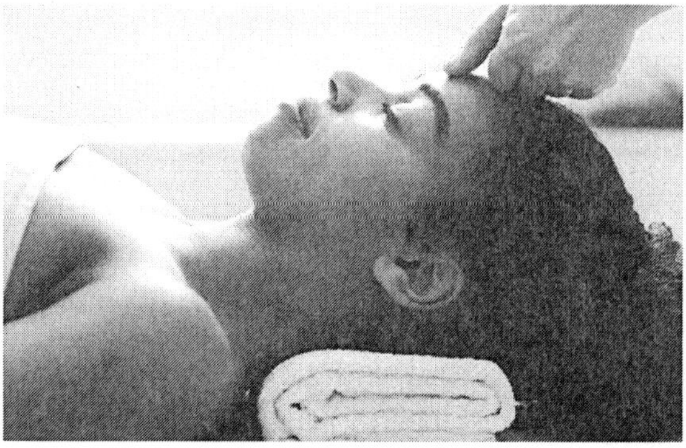

Marma points is a term that comes from an ancient form of energy healing, originated within the 5000-year-old Ayurvedic system of medicine. These energy points, also known as acupuncture or acupressure points in Chinese Medicine play a direct role in both Ayurvedic and yogic healing practices.

Marma Points

In the ancient Vedic era, marma points were considered mystical points situated on the outer self in the physical body (annamaya kosha). When these points are pressed, they are thought to activate a passage to the inner self.

Marma points are generally engaged nowadays in massage, or therapy, within the context of ayurvedic healing and medicine.

The Vedic scripture tells us the body encompasses a total of 107 marma points, each serving a specific purpose, with its individual name and exclusive massage technique.

These physical marma points are positioned at the convergence of tendons, bones, muscles, joints, veins, nerves, and other tissues. The choice of Ayurvedic massage oils when it comes to massage is determined by an individual's Ayurvedic dosha type.

In total, there in fact exists 108 marma points-107 on the physical body as mentioned, and 1 in the mind.

Phana marma	found symmetrically at the base of the nostrils, measuring half a finger point
Apanga marma	found symmetrically at the outer sides of both eyes, measuring half a finger point
Vidhur marma	found symmetrically behind and below both ears, measuring half a finger point
Shankha marma	found symmetrically at both temples on the head, measuring half a finger point
Utkshepa marma	found symmetrically where the hair meets the forehead on either side of the head, measuring half a finger point
Avarta marma	found symmetrically midway above both eyebrows, measuring half a finger point

Marma Points Found in Your Head

The age-old Ayurvedic healing system emphasizes that healing originates from within the body itself. Stimulating these marma points, through this passage to the inner self, encourages the body to address illness and pain.

It also tells us these points play a pivotal role in promoting overall well-being. Each marma point is linked to a particular name and health benefit and comes with its own appropriate massage technique for activation.

While marma points can be highly effective in promoting good health, they should be approached with care as they can also be used to inflict pain or paralysis in certain martial arts.

In the realm of Ayurveda, however, marma points are exclusively employed for their therapeutic properties and are never intended for harmful intentions.

Marma points are measured in 'finger units' with each point having distinctive features. For example, the Hridaya marma, symbolizing 'heart,' is situated at the sternum and extends four finger units. The optimal technique for this particular marma point involves gentle palm massage with oil, nurturing the heart's energy. This oil can enhance circulation, while acupressure at this juncture assists in alleviating stress and negative emotions.

Ancient healing experts meticulously charted the precise locations and effects of marma points on various body parts.

How Marma Points Work

These marma points, or junctures of the body, function on the vital energy force of prana, joined by energy channels throughout the body, called nadis.

Here, we outline the principles of how marma points work:

1. Pranic Flow In Ayurveda, the concept of pranic flow suggests that vital energy, known as prana, flows through the body, nourishing and sustaining all aspects of life.
2. Energy Centers Marma points serve as gateways, facilitating the entry or exit of prana within the body. These marma points are regarded as energetic centers, acting as intersections that link the physical body with the mind and spirit, where both the physical and subtle energy bodies converge.
3. Influence On Doshas Each marma point is associated with specific doshas (Vata, Pitta, and Kapha), and its stimulation can influence the balance of these doshas in the body.
4. Healing And Stimulation Through the application of pressure, massage, or other therapeutic techniques to these marma points, it is believed that the flow of prana can be stimulated or harmonized, leading to various health benefits.
5. Release Of Blockages Marma point massage is thought to be effective in releasing blockages and imbalances in the pranic flow, thereby alleviating physical and emotional discomfort.

6. Integration Of Body And Mind Stimulating marma points is believed to enhance the connection between the physical body and the mind, fostering a sense of well-being and harmony.
7. Specific Functions Each marma point is associated with unique functions, and Ayurvedic practitioners leverage this knowledge to address specific health concerns or promote overall vitality.

How Marma Points can be Affected Negatively

The flow of prana from the nadis to and through the marma points is essential for overall well-being.

On the other hand, if the energy becomes stagnant or its flow is disrupted, it can lead to health problems.

Numerous common practices have the potential to disturb the natural prana flow through the marma points, including:

- Overexposure to UV
- Sedentary lifestyle without exercise
- Artificial lighting over natural lighting
- Consuming unhealthy food
- Poor sleep patterns
- General stress

Despite maintaining a relatively healthy lifestyle, living in our current day and age can still impact the healthy flow of life force into your body.

Ayurveda attributes several aging-related processes, such as fatigue, stiffness, memory loss, fragile bones, and sensitive digestion, to the degradation of the body and mind caused by the stifling of these marma points.

Marma Point Ayurvedic Massage or Therapy

Marma points are generally used in Ayurvedic massage to influence subtle energy or prana, but they are also highly useful for physically easing sore muscles and increasing circulation.

The Ayurvedic practice of marma treatment is widely practiced and is seen as crucial to self-healing and self-care.

The secret to better health and happiness doesn't always reside outside of ourselves, but as we learn through the practice of yoga, be it in asana practice or Karma Yoga and so on, the key is within.

At the core of marma point therapy lies an elaborate and intricate energetic framework, which is believed to have laid the foundation for other popular point-based therapies such as acupuncture, acupressure, and reflexology.

Every cell in the body has a memory, and according to Ayurveda, these memories get retained, causing blockages that prevent prana (life force energy) from freely flowing through this framework.

The generation of hormones and the condition of the important organs are both thought to be impacted by stimulating the marma points and moving this stuck energy.

Initially, the knowledge of Ayurvedic vital energy points served dual purposes: ancient warriors utilized specific marma points to incapacitate opponents in combat, while Ayurvedic physicians applied other marma points to facilitate healing.

Interestingly, the term "marma" itself translates to 'a point that can kill,' underscoring the importance of some of these points in martial arts as mentioned before.

In the realm of marma point massage, these specific points serve a singular purpose - harnessing their therapeutic qualities. Termed also as neurolymphatic points, they actively contribute to lymphatic drainage and optimize the functionality of the body's organs.

A marma master would possess the rare and profound knowledge of manipulating or directing prana (life energy) to achieve either specific violent or therapeutic outcomes via these marma points, as a combatant, or as a healer.

Benefits of Marma Point Ayurvedic Massage

1. Energy flow and balance It stimulates the flow of prana (life force) throughout the body, releasing energy blockages and restoring balance and vitality.
2. Relaxation and stress relief Through gentle and precise techniques, marma point massage induces a sense of tranquility, calming the nervous system and reducing stress.
3. Improved circulation By massaging marma points, blood circulation is enhanced, leading to better oxygenation and nutrient delivery to tissues, supporting overall health and healing.
4. Pain relief Specific points are targeted to alleviate physical discomfort, tension, muscle soreness, and joint stiffness.

5. Enhanced immunity According to Ayurvedic principles, stimulating marma points can strengthen the immune system, increasing the body's resilience against illnesses and diseases.

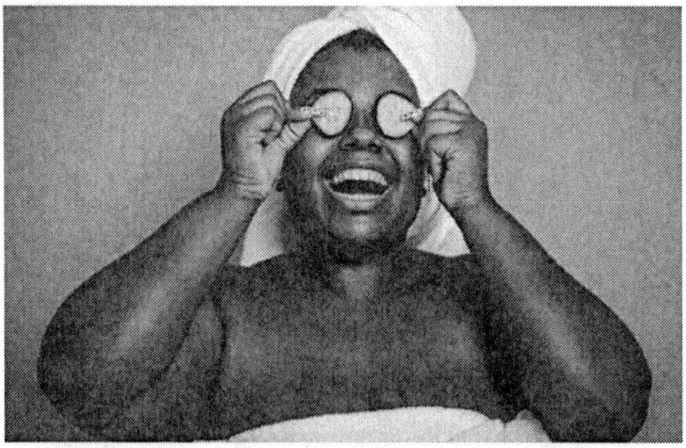

6. Emotional balance Marma point massage is believed to promote positive feelings, reduce anxiety, and ease emotional imbalances, supporting emotional well-being.
7. Detoxification By improving circulation and energy flow, the massage may assist in eliminating toxins from the body, aiding the detoxification process.

8. Improved sleep quality Many individuals experience better sleep after a marma point massage due to its relaxation and stress-reducing effects.
9. Headache and migraine relief Specific marma points on the head and face are targeted to alleviate headaches and migraines.
10. Enhanced mental clarity and focus Regular marma point massage may help improve concentration and mental clarity, leading to better cognitive function.

Marma Points of the Feet: Importance in Health and Healing

Marma points are considered the vital points where the force of life (prana) dwells. Many of these vital points (marma) are situated on the foot. So, caring for the feet has high therapeutic importance that goes beyond cosmetic purposes.

Marma points, often referred to as vital energy centers, are crucial spots where the life force, known as prana, resides. Among these significant points, many are located on the feet, making foot care more than just a cosmetic concern. In this blog, we'll explore the marma points in the feet and how stimulating them can enhance your overall health.

These points are considered life-giving, and their importance extends far beyond aesthetics.

According to vagabhatta, marma points are specific areas where any injury can result in various types of pain and even tremors. This concept of marma forms the foundation of martial arts, acupuncture, and acupressure anesthesia. Sushruta Samhita explains that damage to the "mansa marma," or muscle-related marma point, can lead to a loss of touch sensation. Remarkably, this information can be utilized to induce local anesthesia by stimulating the mansa marma.

In one leg alone, there are 11 marma points, and the same number exists in the other leg, summing up to a total of 44 marma points across both the upper and lower extremities. Furthermore, there are 12 marma points in the thorax and abdomen, 14 in the back, and an additional 37 marma points situated above the clavicular region, encompassing the neck and head.

So, as we go deeper in learning about marma therapy, you'll discover the incredible potential these points hold for enhancing your well-being.

The 5 Marma Points of the Feet

Before delving into the practice of marma therapy, it's crucial to pinpoint the exact location of each specific marma point. These locations can vary from person to person, depending on their unique body measurements and structures.

The descriptions of these points often reference bony prominences, joints, and other anatomical landmarks. The distances are typically measured in terms of finger lengths specific to the individual. Additionally, marma points come in various sizes, ranging from as small as a pinhead to half a finger's width, four fingers laid laterally, or even the size of one's palm.

Marma therapy holds the potential to significantly enhance physical, mental, and spiritual energies. On a physical level, it acts as a rejuvenating force, revitalizing the body's tissues. At the cellular level, it enhances vital functions such as digestion, respiration, blood circulation, and excretion. On a psychological plane, marma therapy improves mental faculties by channeling them in a positive direction. Remarkably, it provides a drug-free approach to address many psychosomatic ailments and harmonizes the nervous and endocrine systems to manage psychological disorders.

Spiritually, marma therapy involves the reasoning of the mind, regulating and transforming thoughts towards a positive orientation, thus aiding concentration on life's ultimate goals. It serves as a preventive measure, helping individuals cope with challenges that arise due to various diseases. Furthermore, marma therapy plays a pivotal role in perceiving psychic centers within oneself, ultimately guiding individuals toward inner consciousness transformation.

For those who embark on the journey of self-marma therapy, the experience is transformative, leading to the accumulation of physical, mental, and spiritual energy. The ancient Ayurvedic sage Sushruta defined marma as the anatomical site where muscle (mamsa), vein (sira), ligament (snayu), bone (asthi), and joint (sandhi) meet.

There are 5 marma points located at the foot. These are kshipra marma, talahridaya marma, kurcha marma, kurchashira marma, and gulpha marma. These marma points are the mirror image of those situated on the palm region in number and location. They also have the same names. They come under the category of marmas of the limbs (Sakthi marma points). Here is a detailed analysisof the marma points of the feet along with their importance in health and healing.

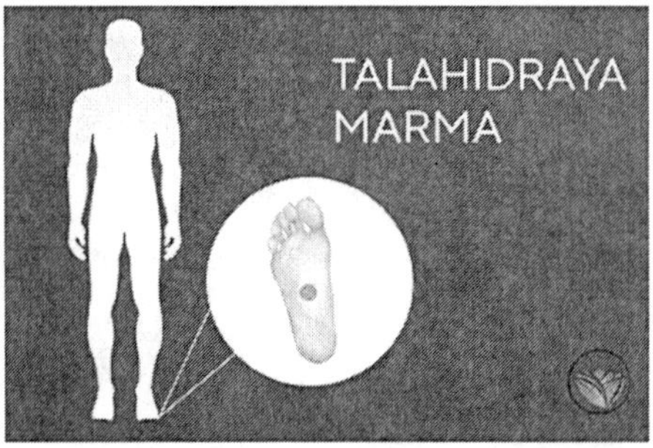

Talahidraya marma is associated with respiration and circulation. It boosts the immune system. It controls the right foot and left foot along with the power of circulation particularly for the lower part of the body (below the navel).

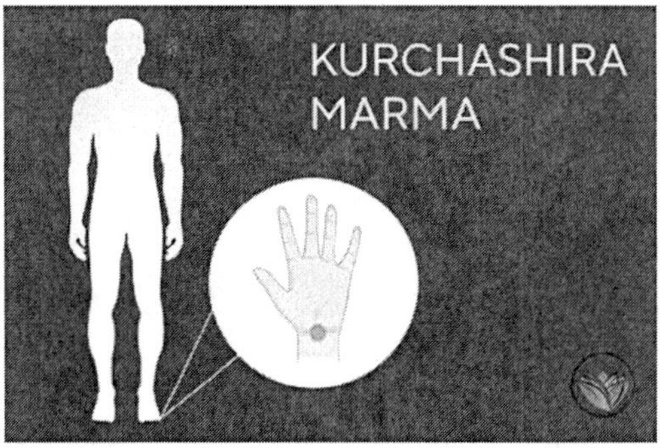

Kurchashira marma located on the hands as well as feet helps to control the muscular system of the body. In particular, it helps control the muscles of the foot and bodily posture. It boosts digestive power, promotes visual activity, and reproductive stimulation.

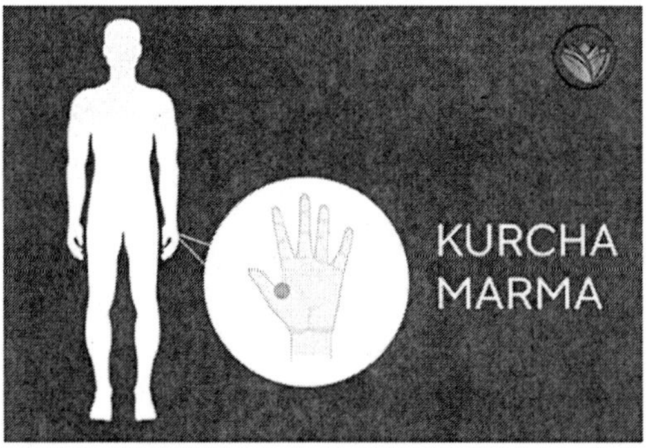

Kurcha marma located on the hands and the planter sides on the feet. It is related to the force of life and with the digestive process. It improves the flow of prana for sensory activity.

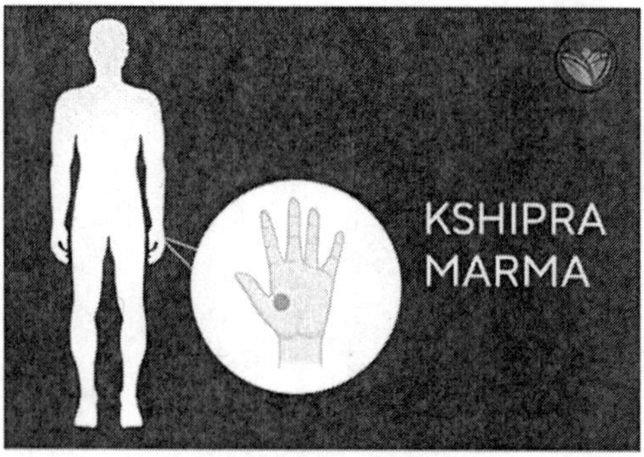

Kshipra marma is associated with the functioning of the heart and lungs. It controls the lymphatic (circulation) and respiratory system and supports functioning for the heart and lungs.

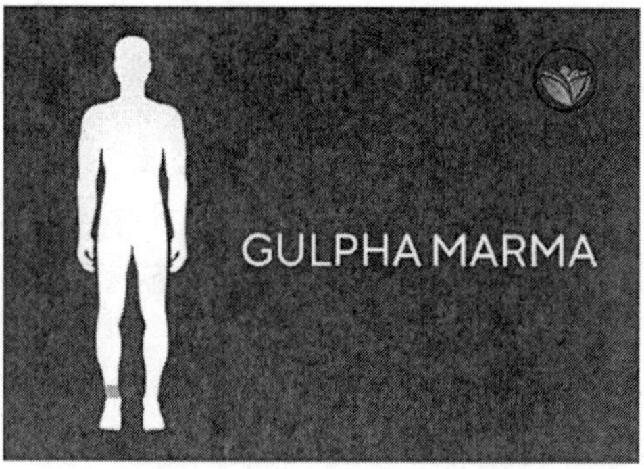

Gulpha marma is responsible for joint movements. It helps in the management of joint injury, muscle sprain, and pain. It controls fat, bone, and reproductive systems, lubrication of the joints, and movement of the feet.

Marma points of the feet: Marma therapy and reflexology

As mentioned above, marma therapy is an ancient non-invasive practice that focuses on the manipulation of life force or subtle energy (prana) in the body for supporting and healing process.

It is based on utilization of 107 marma points which are considered to be the access point to the body, mind, and consciousness. Marma points help to balance the three biological humors (Vata, Pitta and Kapha) which are the integral components of the human body.

It balances triguna (sattva, rajas, and tamas) which are integral components of the mind. They are also helpful in healing the human soul as all these life forces (prana) are considered to reside in these marma points.

As marma is related to life force which is associated with Vata Dosha so marma mainly deals with Vata.

Marma therapy helps to move positive prana through the various channels of the body by applying moderate pressure on Marma points. This prana may be instrumental in managing health conditions like headache, joint pain, paralysis, heart diseases, mental stress, and muscular sprain. It is the art of touching at exactly the same point so that the energy blocked at that point can be released.

The therapeutic regions like marmas on the arms and legs, are the most important for treatment purposes. While doing marma therapy on the feet, points are stimulated to open the channels of the body.

Foot Reflexology and Marma Therapy

Reflexology is a science that seems to be derived from the core of ancient Ayurvedic knowledge. Foot reflexology is a form of foot massage that targets points on the foot which are believed to correspond to another part of the body.

Reflexology practitioners rely on the reflexes map of the feet and hands which are connected to all the internal organs and other human body parts. Like marma therapy, they also believe that by applying the appropriate pressure and massage on certain spots on the feet and hands, all other body parts could be energized and rejuvenated.

Marma points are similar to the pressure points used in reflexology and acupressure techniques. Many marmas and acupuncture points share similar locations.

It is said that reflexology and acupressure evolved from the marma system of Ayurveda.

Marma Points in Massage and Oleation

Marma points are energy points which play an important role in regulating the body and keeping it in a harmonious and balanced state. So, the utilization of these points in oleation therapy may enhance the effectiveness of the therapy for wellbeing.

As marma points are related to various internal organs, doshas, and channels (srotas), these points when pressed, may be useful in influencing the functioning (stimulate/inhibit) of internal organs, treating various disease conditions and help in promoting health. Marma therapy can thus improve the functioning of body organs by achieving homeostasis.

In massage therapy, marma points can be used in three ways.

1. To treat nerves (nadis) and thus the vital force of life (prana)
2. To treat a specific organ or system
3. To treat specific dosha imbalances

Foot massage with oil (padabhyanga) and marma points of the feet

Foot massage with oil (padabhyanga) is considered a part of the recommended daily Ayurvedic routine. It also has its importance in reflexology and acupressure techniques.

TRY these oils and tools for foot massage: Balaayah Black Gram Body Booster | Kansa wand and Marma tools

What are the Benefits of Foot Massage with Oil

In the Ayurvedic classics, it is mentioned that by regular foot massage with oil, roughness, immobility (stiffness), dryness, fatigue, and numbness of feet (loss of sensation) are immediately cured. After massaging, the feet become soft, strong and steady. All diseases related to the power of circulation or an imbalance of Vata dosha are resolved with oil massage. That is, the person who does regular oil foot marma massage will not be affected by sciatica or constrictions of the vessels. Massage to the feet brings sound sleep. It is relaxing, refreshing, and invigorating to the body and the eyesight.

Presently therapists are focusing on marma points during foot massage (padaabhyanga) with application of different kinds of Ayurvedic herbal oils and aromatics or essential oils, as needed.

Stimulation of these specific marma points of contralateral and affected feet treated with rubbing, pressure, and oil massage has also shown relief in specific groups of conditions.

1. Kshipra, talahridaya, kurcha, kurcha-shira, and gulpha marma points are useful in the treatment of vertebral column injuries, spinal cord lesions, and trauma to the peripheral region.
2. Marma of the lower extremities are useful in treating cerebral palsy.
3. Kshipra, kurcha, kurcha-shira, and gulpha marma points are useful in cases of tingling sensations in the feet.
4. Kshipra and gulpha marma point massage are responsible for the relief of pain in the leg, knee, and sciatic pain.

So, we see that feet are an important part of the body where some important marma points exist. They should be taken care of properly. With regular massage and pressing of these points one feels relaxed, energetic, and healthy and does not suffer from several health problems.

Marma Science

Marma science and Marma therapy is an untouched chapter of Indian surgery. With the exploration of Marma science, the whole scenario of Indian surgery may change in multidimensional approaches. As previously Yoga was the means of achieving spiritual gain and these days Yoga is a tool for health promotion, in the same way, the implementation of Marma therapy may help in different medical and surgical lesions and to combat most of the diseases from which man suffers.

Among the hidden sciences (Gupta Vidya) of India, Marma science is the most important. The human body is the basis of all types of activities. One can achieve many mortal and immortal gains from this body. In another reference it is said that the human body is the seat of diseases. Can any individual be able to get any gains from ill-health? Is there any means to keep the body healthy? In answer to these questions we can confidently say yes, and with the knowledge of Marma, one can achieve it. According to Ayurvedic texts the Marmas are the points, when injured, may be life-threatening. Marmas are not superficial landmarks on the body surface but these are deep seated important physio-anatomical structures. When stimulated appropriately, they can preserve health and cure disease.

The knowledge of Marma is the oldest hidden treasure of Vedic surgical skill.Many ancient saints got the knowledge of Marma and practiced this knowledge for the betterment of suffering humanity. Ancient Rishis, the experts of Marma knowledge, developed the Marma science and therapy for suffereing humanity, and for those people who are engaged in the activities of service to humanity and are seekers of achieving the highest state of consciousness. However, it gradually became a hidden science and only the kings and warriors knew it. Why did it become a hidden science?

To reply this question, it is important to know what Marma is . Accoding to medical definition, the specific part of the body, which are very vulnerable to trauma, is known as Marma. Any trauma to these places mat lead to death and many other complications regarding the physiological and anatomical functions. These places are know as vital points and are the source of energy, and by stimulating them, there can be many physical and spiritual gains. So these places should be preserved and not be exposed to any trauma. Therefore the Marma science was obscured and hidden for a long period of thousands of and know only to kings and warriors years.

In the present times, with due precaution, this hidden treasure of Vedic surgical skill can help greatly to relieve the suffering of humanity. However, till date, the knowledge of Marma science is not well-known to the practioners of Ayurveda so this science has not flourished like the other specialities of Ayurveda.

Persons engaged in higher spiritual practices cannot practice Yoga, pranayama, and other physical practices to keep their body fit due to their specific lifestyle. They can, however, attain the same result and enjoy a similar outcome with Marma therapy, which enables them to attain physical well,being, mental calmness and spiritual gains and self-realisation.Ancient Rishis had devoped this knowledge and it is inherent even in many day to day spiritual practices and given as instruction in religious texts.

Bibliography

Apte, V. M.: *Social and Religious Life in the Grihya Sutras*, Rawat Press, Bombay, 1954.

Baba, Pagal : *Temple of the Phallic King: The Mind of India*, Simon and Schuster, New York, 1973.

Beyer, Stephen : *The Cult of Tara: Magic and Ritual in Tibet*, University of California Press, Berkeley, 1973.

Chattopadhyaya, Sudhakar: *Reflections on the Tantras*, Motilal Banarsidass, New Delhi, 1978.

Comfort, Alex: *The Koka Shastra: and other Medieval Indian Writings on Love*, George Allen and Unwin, London, 1964.

Cozort, Daniel : *Highest Yoga Tantra,* Snow Lion Publications, New York, 1986.

De Ropp, S. R. : *Sex Energy: The Sexual Force in Man and Animals*, Corgi Books, London, 1972.

Douglas, Nik and Slinger, Penny: *Sexual Secrets: The Alchemy of Ecstasy*, Destiny Books, New York, 1979.

Eliade, Mircea: *Rites and Symbols of Initiation*, Harper Torchbook, New York, 1965.

Farrow, G. W. and Menon, I. : *The Concealed Essence of the Hevajra Tantra,* Motilal Banarsidass, Delhi, 1992.

Gambhirananda, Swami: *Brahma Sutra Shamkar Bhasya,* Adavita Ashrama, Calcutta, 1977.

Hopkins, W. E.: *Ethics of India,* Yale University Press, New Haven, 1924.

Jacobs, Hans : *Western Psychotherapy and Hindu Sadhana*, George Allen and Unwin, London, 1961.

Kaushalayan, Bhadant Anand: *Swami Vivekananda and the Great Buddha*, Buddha Bhoomi Prakashan, Nagpur 1994.

Kramrisch, Stella: *Manifestations of Shiva*, Philadelphia Museum of Art, Philadelphia, 1981.

Lessing, Ferdinand : *Introduction to the Buddhist Tantric Systems*, Motilal Banarsidass, Delhi, 1993.

Majumdar, A. K.: *Caitanya: His Life and Doctrine*, MacMillan, Bombay, 1969.

Mulin, G. H. : *Meditation on the Lower Tantras*, Library of Tibetan Works and Archives, Dharamsala, 1983.

Narayanananda, Swami : *The Kundalini Shakti*, Rishikesh, 1950.

Panikkar, K. M.: *Himdnism and the West*, Panjab University Publication, Chandigarh, 1964.

Payne, E. : *The Shaktas: An Introduction and Comparative Study*, Calcutta, 1933.

Rajneesh, Bhagwan : *Tantra: The Supreme Understanding,* Chidvilas, Boulder, 1993.

Ranade, R. D.: *Mysticism in Maharashtra*, MacMillan, Delhi, 1933.

Ranganathananda, Swami: *Science and Religion*, Advaita Ashram, Calcutta, 1978.

Rastogi, Navjivan : *The Krama Tantricism of Kashmir*, Motilal Banarsidass, Delhi, 1979.

Schmidt, Toni : *The Eighty-Five Siddhas*, Stat Etnografiska Museum, Stockholm, 1958.

Singer, June : *Androgyny: Toward a New Theory of Sexuality,* Anchor Press/ Doubleday, New York, 1976.

Singh, Kirpal: *Jap Ji: The Message of Guru Nanak*, MacMillan, Delhi, 1964.

Sircar, D. C. : *The Sakta Pithas*, Indological Publishers and Booksellers, Delhi, 1973.

Taylor, A. E.: *Elements Metaphysics*, Methnen & Co., London, 1924.

Trevor Leggett: *Realization of the Supreme Self: the Bhagavad Gita Yogas*, Kegan Paul International, London, 1995.

Van Kooij, K. R. : *Worship of the Goddess According to the Kalikapurana*, E. J. Brill, Leiden, 1972.

Vidhushekhara Bhattacharya: *The Agamasastra of Gaudapada*, Motilal Banarsidass, Delhi, 1989.

Wayman, Alex : *Yoga of the Guhyasamaja Tantra*, Motilal Banarsidass, Delhi, 1977.

Wheeler, Robert Eric Mortimer: *Civilization of the Indus Valley and Beyond*, McGraw-Hill, New York, 1966.

Winternitz, M. : *Notes on the Guhyasamaja Tantra and the Age of the Tantras*, IHQ, Calcutta, 1933.

Woodroffe, Sir John : *The World as Power*, Ganesh and Co., Madras, 1966.

Yogananda, Paramahansa, *Autobiography of a Yogi,* Self-Realization Fellowship, Los Angeles, 1946.

Yogananda, Swami : *Autobiography of a Yogi,* Fellowship, Los Angeles, 1946.

Zimmer, Heinrich: *Myths and Symbols in Indian Art and Civilization*, Joseph Campbell, Delhi, 1946.

Zvelebil, Kamil. V. : *The Poets of the Powers*, Rider and Co., London, 1973.

Index

M

N

P

R

S

T

V

Y